By Agnes Newton Keith

LAND BELOW THE WIND

THREE CAME HOME

THREE CAME HOME

Sketches by the author and Don Johnston

An Atlantic Monthly Press Book

Little, Brown and Company · Boston · 1947

THREE CAME HOME

by *Agnes Newton Keith*

ATLANTIC–LITTLE, BROWN BOOKS
ARE PUBLISHED BY
LITTLE, BROWN AND COMPANY
IN ASSOCIATION WITH
THE ATLANTIC MONTHLY PRESS

Published simultaneously
in Canada by McClelland and Stewart Limited

PRINTED IN THE UNITED STATES OF AMERICA BY
KINGSPORT PRESS, INC., KINGSPORT, TENNESSEE

For My Husband — for Every Reason

I HAVE written this book for three reasons:

For horror of war. I want others to shudder with me at it.

For affection for my husband. When war nearly killed me, knowledge of our love kept me alive.

And for a reminder to my son. I fought one war for him in prison camp. He survives because of me. He belongs now to peace. I remind him that it is better to give more and to have less — and to keep the peace — than to fight.

The Japanese in this book are as war made them, not as God did, and the same is true of the rest of us. We are not pleasant people here, for the story of war is always the story of hate; it makes no difference with whom one fights. The hate destroys you spiritually as the fighting destroys you bodily.

If there are tears shed here, they are for the death of good feeling. If there is horror, it is for those who speak indifferently of "the next war." If there is hate, it is for hateful qualities, not nations. If there is love, it is because this alone kept me alive and sane.

A. N. K.

Foreword

ONE day after we were imprisoned on Berhala Island, North Borneo, a little short man, very clean and neat, and very military, arrived on the broken-down wharf. This, we were told, was Major Suga, the Japanese Commander of all Prisoners of War and all Internees in all Borneo.

We were mustered at midday in the sun and stood for two hours waiting, while women had hysterics and fainted, children wept, and men looked very weary. Then Suga came to the prison compound and spoke: "Try to be happy and content, keep up your morals, and be healthy. I am sorry for you. You must learn to live under discipline. You may be moved to Kuching, Sarawak, where my headquarters are. The prisoners there are happy. It will be a long war, so make up your minds to do as you are told. Don't complain, be good, obey, keep up your morals, keep well, and be happy."

After this speech the representatives of the two camps asked for interviews with him. They complained of the conditions we were living in. Major Suga said, "Is zat so? Well, you are well treated now!" They said we could not endure the life. He said, "Is zat so? Well, you will learn!"

He commanded me to a private interview at the guardhouse. Being guilty of many misdemeanors, I feared it might be for punishment. I took George with me as a maternal touch, and because George wanted to go. I expected sternness, if not violence. Instead Suga treated me with courtesy, one of the few Japanese officers who ever did.

While he talked I studied him with interest. He had the brief stature which we consider Japanese, and was built without angles, but not fat. His head was round and his face elliptical in contrast to the rectangular block of the average Anglo-Saxon head. His forehead was unlined and low, and he had well-defined, rather thick lips. His hair was stiff and black and shaven close, his mustache military, and his beard incipient only. When he spoke of abstract subjects his brown eyes were pleasant and straight, but when he talked of the war they glittered and became cold. By watching his eyes I could tell what subjects to avoid.

He told me that he had read my book, *Land Below the Wind*, in the Japanese translation, and that he liked it, and asked me if I had the Western edition. I told him that his soldiers had stolen it from my house, and he said, "Is zat so? Then I take it from my soldiers."

He told me that he was a graduate of the University of Washington in the United States, and asked me why Americans were prejudiced against the Japanese. I told him it was because cheap Japanese labor threatened ours, and that it was an economic prejudice. He replied that this was only a small part of it; he said, "They exclude us because of labor, but they despise us because we are Japanese. You know that this is so."

I did know it. I could only answer that I myself had no racial prejudices, that before the war I had believed that I had real friends amongst the Japanese, that they had rejected me after the war, rather than I them.

I said that in wartime we were all trained by national propaganda to hate the enemy, as otherwise we were unwilling to kill, and be killed. He and I were now being trained thus to hate each other, but perhaps after the war we might meet as human beings again.

He then said to me, "You are writing a book about your life here?"

I said, "How can I? You have taken my pencils and paper away."

"Ah, so. I will give back to you. You shall write a book for *me*, and I shall censor it."

"I work too hard here in camp to write. I don't have time or energy to write."

"But that is the best time to write, when you are busy. When many good and bad things happen to you, then you have good and bad thoughts. Then is the time to write. Yes, I think you intend to write a book here. Some day you shall write one for me."

In time we were moved to Kuching, and there I saw Suga, who was Colonel Suga now, frequently. At every meeting he brought up the subject of my writing for him, and nagged me constantly to do so.

I told him this was impossible because of the heavy work we had to do and because I had no materials. He said he would make it possible — he would lessen my work, he would give me writing materials; that I would write for him, and he would censor the product.

Always he stressed the fact that he would censor. Always he questioned me if I was writing myself.

One afternoon he called me to his office and produced an American copy of my book with my name in it, taken from my house by Mr. Maeda, and taken from Mr. Maeda by Suga. He opened it to the foreword about the lion and the lamb, and asked me to explain the meaning of this. I did so. He then requested me to "give" the book to him by writing his name in it, and drawing a picture on the flyleaf. He pulled Harry's fountain pen out of his pocket, and handed it to me to draw with.

After the purpose of art had been served, the orderly produced pineapple, biscuits, and very sweet coffee for us. Then Suga broke the news.

"You are going to write 'The Life and Thoughts of an Internee' for me in your spare time. That is my wish. Do not argue," he said.

I replied that I had no spare time, no materials, no thoughts, etc., etc. For a few minutes the tone of the conversation remained friendly, then he became Colonel Suga, Commandant of Prisoners of War and Internees in Borneo.

"It is my command that you do this," he said. "I order it. I give you all materials. If need be, I release you from other camp work. Do not talk further about this. It is my order."

I said, "If you order me to write, I must write. But you cannot order me what to say."

"All right! All right! All right! All right!"

Then he gave me pen, ink, pencil, and paper, and ordered the office to release a confiscated typewriter to my use, and told me to go.

I did not sleep easily that night. I did not know what use he might intend to make of what I wrote, and I feared that my words might be turned against me by one side or the other. I knew that I was needed for community camp work, as we never had enough able-bodied people for the jobs, but I knew also that I could not do the work and produce written material for Suga at the same time. But experience had taught me that the choice was not mine to make.

The next day an order came to our camp master that I was to be released from community camp work by Suga's order. The Japanese office was to pay three dollars a month into our community fund as my salary. I was to continue doing part-time work in camp as a substitute for women who became ill.

So I wrote for Colonel Suga. I titled it "Captivity," and I told the truth, but not all the truth. There was much which for my own sake and that of others in camp I could not say, and there were also things that I did not dare to say to Suga; he could be very much the Oriental Potentate at times.

But he stood more than I believed he would. I complained persistently of wrongs and mistreatments, I constantly asked for better food and less work. I said that I believed trouble between our races was based on misunderstanding, and that I hoped for tolerance and sympathy in time to come, between our peoples. I said that I believed Suga did what he could do for our women's camp. And that, as he was kindhearted to women and children, please could we have some more food? This story was submitted to Suga at given intervals.

But there was another story also that I wrote in captivity.

This story I wrote in the smallest possible handwriting, on the backs of labels, on old Chinese papers that our tobacco came in, on the margins of old newspapers given us by the Japanese . . . and when I could get it, on Colonel Suga's paper. I stuffed George's toys with these notes, I sewed a layer of them in his sleeping mat, I stuffed his pillows, and I put them in tins which I buried under the barrack.

The Japanese searched my things frequently, turning inside out my suitcase, reading my papers upside down, when they did not read English. In time I lost everything with writing on it: documents, passport, wedding lines, bank receipts — everything except my notes.

From these notes I have reconstructed the true story of my captivity. This is not the story I wrote at Suga's command, it is my story.

Contents

THREE CAME HOME

1

To Us a Son

WE had always wanted a son. On our honeymoon we had fed coppers to the golden Buddhas in the temples of fecundity all over Japan, for one. We had planted bamboos in the garden at home, and waited for them to shoot, as a symbol to us of a son. We had even gone so far as to ask a doctor. "No reason," he said, "why not?" But Buddhas, bamboos, and babies were slow, there was something wrong with communications; it took six years from prayer to answer.

On April 5, 1940, in Sandakan, North Borneo, Henry George Newton Keith, called George, was born. To quote a masculine friend, this was accomplished with the minimum amount of effort. Certainly not as much effort as it had required to finish *Land Below the Wind* the year before.

Land Below the Wind was a book about Borneo, written because I was happily married to a man, a country, and an idea. The Conservator of Forests and Director of Agriculture in Civil Service in North Borneo was my husband; Borneo was the country, and The Far East Is Human was the idea.

I had lived in Borneo with my husband, an Englishman who doesn't like being described, since 1934. When I started to write a book, he said he hated travel books by women because they were full of women instead of travel, and they were inaccurate. I had to admit that after four years in Borneo there was a lot I didn't know that he did, but what I did know had hit me in the eye.

In the warm, sticky, sweet-smelling heat of the equator, Borneo was more fantastic than fiction, because it was real. I felt the monsoons blowing, half the year one way, half the

other, but always blowing; I felt the warm rain coming in streams, the hot sun steaming through; I saw many shades of human beings, drinking, eating, sleeping, sweating, loving, hating, living their private lives like me, under a moon like a yellow melon, under a sun like a pale grapefruit, on the equator, and in the impenetrable, much-penetrated jungles.

I saw a civilization where the head-hunters of Borneo still hunted heads, the Moro pirates still came down from the Philippines to loot, the Muruts still wore their hair long and went naked; where civil government was a Chartered Company, the Crown ruled but the Company paid salary, and letters from home were six weeks on the way.

Here British Colonial life lived itself placidly and without confusion as British life should, on the edge of the Borneo jungles, by the blue tepid waters of Sulu and China Seas. Here

Social Club, Golf Club, Tennis Club, Squash Club, Bridge Club, Rugger and polo and soccer, made British the day; but the heavy scents of night-blooming tropical trees, *kenanga*, *chempaka*, frangipani, *Cassia fistula*, and *sundal malam*, made exotic and languorous the nights.

Here rogue elephants, monkeys, apes, otters, and musangs, natives of Borneo, Muruts and Dusuns, went their unclad, uninhibited way regardless, while Empire builders and their consorts drank tea, wore black ties, played cricket, sang hymns, and kept Christmas, and grew more Scotch, and more English, the longer they lived from home.

Such was the town life of North Borneo in its capital, Sandakan, with fifteen thousand Asiatics, seventy Europeans.

When the life of a lady palled on me, and being a gentle-man made my husband into the opposite, we would be called out of town. Then together we went up the cool Borneo rivers, white rapids and streams, through its jungles, across its mountains, over its plains; meeting and knowing its people; seeing, feeling, tasting adventure; sick and tired sometimes, sometimes hating it, swearing I'd never go again — but always going, and loving it, too, while the Conservator of Forests and Director of Agriculture made trees grow where before they were not.

It was a good life, it was a life of joy to remember, it was my first four years in Borneo; it was the Land Below the Wind.

Then leave came, eight months at home; I could just get there. I had malaria and typhoid, I had my book in a suitcase half-done — half-done, like me.

We arrived home, I came to life and finished the book, and it won a prize. Before it was accepted, the publishers in-sisted on a chapter of autobiography and data, saying that the American reading public was fact-loving, and liked to know its authors. Harry was nervous. He said that writing auto-biography truthfully was like letting a stranger into bed with you. I could only reply that my experience was more limited about that than his.

The book crisis finally being solved by letting the stranger into bed with us, the following facts were sent to the publishers:

Although my birth certificate has vanished, my parents are sure that I was born, and the evidence points to Oak Park, Illinois. While still helpless, I was carried to Hollywood, California, and there grew up amidst lemon and orange trees, and innocently pushed my doll carriage down dirt lanes which were soon to be made famous by celluloid passion.

When I was ten we moved to Venice, a near-by beach resort, for the health of my brother, Al. Here free passes enabled us to ride the roller coaster and Ferris wheel until we could not stand up, and gave us an early training in stomach control to which we attributed our later ability to sail the sea unmoved. Our home life was ideal because our parents loved each other and us, and we loved them, and there is nothing more important that parents and children can do for each other.

Meanwhile I attended school frequently enough to get credits to admit me to the University of California at Berkeley. From there I graduated with two engagement rings, a sorority pin, a prize for essay writing, a respect for learning, and a promise of a job on the *San Francisco Examiner*. I got the job and started work as the lowest paid person on the staff; I used to sit in the city room praying for fires, murders, suicides, without knowing that I was to be the central figure in one.

I worked on the paper eight months and two things happened: I was almost murdered by one man, and my heart was broken by another. The experience of a broken heart was not without benefit because I learned through it what qualities I wanted in a husband when I married again, but the broken head was totally destructive.

A loafer on the streets of San Francisco whom I had never seen before, crazed by drugs and alcohol, decided that the *Examiner* was persecuting him by printing the cartoon called Krazy Kat: Krazy Kat, he said, was himself. He decided to kill the first person who came out of the *Examiner* office, and I was that person. He swung on me with a two-foot length of iron pipe, and struck my head twice before anyone could stop him, and fractured my skull front and back. With this injury I nearly lost my life, my memory, my eyesight, and I did lose the idea that God had created the world primarily for me.

After my assailant had been sentenced to prison, I went home to recuperate, broken physically, mentally, emotionally, if I would have admitted it. But I would not; I was living up to a picture I had painted for myself in which I was brave and courageous. Nobody knows how much I wanted to break down and weep in the corners, and cry out, "It's no use! I know I'm done for! I can't go on!" Instead I went to parties, rode horseback, swam, drove a motorcar, and pretended to have fun and be human, believing throughout that I was losing my mind.

After two years of illness, hoping that a change would help, my father sent me to Europe with Al, who was going to study an engineering project. The night we left home Al said to me, "Don't die on me, Old Scout! I could never explain it to Pop!"

But I didn't die; instead I began to live. Al was the best traveling companion in the world because he let nothing interfere with enjoyment. If we were enjoying ourselves at the time our train was leaving, we let the train go without us. Working on this principle we toured on foot, horseback, by Ford and train through England, France, Germany, Austria, Hungary, Czechoslovakia, Albania, Montenegro, and I ceased to need to forget. When I came home everybody said, "Well, you just must be strong!"

By the time we returned to the United States I was sure of myself again; I rented a garage and typewriter and settled down to be a writer. Then without warning I lost the use of my eyes, as a result of the frontal fracture to my head, and for two years I could not read a page of print. While having treatment for my eyes I started to study dancing in a Hollywood studio, and while dancing I injured my foot. Then, as I had a clotheshorse figure, I tried modeling clothes, and because of a photogenic face I did bits in the movies. Meanwhile everybody said, "Poor Agnes! A girl of such promise!"

Out of that specialized training I learned one thing — that none of it was what I wanted.

Then a young Englishman who had been a friend of my brother's and mine since childhood came home on leave from British North Borneo, where he was engaged in Government Service. Harry Keith had been at school in San Diego, California, and I had met him first as a ginger-haired schoolboy swimming in the clear pool of the Coronado Hotel. Standing dripping in blue bathing trunks one day, he had grinned at me and dared me to go down the slide in his arms. I did so, and never really got free of them afterwards.

We had not seen each other for ten years when Harry returned to the United States on leave in 1934. As soon as we came together again we made up our minds to be married, and after three days waiting for the license to mature, we were. This was completely satisfying to both of us. In that ten years apart we had both known different lives, but we had come back to each other with renewed desire. We believed now that we were fated to be together.

We were married, I had an operation on my head which cured my eyes, and we returned to Borneo. On the way out, when we had cut loose from my world and not yet touched his, I said to Harry, "I am doing what I would rather be doing than anything else in the world, with the person I'd rather be doing it with."

He said, "I hope you feel that way after four years in Borneo."

And after five years in Borneo, I still did.

Those were the facts which I gave to the publishers in 1939.

While home on leave that year we flew from the Pacific Coast to Boston for Harry to deliver some Borneo bones to the Harvard Museum, then back to Los Angeles where we purchased a secondhand car, then, accompanied by biliousness of unknown origin on my part, and malaria on Harry's, we drove down into Mexico, then up north to Canada. By August 1939 we had arrived at Victoria, British Columbia, where Harry owned a small home.

Here we intended to wait for our sailing date to England. Harry had been given extended leave in order to take a refresher course in Forestry at Oxford, and we were looking forward to three months of study and play in the England we used to know.

But before we sailed, September third came; war began, European states vanished, Germany rolled forward, and the British Empire mobilized. From that day on, Harry was under government orders. Our leave in England was canceled, and he was ordered to report in Borneo immediately. He was enjoined not to enter the armed forces; his job was Borneo, his war was there.

Every war has its tune, a song to make forever sad the hearts of those who have listened. "Roll Out the Barrel" was the enlistment tune in Victoria, played by the Canadian Scottish on every street corner then. It followed us everywhere — into the Canadian Pacific steamship office getting our tickets changed, into the telegraph office writing cables, standing on the streets looking up to read the news bulletins above our heads, news which made our hearts stand still. Into the bakery and the liquor store it followed us, onto the bus and the tram.

And it followed us into the doctor's office, where I learned that the biliousness I had been treating with calomel and salts was a baby. Heartsickness and morning sickness are forever inseparable now in my mind from "Roll Out the Barrel."

The doctor's report on me was upsetting. Because of acute anemia developed in the East as a result of prolonged malaria and much quinine, he said that I should not have the baby; in any case not to have the baby in Borneo, and in fact not to go East at all in the teeth of war.

But none of this medical advice took into consideration the fact that I was first of all my husband's wife, both believed our lives were cast together; both were now determined to live them through side by side. Faced by the war, we were especially anxious to stay together. And both wanted that son.

So, stocked up on iron and liver compounds and calcium, to supply what the Borneo vegetables didn't, with a book entitled *The First Five Years of Life*, with a trunkful of tweeds, woolens, and a velvet dinner gown for the winter in England for which we had prepared, the nicest clothes I ever had, but without baby clothes or tropical cottons, we boarded the *Empress of Russia*, the first transpacific steamer to sail after the war began.

Once on board we relaxed, though conditions were not relaxing. At least our decision was made. And the ship cut us off from the past and the future.

In Victoria we had listened to the terror of war far away. Now in the ship we were in it. It was easier there, with the submarine menace, with airplanes expected, living in life belts, and being with Harry, than waiting on shore alone, to hear. Even more I became convinced of my theory: the war was our time — we could not now escape it. To try to do so was to fail our time.

I was traveling on a British passport, as American passports were not allowed East. The *Empress of Russia* passengers were all civil service and military people returning hastily from England to their posts in the Far East, routed via the U.S.A.

because they could not get through the Suez Canal. They were all one-minded. I was the only alien idea.

I fought the war two ways, on that boat. In every smoking-room conversation America was condemned for her isolationism: if America entered the war speedily, it might be a saving factor; it was life against death. But from the American point of view, if America could stay out of the war I knew she should do so. No nation fights to save another nation; the British were engaged in battle to save themselves, and I believed that the Americans would have to enter that battle to save themselves. Only time could prove that point. Meanwhile because my heart, my life, and my material interests were with my husband, and he was British, I longed for *anything* to happen which might save the British Empire. But I saw the American point of view.

From the point of view of conversation, that was the best boat journey I have ever had. British social conversation ceased to be social and we talked about things that mattered. For once, we were not afraid to be honest with ourselves, intellectually or emotionally. On that boat in danger I got closer to the heart that is England than in four years in Sandakan.

We were caught in a typhoon off Japan, and cut off from radio communication for three days. When we finally arrived some days late at Yokohama, we read in the newspapers that the *Empress of Russia* had been sunk by a German submarine. While sending cables home to assure our family that we were not drowned, we were interrupted by the Yokohama police and taken to police headquarters. We had been unable to get Japanese visas on our passports before leaving Victoria, and had thought to get them at Yokohama, as we had done before. But this time the Japanese were not being co-operative; they successfully refused to understand anything we said, and held us in the police station throughout our stop in port.

At Nagasaki, however, we overpowered the officials with American cigarettes, and raced ashore in time to grab a broken-down taxi and motor along the magnificent coast line with the choppy bright blue waves that Japanese prints always have, and which do really exist. We drove to a mountain resort with an extinct volcano and a very alive inn, and once away from official uniforms and brass buttons we found the people of Japan were as friendly and courteous as ever.

In drydock at Nagasaki, the mystery ship was building — said to be designed as the largest, fastest, and most heavily armed ship of war in the world, walled in for secrecy. We looked at the high walls with apprehension.

Arrived at Hong Kong we were immediately in the midst of war, and the one topic of conversation was, When will the Japs start it? Most people said within six months. Women were expecting to be evacuated at any time, and wives who wished to remain with their husbands were taking up emergency nursing as an excuse for staying.

By the time we reached Borneo, the new member of the Keith family had seen the world through as many portholes as a Marine and was kicking at it. He was now known as "Little Jo." Little Jo had hung on for dear life despite many hazards. Conceived in Boston, diagnosed as biliousness, flown across the continent twice, motored from Mexico to Canada, almost sacrificed to medical caution, cradled in a Pacific typhoon, nursed in a Japanese police station, landed in a Hong Kong heat wave, delivered to Borneo in a freighter in a squall, he hung on still. It seemed that prenatal training was already trying to make Little Jo tough.

Meanwhile Mama went from strength to strength, flourishing on iron and liver compounds, vitamins, and pregnancy. Everybody said I had never looked so well, but nobody guessed the answer. Harry said it was like walking by an empty bottle in the road for years; then one day it is full of whiskey, but nobody stops to pick it up, supposing it still to be empty.

*   *   *   *   *

And so on his father's birthday in Sandakan, North Borneo, our son was born. George was nicely tanned from the moment of birth, so much so that everyone commented on it. The doctor called it jaundice, but it gave him a well-done look. He had yellow hair like Harry's but without the ginger streak and the curl. He had two complete facial expressions, both

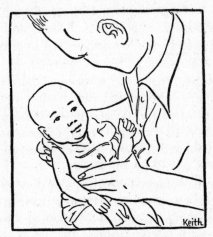

like Harry, one being acute amusement and the other acute distress, and, as with Harry, there was no doubt which was which. He had a long head shaped like mine, and my fore-head and gray-blue eyes. He had no prickly heat, and no nose. I don't know what happened to the nose because both Harry and I have quite a nose. But Harry said that a *baby* with a Roman nose would be revolting. If I ever criticized George, to hide my pride, Harry didn't like it. He didn't hide his pride; he said George was wonderful.

For others, that was the awful spring. Through whiffs of chloroform, the scent of tropical flowers, the excitement of fan mail from my book, the sizzle of whiskey sodas, the sizzle of George in his basket, the hiss of mosquitoes, the hum of cicadas, lying in the hospital, I listened to thunder over Europe, the retreat across France, the invasion of Norway and Denmark. Every radio, every paper, every visitor, told me the same thing. . . . Slowly, surely, inescapably, impending disaster settled over us. We knew we were for it; Europe was far, but Japan wasn't. There was only one good thing in our world then. That was George.

That spring for the first time Harry and I got a radio. Radios are not much good in Borneo because the island is surrounded by layers of loud noises. Everybody says, "Come and listen to my new radio. You can hear Raffles's Orchestra in Singapore, the Hong Kong Hotel, and Big Ben striking the hours!"

You go and listen, and what you hear is electrical storms enlarged, and the voice of your host saying, "I can't understand what's the matter — I got it perfectly last night!"

But Harry and I got a radio; it was awful to hear the news, but it was worse not to know, and somehow the war always came through. That radio collected violence, outrage, terror, suffering, from the corners of the whole world, and laid them at our feet in Borneo. As we sat barefoot in our living room on the hilltop, with every window open to the hot night air, to the scents of flowers and trees, with the wind coming up from the harbor with the sound of the town below, with George safe asleep upstairs in his mosquito room, with the servants' wooden clogs clattering in the back, the agony of all Europe came to us.

Homes like ours were being blown to bits, babies like George were being killed, lives like our own were destroyed and loves like ours were torn apart. Thus in the shadow of Europe's destruction, we waited with dreadful certainty for Pearl Harbor.

Again we went through the decision: Should I go home, or stay? Again I knew that my life was with my husband, and George was part of us now, he was fated, too. If we were born to war in our time, then we would face it together, all three.

*   *   *   *   *

The same year that George was born there were seven other white babies born in Sandakan, an accomplishment for our small European community where usually there was only one poor lone child. We mothers all said, "What fun! Our children won't be alone! They can have birthdays, and Christmas parties, and lots of fun together — if — if — the war doesn't come!" That was behind all we thought and said.

We were a simple group of mothers. We wheeled the kids about in their prams, compared them daily, talked about prickly heat and wet pants, brought them up by the book, had formulas for their milk, boiled their dishes, fussed about their strained foods, and wanted them to have the best of everything. We couldn't send home for much, because things always got sunk between England and Borneo, and financial regulations forbade us to shop in the U.S.A. Perambulators, powdered milk, vitamins, diapers, came from Australia.

George didn't wear clothes much. First, because I didn't have them, and couldn't get them or the material in Borneo. Second, because I believed in no clothes for babies, in a hot climate. So George always kept his infant tan.

The first year and a half of George's life nothing happened. Europe crashed, civilization teetered, the world rocked, but nothing happened. It's what goes on inside his perambulator that counts to a baby.

Only once in that eighteen months was George's future at stake. It happened like this. George slept every morning in the garden in the pram. Changing diapers in a perambulator under a green canvas tropical-top shade shelter, inside a mosquito net, is a trick for Houdini. I always warned Harry to be careful with the safety pins, for little boys are exposed, and a part of George usually got in the way.

One day I was doing the changing, working at arm's length, touch system, inside folds of mosquito net, one pin in my mouth, the other plunging through depths of diaper, when George gave a yelp. The depths had not all been diaper!

In horror I examined: the pin had gone in one side and come out the other like an aboriginal phallic decoration.

I withdrew it in horror, begging George to forgive me. He did: he only gave that one yelp, then looked at me in reproach. But the yelp brought Harry and the Chinese amah, Ah Yin. It was no use my trying to explain to them; they had felt all along that I wasn't to be trusted with George.

The wound never festered, or became infected, or even seemed very sore; I decided that despite testimony to the contrary, that must be an insensitive region. George never mentioned the matter to me again. But it took a long, long time for Harry and Ah Yin to forgive me.

George's name was "Mistah Groge." So said Ah Yin, the Chinese amah, Ah Kau, the Chinese cook, Arusap, the Murut boy, Usin, the native gardener, for "George" they could not say. Harry was the Mastah or Tuan, I was Missee or Mem, and those honorifics by which we were all carefully referred to were symbolic of the Borneo we lived in then. Mistah Groge was wonderful, all our household said. The house just opened and closed for him; he was the reason for our being. He fed well, slept well, howled well, and never mewled or puked.

But Anjibi and Herman, her husband, our Borneo gibbon apes, never forgave me. Anjibi, the big female, silver gray with black cameo face of velvet and eyes of beauty and sorrow, and small Herman, grown large now, had been ours for years. They lived in a large wire house in the garden built around the great *chempaka* tree.

Although we believed they were happily wedded, these two had no offspring. Apes seldom breed in captivity, and they saw no reason for our doing so.

I wanted George to know them and love them, I wanted George to not be afraid. On my visits to the apes now I carried a naked baby: when I held Anjibi's limp black hand in mine, there was a pink fist fastened to my arm; when I talked

Keith

with her of mature grown-up things that we understood, there was a baby's gurgle to interrupt; when I told her that she was beautiful, very beautiful, she knew that her beauty was nothing to me, compared to George's mere being.

Where once I had held Anjibi, I now held a small hairless thing. This thing couldn't move, act, or do the things that Anjibi could; it wasn't beautiful or strong; but she knew that it was bone of my bone, race of my race, belonging to the group of men — and it was mine. Without one lift of its powerless fist, this hairless soft thing had destroyed her charm.

And Anjibi remembered that something had once existed between herself and me — some bond, some tie, not of blood, but of sympathy and love. Was it there now still? This was the enigma of her existence. Anjibi didn't think so, but she was always trying to find out.

One day when the door of her house was carelessly closed, Anjibi unfastened the gate and came out. She started to look for George. To the pram first in the garden to see; then, as he wasn't there, upstairs. Long, loping, silent steps and swings, through the house that once had been hers, into the bedroom she had let me share with her, then across the hall to the other side, and there he was!

There was this hairless ape that had taken Anjibi's place, but he was installed in a wire mosquito house inside that room. Now here was Jibi loose, and the baby captive in the cage! Jibi's melancholy face presses against the wire of his cage, her eyes black and questioning. George stares back. He doesn't care.

Then Jibi sings. The long, high melody sweeps the room. There is no other call like it in the jungle; it has the madness and beauty and sadness of every living wild thing. It thrills you and frightens you, and takes your heart. George sucks his thumb. Anjibi sings.

Arusap, Ah Yin, Harry, come running. Ah Yin calls, "Jibi's

loose! Mastah! Missee! Get Mistah Groge! She'll hurt him. Go, Jibi, go! Bad Jibi! Bad, bad Jibi! Go 'way!"

Harry to me, "Oh, you're here, are you, Agnes? Better get Jibi back to her house. I'll take George."

So I am relegated to the apes again! I sulkily say, "I'll take George. I'm *his* mother, not Jibi's."

But then I am ashamed. I look at Jibi, now perched on top of the walled partition between the rooms. She looks at me; even if she could speak, there is nothing we could say. Poor beautiful sad wild thing. Hers is the fate that comes to every living being, animal or human. The king is dead, long live the king.

In 1941 the Sandakan Junior League was formed. Its members met daily on the wide green lawn of Government House, where black and white trousered Chinese amahs pushed large Australian perambulators bulging with the British offspring of Sandakan society. A casual visitor would have thought our governor very prolific; in fact, I believe they did.

Here in the ample Government House grounds, under the pleasant trees, surrounded by bright blooming balsams and canna, was *the* place to be. This was the infants' smart club life, and the amahs' mecca: this was society.

Every afternoon Ah Yin put on her starched white trousers, her neat, tight, high-throated blouse, put George in his handsomest breeks, placed him in the pram surrounded by stuffed elephants, zebras, rabbits the biggest she could find, said "Good-bye Missee, I take Mistah Groge Gov'ment House now," and did.

The participants in that swank club life were: Susan, Alastair, David and Derek, Sheena and Ranald, Carol and Michael, Edith and Eddie (the Chinese Consul's children), Jimmy, Fenella and Fiona, Carlotto, and George.

It was the year for birthday parties, too. The first one was at Susan's house in the garden behind the high hedge. The mothers came. Each child brought the best present it could find. We had ice cream, cake, sandwiches, sweets, and tea. The children were round and plump, well-fed and satisfied — they had to be urged to finish their plates. The mothers

swapped stories. The amahs had their own party after we finished eating. The children went to sleep in their prams.

The biggest birthday party was at Alastair's house. Here on the hill was a beautiful garden; the native gardener cut lawns, hacked hedges and trees, but Teresa Mitchel, the British hostess, made the flowers bloom there. Here were spectacular azaleas, orchids, roses, begonia, cosmos. Here Teresa dug holes, said magic words over seeds, sprayed love and caution where I sprayed insecticide, patted with charmed hands at the roots, and the next day came out and found a flower that nobody else could grow.

Here in this garden Alastair celebrated his first birthday.

That was September. All the children were invited, all the amahs, all the mamas, and the poppas were to come and collect us and take us home. None of the mamas called each other by their first names then. To each other we were still Mrs. Mitchel, Mrs. Robinson, Mrs. Cho, and so on. I hadn't seen Mrs. Cho, the Chinese Consul's wife, since she had changed Eddie's food, and I asked her how he was doing on Lactogen; she said he was doing fine.

After the poppas came, we sat in the twilight and looked out over the valley. "The Japanese will be sitting here looking out over this valley a year from now," Harry said. After that the party broke up.

There was little formal social life now, men were working too hard. Many younger men had enlisted despite regulations, and it left Borneo very short-manned. Government men were working all day on their jobs, and all night on emergency war work. Our community was limited, hemmed in, cut off. We couldn't get extra help, or supplies.

No one dressed any more for dinners; no one gave dinners, we couldn't afford to waste food. People dropped in for conversation only, something they had never done before in Sandakan. Men sat down with their shirt collars open. Everybody said, "Let's never go back to the old formal life again. This is one good thing the war has done!"

About this time I did the smartest thing that I ever did. I ordered from Singapore at great expense a concentrated form of haliveroil especially suited to infant feeding, and contained in very small vials. One small vial was a month's supply, one drop being the daily dose. I purchased sufficient dosage for a year and a half, although I couldn't believe that if the Japanese did take Borneo they would hold it more than six months. But I just thought I'd be safe for once. I also purchased three hundred calcium tablets. These, if we were cut off from proper food, would insure George's teeth and bones. I packed these supplies away for emergency.

Early in 1941 the American Naval Observer, Commander

Murphy, with his young secretary, Rogers, came. We assumed they were American Intelligence Service. This set everybody by the ear. "If America is doing this, she must be scared! They must expect something soon. It won't be long!"

Murphy and Rogers were very American; they *would* play golf with their shirttails outside their trousers, just because it was cooler. This was almost as upsetting as the war, in Sandakan.

But in the end everybody agreed that they were grand people. Of course they were crazy, but then they were Americans. And what American Beauty cocktails Commander Murphy mixed! And what heroic "small eats" they served with all their drinks — olives, anchovies, salted almonds, fish eggs, *pâté de foie gras,* all things that had to come out from the States now. *We* couldn't get them at all, because we couldn't buy out of the sterling bloc.

In the last months of 1941 Commander Murphy became a disturbing element in Sandakan. He told the women they ought to get out, go home, leave the East — and soon! Unrest was already in us, and he urged it on.

Harry and George and I went down by the *Baynain,* a tiny coastal steamer, to Dutch Borneo for a trip. That was George's first boat trip and he liked it. We visited the oil fields at Tarakan. Every hill, nook, cranny, tree, field, hole, house, shrub, hid a gun; every inch was defended, or mined to be blown up, when the end came. The European women had been evacuated.

The Dutchmen talked to us. "We are ready. We expect them soon. We will fight for every inch, and then we will destroy and burn until we are killed." The iron was in their Dutch souls.

Shortly after George was born I had been asked to take an emergency job in Sandakan in order to relieve man power for war work. The men in responsible offices were overworked and overworried. Their children at home in England were being bombed, their sons were being killed, their homes destroyed. They had a real war, a much worse war than Harry and I, who had our people on a safe continent.

I didn't want to do war work; I wanted to finish the Borneo novel which I had started. But with the world crashing about us I couldn't sit and do nothing. I hated Red Cross, and knitting, so I took a war job instead.

Now in Sandakan invariably when people met, both civilian and government, we argued the question of whether or not women and children were going to be evacuated by government order. Evacuation would remove the responsibility for the decision from us. As I was determined to stay, and felt I had a good excuse now, as I had a job as well as a husband, I hoped that no evacuation order would be given. It never was.

I believe, however, that this was wrong; I believe that the women and children should have been evacuated by order. The decision should not have been left to the individual. In wartime the individual is not in a position to know military or defense facts. Those who know these facts should take the responsibility of deciding who may stay in a war zone. It is evading responsibility to refuse such a decision.

In my own case I take full responsibility for staying. I was under no delusions about security. I knew the war was coming to the East, and that the Nipponese were coming to Borneo. The Japanese themselves had been writing pamphlets for us in English (the *Bulletin of the South Seas*) and sending them to us for several years back, mentioning just those facts. But what I did not know, or even dream of, was that the Nips would be in possession of Borneo for three and two-thirds years.

At this time I also considered the possibility of hiding with George in a jungle camp, beyond reach of the invaders, when the Japanese came. By this plan I would be able to stay on the job with Harry until the very moment of the country's surrender. The success of this escape theory was based upon the supposition that the Japanese would not be able to hold Borneo longer than six months, or a year.

With this in mind Harry and I established a jungle hide-out deep in a forest reserve, and stocked it with food, medicines, bedding, and clothes. We also sent out a number of cases of valuable books, and some silver.

I wrote an article telling of this jungle camp and my plan for escape to it, not giving its location. I sent this to the *Atlantic Monthly*, where, ironically, it was published the very month the Japanese took us captive in Borneo.

Future events proved that if we had hidden away we would certainly have been found and brought back to captivity. Our books and goods which we had hidden were in time revealed to the invaders, and brought in to Sandakan and confiscated by the Japanese. If we had been captured likewise, our fate would have been problematical: time has disclosed two versions of what happened to people who tried to escape. In one version they are well-treated, but in more cases ill-treated, and in most cases murdered.

As weeks went on and the war came closer I gradually abandoned any idea of escape. Since I had chosen to stay in the tide of war, it was futile to paddle with my hands against the flood.

During this gradual descent of disaster I had two comforting facts to hold to. First, I believed completely in the rightness of my staying; it wasn't unselfish, it might not be wise, it might prove a mistake — but it was the only thing for *me* to do.

Second, I had a few good friends on whom I could rely. Two of these had chosen to stay, as I had, and were just as convinced of their rightness as I. And whatever fate came to the women after the Japanese came in, these two women and I would share. Neither of them had children, and both were very good to George.

Violet Rutter was George's godmother. She was tall and stately, with a graciousness which came partly from tremendous faith in the goodness and rightness of people and God, and partly from being born and bred in the right places. Her ash-blond hair was short and curly all over her head, her fair skin and blue eyes were all England. Her hands, long-fingered, sensitive-tipped, touched naturally and beautifully the stringed instruments which she played, her violin, violoncello, and viole d'amour.

Her husband was a government man, brilliant and sardonic. He was much too subtle for Violet and me, we both agreed; Reggie was thinking circles about us while we were still trying to find the point from which he began.

The other friend was Penelope Gray. Penelope spoke through her garden. Her strong, green-tipped fingers made buds and blooms come from every plant she touched. Penelope had lived in more different government houses in Borneo than anyone else, and in every one she left a typical garden. People who came after her looked at the garden and said, "Oh, Penelope Gray has lived here." With well-shaped beds, and well-laid-out borders, in her garden flourished all the sweet, deep-shaded, delicate-scented, fine-foliaged flowers that liked the fogs and dews of England; somehow even in Borneo she fooled them into thinking they belonged.

Penelope looked like her English garden and dressed like it. She was delicately made, fragile but resistant, fresh and bright and real. Every birthday, Christmas, anniversary, would come a bouquet of English flowers from her to me.

It was boat day, and mail day, and Monday. And it was the day after Pearl Harbor. Harry and I had heard the news at 6 A.M. on the radio, while we drank early coffee. We told Ah Yin and the servants. Ah Yin said, "Maybe very good, Missee. Now America fight."

Then suddenly, "Missee! You take Mistah Groge and go home! Singapore boat go today. If Japs come here, very bad!"

Harry and I went down to Sandakan to work that morning. It was very hot, everybody was writing mail madly in order to get it out on what would probably be the last Singapore boat. Also people kept an eye on the sky, and ears cocked for planes. A few women were packing hurriedly; they were getting out by the boat.

Would the boat leave, or not? Yes, it would. No, it wouldn't. But it did leave as usual, at midnight. It was the last boat to Singapore. It never returned.

We settled down then to waiting, and listening to bad news. The Japs weren't Japs, now, they were Nipponese Conquerors. They poured over the East like hot lava.

Every time I met Commander Murphy he spoke his refrain, "Get out, get out, get out."

And it still wasn't too late to get out. Shortly before Christmas the small coastal steamer *Baynain*, the one on which we had gone to Tarakan, was ordered to leave for the Dutch East Indies, in order to keep it out of the hands of the Nipponese. It was made available to evacuate any local women who wished to go.

That was a hard week end. We went through the problem again and again. I was determined to stay. The more I waited, the more I was determined.

I met Susan's mother, Alastair's mother, Carol's mother, Sheena's mother, David's mother, all of the mothers. The unspoken question was there: "Are you going? Are you staying? Are you afraid?" But nobody spoke it. We wouldn't put it in words.

Then night came, and the *Baynain* sailed. Only six women were on her. That was the last ship out of port. After that, fate really closed down.

Hong Kong fell. That was all right. We'd made up our minds to that. Malay Peninsula sweated and trembled. That wasn't so good. We hadn't made up our minds to that. Singapore itself seemed unsound. Oh, no, Singapore *couldn't* fall!

The radio air was full of messages of condolence from

Home Offices to besieged garrisons and falling states that were crumbling to bits unaided: "Good-bye. Be of good cheer. We are sorry we cannot help you. You are doing your duty. God bless you."

The Japs took Kuching, Sarawak, Borneo on Christmas Day. We smelled smoke and saw flames. Then they went north to Miri. They didn't get tired at all, just kept going, and walked into Jesselton, North Borneo, our own state, in early January.

At home in Sandakan our government orders were: "Destroy all resources. Follow policy of denial and passive resistance. Remain at your posts. Meet the enemy, resist passively, do not co-operate. We cannot defend you. Good-bye!"

So we destroyed. All over the golf course went high-octane gas and petrol. Launches and boats were sunk. Machinery was destroyed, sawmills were dismantled, saws were sunk in the sea. All bridges were burned behind us, with no place to go in front.

Commander Murphy called up one night at midnight. His voice was excited. Standing by Harry at the phone I could hear Murphy's voice as plainly as Harry's:

"We're getting out tonight on a small boat. Will your wife and George come with us? Get her out, I tell you! Get her home! Well, ask her. . . . She doesn't want to come? Well, I'm telling you, she ought to. I wouldn't trust these Japs. Well, all right then, tell her good-bye. Tell her I wish she'd come. If she doesn't . . . I don't know! Well, good-bye. Good luck. We'll come back for you with the Navy as soon as we can!"

That was the last link with the outside.

One morning in the middle of January Harry telephoned me. "There are some Americans in town. They escaped from Manila on New Year's afternoon, an hour before the Japs got in. They came down to Borneo by native boat. They're here in my office. Come down and see them."

Those Americans were George and Marjorie Colley, mar-

ried two weeks before, Betty and Harry Weber, and Dr.
Ashton Laidlaw. George Colley and Harry Weber were en-
gineers, used in building Manila defenses, and Ashton Laidlaw was an American dentist who had left Shanghai for the
United States via Manila, and had been almost caught there.
George and Marjorie, the honeymooners, had been married
in Manila. George, who was bursting with vitality, was, I
learned, a graduate of the University of California from my
year. Marjorie was very young, with the extreme slenderness
of the American girl, a mark not of frailness, but of speed
and vitality. I found her fascinating to look at, with golden
skin, long rope-colored hair, and hazel eyes.

Betty Weber was backbone-of-the-country stuff — sound
looks, warm heart, downright, and a swell cook, they said.
Weber was tall and fine-looking. Dr. Laidlaw was convincing
and pleasant, the kind that wears well.

They had beaten their way down to Borneo in a small boat,
and were fed-up with seasickness and escape. They were prepared to relax momentarily in the peace and security of Borneo, which, they assured us, nobody wanted except the English!

Harry quoted Murphy then, and said, "Get out! Get out!
Get another boat and get out. Keep going. Don't stop here.
We have to stay — you don't!"

"Aw, nobody wants Borneo but you!" they said.

So they rested and relaxed, and two days later the Japs
moved closer. Harry warned them. Hastily the Colleys,
Webers, and Laidlaw got together a boat and crew, and
headed out of the harbor. Too late: they couldn't get far
enough away; they got caught.

Saturday afternoon Harry heard that the Japs had been
sighted off the coast of Borneo in small launches, fighting their
way through a heavy storm, headed in our direction.

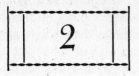

2

Dark Hours

THE darkest hours of all my life followed.

In Sandakan there were then forty-five European men, twenty-four wives, and eleven children to offer passive resistance. The plan was that, when warning of a Japanese landing came, the women and children were to go immediately to one of three different places, in various parts of the town, as it was feared to leave us alone in our homes when the soldiers came in. When this plan was made I had asked to remain at my own home, and had been refused. The government men were of course to go to their posts.

Three residences were chosen for the women to stay in: the Mitchel place on the hill where the children had their biggest and best birthday party, the home of Mr. Phillipps on the waterfront at the other end of town, and Government House, which was my place to go. Government House was only five minutes' walk from home, and my suitcase was already there.

All day Sunday the rain poured down. Gray sheets of it closed us off from the harbor, from the hills and the road, from everything but the dripping trees in the garden. There was no sound of the town, of the apes, of the servants, of anything but the rain all day.

Then the telephone rang. "There's a vile storm at sea. Perhaps they won't make it, in those small launches! But be ready. The Japs have passed Kudat, we know."

Six o'clock came, and again the telephone rang. "Go to Government House immediately, please."

I told Harry good-bye in our bedroom. I am very bad at good-byes. Every nasty thing I have ever said reproaches me then, and all my love overwhelms me: I want to put it all in one moment. I said good-bye, and I added, "If only we could be together!"

Harry said, "We will never part like this again!"

George had his best blue checkered pants on, and his blue pullover jersey, and there was milk on his chin. He carried his panda bear, and a cigarette tin with shells in it. He was excited and his blue eyes were very bright. His round forehead was smooth and unworried. Thank God he's so young, I thought, too young to know!

I took George and went downstairs. Harry followed. He didn't say anything to George; he couldn't.

I put George in Harry's arms for one moment; then I put him in the pram and tucked the waterproof cover over him, and put up the hood. Then with Ah Yin holding the umbrella over us we trundled down the road. Harry watched from the veranda. George popped his head out and shouted good-bye, as usual. But from behind him there came no answer.

At Government House that night I sat with the other women in the long living room while we talked about things that meant nothing to us. Some sewed, some knitted. I just sat. Then we went up to bed.

I got up several times that night to look at George. He slept. I wondered if Harry was still at home, waiting the signal. I looked out of the window; the rain had stopped. I went to bed again. And I learned to pray.

We got up early the next morning, and the women met before breakfast on the veranda; we were gray in the face. The children were fine: quarrelsome, hungry, and noisy.

His Excellency the Governor and the Government Secretary were in the reception room waiting. Waiting for the

Japanese to find out what we had done to the town and its resources.

That was seven o'clock on Monday morning, January 19, 1942. The storm-battered Japanese launches had anchored offshore the night before in the dark. Now they came to the wharf, they were landing. The British Resident, East Coast, was at the wharf waiting for them, standing alone, unarmed. In the prow of the first Japanese landing launch was the British Resident, West Coast, unarmed. The Japanese had brought him along and placed him there to get shot first, in case we shot. I always wondered what these two Englishmen said as they passed each other.

Then a shot was heard. We thought it was the Resident being shot by the Japanese. It turned out later to have been a European who had committed suicide in his home.

After the shot, noise, excitement, confusion came up to us from the town. Before this, the stream of Chinese women, coolies, and market people on the road had been flowing past Government House into Sandakan; now the stream started to flow the other way, out of town. Faster, faster, faster; soon the people started to run.

The phone rang. The Governor was to go immediately, quickly, without delay, down into town, and be interviewed by the angry Japanese generals.

Now on the crest of the stream of Asiatics racing past Government House came the Japanese troops. Baggy-breeched, heavy-booted, small men with big guns, bayonets fixed, they poured over garden and lawn. They surrounded, entered, raced through Government House, and stationed themselves inside and out. They were shock troops; they needn't have been, there was nothing tough about us.

They threatened and browbeat, bullied and frightened us; they moved in with us. In the first few days they took our watches, fountain pens, knives, and any other belongings they wanted, if we didn't get them hidden first.

They tried to get drunk; we locked up the liquor, then poured it out. Sometimes we bluffed them; more often they called the bluff. Sometimes they were kindly, sometimes they played with the children, but always it was with a gun by their side. Charming them was like charming a cobra: you never knew when it would strike. But they didn't kill us, or rape us.

From that day until September 11, 1945, we were to live in captivity. Violent things happened about me, and to me. But in all of my life there is nothing for sheer mental terror to equal those forty-eight hours before the Japanese came.

When the Japanese fully realized the lack of supplies on hand, they didn't like it a bit. They said it was an act of war on our part to destroy these things, and that this had washed out their first idea of making a peaceful occupation. It seems they had expected us to save our oil, petrol, scrap iron, motors, launches, industrial machinery, and high octane to trade with them, in exchange for our lives, and the spirit we had shown in destroying them was not friendly.

One young man was actually caught red-handed on the golf course, pouring out petrol while the Japs marched in. They sentenced him to immediate death. But somebody forgot to execute the sentence. A few days passed, the Governor pleaded for him, and the young man, who drew marvelously well, made funny pictures for his guards. More days passed and nothing happened. He was never reprieved, but he just wasn't executed.

They interned all the government men in the second-class ward of the Sandakan Civil Hospital, while they decided whom to shoot. They argued about this for a week. During this period the men became familiar with the Japanese methods of extorting information, and their guards went through the ward hourly throughout the night, deliberately awakening all the men. Then as the Japanese generals could not agree on whom to shoot, they decided instead to ask certain of the men to come out and work with them.

I remained at Government House two days. Then, as I knew my home was being looted, and I was at that time making attempts to save things, I asked the Japanese military authorities to permit me to reoccupy my house. In those days, the Japanese termed their relationship to women "protective custody," and under this relationship I was granted permission to reoccupy the house on the hill.

The reason for this may have been that I had been introduced to the enemy through my book, the Japanese translation of which had been widely read in Japan. Its subject, Borneo, was a country they were determined to take, because of its oil. I thanked God then that I had made no rash statements about the Japanese. If everyone who writes a book knew he would sometime be helpless in the hands of his characters, literature would grow tame.

So I reopened my house, with George, Ah Yin, and Ah Kau beside me. Soldiers were billeted on both sides of me, but my house, the military police said, was to be left alone. This meant that once in every forty-eight hours, when I called the interpreter, the soldiers were turned out; the rest of the time I held the fort with difficulty. The military police told me to tell the soldiers not to come in. I took this seriously and tried it at first; then I realized it must have been a joke. Ah Yin and Ah Kau were brave as lions, practically spitting in soldiers' faces, but in spite of them the soldiers moved the furniture out from under us.

At this time I asked the military police if soldiers were authorized to remove what they wished from my house. They answered that they had the right to take anything they needed for the prosecution of the war. I found that colored shirts, pens, clasp knives, silk stockings, pillows and drapes, sweaters, cheese and alcoholic drinks and cigarettes, all came under this head.

One day I took a hammer and nails and nailed up the downstairs windows and doors with bars of wood. Then we retreated upstairs to live. A Japanese came slumping across the lawn from the billet next door. He was wearing a blue silk shirt of Harry's, and Harry's gray trousers and slippers. He tried all the doors, then pounded and roared. Seeing no uniform, I stuck my head out of the window and shouted in English, "Get out! Go away! This is my house. I have permission to live here."

He understood. He went away. He came back with a soldier with a bayonet who started to knock in the door. I went down and opened it. I had George in my arms. The man made violent motions with his fists at me, but didn't really hit me.

I put George down in the next room with his blocks, and returned to try again to explain that I had permission to be here. The man became more angry. I went to the telephone to call the military police, thinking they would explain to him on the phone. He struck the phone from me, and struck me. George picked up his blocks, and started to heave them at him through the door, one by one. The man bellowed like a bull and tore at George with his fist open. Ah Yin grabbed George and faced the man, both of them livid through their yellow skins. He subsided. But I am sure he would not have struck George; the Japs were not brutal to children.

Then he called the military police. They came. They explained to me that the man had read *Land Below the Wind* and had intended to make a friendly call on me. When he found the doors were barred, he was insulted. When I stuck my head out and shouted at him, both he and the Emperor were insulted, as he was a Japanese captain, just relaxing temporarily in Harry's silk shirt and gray trousers.

It took me three hours to apologize adequately for a captain. At the end of that time, both the military police and the captain advised me again to close my doors tightly, and not to let the soldiers in!

Sandakan was now being looted by the criminal element amongst Asiatic civilians, as well as by Japanese and by unemployed coolies. As the sawmills had no machinery, there were large numbers of idle, hungry men about. We always slept with golfsticks on the pillow, as they were the only weapon left to us by the Japanese.

Meanwhile it was decided by the Governor of Borneo, on his own judgment and in concurrence with Japanese demands, that certain men in essential services should be released from internment and should attempt to work with the Japanese for the good of the civilian occupants of the country. The services thus classified were medical, police, city water supply, and food production.

The country had at no time supplied its own essential foods, and it was now expected that it would shortly be cut off from the outside. My husband, as Director of Agriculture, was considered indispensable for the purpose of food production, and he was released from imprisonment for this purpose only.

He returned to our home with me. It was a heartbreaking reunion. We thanked God at being together again, and took new heart. But I found that the nervous strain was worse when he was home. I was ready to put up with whatever I had to from the conquerors, but he was not ready to do so for me. When Ah Yin and I were alone together we could run, fight, weep, hide, evade, plead, and, if the time came, give in. When Harry was home I constantly trembled for fear chivalry would force him to resent something on our behalf.

When living in such circumstances, working with the enemy is impossible, and working against him is also impossible. I learned truly then the abject attitude which best befits the vanquished. We had food enough, and strength enough, at that time, to resent in our whole beings the humiliations which came. Physical disintegration had not started; the complete panorama of degradation was not yet revealed to us.

At first I occasionally walked on the street. I was ridiculed, spat at, struck by soldiers; not always, but frequently enough to soon keep me at home.

One day three soldiers came to the house when I was in bed with an attack of malaria. Ah Yin told them I was sick. They insisted that I come down. I put on a negligee and went down to the veranda, where they sat drinking our beer. They showed me a map, and asked me to name the roads and the houses on it for them. This I did as well as I could.

I was perspiring and the wind on the veranda was cool, and I began to shiver. They insisted that I must name all the houses, which I could not do, as the map was not correctly drawn. I felt very ill then, and was shivering, and sat down almost fainting. They became angry with me for sitting down, and with the map for being wrong. They shouted, and struck me, and when I stood up they pushed me roughly down and struck me again and again. Then they left.

I went upstairs to bed, shaking. I became very ill. I was pregnant at that time. That afternoon I had a miscarriage.

We lived like this for four months. You do not die when such things happen. They are not killing matters. In warfare, they aren't even serious ones.

It was three o'clock in the afternoon and very hot, just a month after I had lost the baby. I was lying undressed on my bed, reading *The First Five Years of Life*. George was in the bedroom pulling out the drawers of my dressing table and investigating the contents. How much like the apes he was in his curiosity, I thought. He was into mischief, I knew, but it was keeping him quiet.

The book advised me not to despair over infant bad habits, which disappear automatically as the child grows, new ones developing with each new stage. As there is always something to worry about, why worry?

"George, take your thumb out of your mouth!"

I returned to the book now, comparing George as he was at two years with George as he ought to be. Almost normal! Anyway, the book says don't worry! Yes, George walks, runs, sleeps, eats, talks when he has something to say, is smart enough to get what he wants from everyone, and to control intake and output. O.K., George!

Ah Yin's bare feet come running up the stairs; she enters my room hastily. "Missee! Missee! Japanese soldier say come quick! I tell him Missee sick, Missee in bed. He say must come."

I knew enough now not to argue with the enemy. I put on my black day kimono, took my lipstick away from George, put the powder box where he couldn't reach it, pushed him inside the mosquito room in which I had been lying, and went downstairs. I never heard the words "Japanese soldier" now without a sickness of heart. George's howls of rage at being left behind followed me.

The soldier stood at the door with his rifle, and handed me a mimeographed piece of paper. I read it. It was an order for all Europeans to appear at the Nipponese Military Administration Headquarters at 3 p.m. on May 12, 1942. Today, this very hour.

I went upstairs and dressed quickly in my white sharkskin suit. Whatever was coming, I knew it wouldn't be good. I told Ah Yin to keep George, and I ran all the way down the hill in the sun, to Japanese headquarters in the old government Secretariat Building.

There I found Harry, and about thirty men and women, the last vestiges of white authority in Sandakan. Harry and I said little. The room was stifling with heat, sweat, nerves, and strained laughter. What was the joke? Nothing. What did we laugh at? Nothing. We only laughed in order not to cry.

When the future is so bad you can't face it — but you must face it, and you wish to face it — what can you do? Human beings are hard put to find the right reaction, when strength is being tested too far: some scream, some cry, some become angry, some laugh. We guessed at the news that we had been assembled to hear that day. We were trying to take it without tears, so we laughed.

There was an hour of waiting, then the Japanese Commander in Chief appeared, and addressed us at length in Japanese. While Japanese interpreters argued with each other as to the exact text of the Commander's words, we got the drift unaided: We were to be ready to leave for prison camp in an hour's time. We were permitted to take one suitcase each. The men would be imprisoned separately from the women.

We knew it had to come. It was one step further along the road to the end.

Harry and I returned to our house under guard. We went

upstairs and finished packing our already half-packed suitcases. In my suitcase I placed a Bible, a dictionary, a *Roget's
Thesaurus*, and writing materials, two pairs of canvas shoes,
a pair of California play shoes, two sharkskin sport dresses,
three pairs of shorts and three men's shirts, two pairs of slacks,
three woolen sweaters, a rose-colored kimono, nightgowns
and underthings, wool socks and stockings, two berets, bath
towels and sheets, sanitary goods, a sewing kit, a few pieces
of jewelry, four pairs of scissors, documents of identification
and nationality, a medicine flask of whiskey and an assortment
of necessary drugs in small quantities. And hidden throughout all my clothing in pockets and hems were George's tiny
haliveroil bottles and the calcium tablets.

We had already packed a separate small leather medicine
case, equipped completely with all drug supplies.

In George's suitcase I packed a number of cotton sun suits,
a few napkins for emergency, two pairs of canvas shoes, socks,
several wool jerseys and shawls, and all his baby bedding,
small blankets, and so on, some cotton material, and a number
of his playthings.

We made up a small bedding roll, and also rolled up separately a small camp mattress. We had been told to bring only
one suitcase each, but hoped we might be allowed more — although I knew I must be limited by my own carrying capacity, and the fact that I had George, in addition to the luggage,
to maneuver.

We filled a packing case with concentrated foodstuffs especially suited to a small child's needs, such as powdered
milk, tinned butter, fortified milk, cereal, sugar, honey, glu-
cose, prunes, raisins, corned beef. We also packed a small
basket with china.

I took George from Ah Yin, who was in hysterics, hugging
George, sobbing frantically, begging me to take her with us,
which I could not do, saying that we would all be killed,
which I thought probable. Then we were ready to leave our

bedroom. Harry and I kissed each other good-bye, and Harry kissed George. Even George knew this time that there was trouble, and whimpered in a puzzled way. I saw lying on my bed *The First Five Years of Life,* open where I had left it. I pushed it into my bag.

We dragged our luggage downstairs. We had done a lot in that hour. There was nothing to do now but wait for the military truck that was coming to take us. We went to the storeroom and unburied from their hiding places two bottles. One was very fine, very old Three Star Brandy; the other was not so fine, not so old. We went out on the veranda. The guard was at the door. We gave him the not-so-fine-or-old bottle, and we sat down ourselves with the other.

We drank our bottle. We wanted something to stupefy our senses and slow down our reactions; something to make these last moments of parting bearable, to make these first steps on the long road ahead of us endurable. We wanted courage, drunken if no other. We drank our bottle. It did absolutely nothing for us. Our strained nerves could not be reached by alcohol.

The guard drank his bottle; he went under the bushes sniffling; he spoke good English now. "I feel so very sorry for you — so sorry that the father and the mother and the child must be parted. It is so very sad. It makes me cry." He cried.

The military truck arrived. We walked out of our home. My mother and father still hung in their photos on the wall, in the dining room were the green crystal goblets of which we were proud, on the shelves were the ancient Celadon bowls. There was no place in our luggage for sentiment.

Thus we turned our back on all our worldly possessions. On things irreplaceable: on Harry's library of Borneo books, perhaps the most complete in existence, his one self-indulgence, collected through sixteen years; on the Chinese pottery we had bargained and gambled for with excitement with peddlers; on our wedding presents with their sentiment and extravagance; on my wardrobe of beautiful clothes — a weakness, but I loved them! On all the pleasant household goods that other people had said to leave at home — "They're too good for Borneo!" But we didn't look at it like that. Thus we turned our backs on these things. They were material. There was just one thing to fight for now . . . our lives.

We left Ah Yin and Ah Kau on the veranda crying, Jibi and Herman in their cages calling, the guard under the bushes sniffling, and we went down the path to the truck.

The Japanese officer in charge allowed us to put our suitcases and the bedding roll on, but he refused the rolled-up mattress, he threw off the leather medicine box, and he threw off George's box of foodstuffs. A tin of powdered milk broke open and spilled in the dirt on the road; life and health in tins and bottles, mixed with the Borneo soil. The truck started. I did not look back.

The next stop was the Hills' house. Susan and her mother got on. They were escorted by a different Japanese officer. Their suitcases were loaded on, bedding rolls, basket with foodstuffs, and Susan's large red rocking horse. George eyed the rocking horse and then me balefully; why hadn't I brought his?

At the wharf the men were separated from the women. We were searched for money and it was confiscated. We women compared notes on what we had brought; some had been permitted more than others, according to the varying whim of each officer. And here on the wharf they were, the children of the birthday parties: Alastair, Sheena, Ranald, Derek and David, Carol and Michael, Susan and George.

Twenty-four women and nine children packed themselves onto a very small launch. It was a twenty-minute ride to Berhala Island, but with Japanese military efficiency, with their backing and filling, we made it in five hours. Like Harry and me, most people had sought for Dutch courage, and on the launch reaction set in. Here in the dusk and the dark, we wept, prayed, laughed, cursed the enemy, and sang lullabies to the children. It was ten o'clock at night, the children had no supper, they were tired, excited, frightened, they cried until they dozed.

Finally we arrived at Berhala. The Lepers' Settlement was on one side of the island and we were on the other, about a mile distant, at the abandoned Quarantine Station. Here on the broken wharf in the dark we unloaded children, selves, and luggage. Most of us had flashlights, and by the aid of these, carrying children and dragging suitcases, we climbed over the broken wharf to the land and followed the path to the filthy wooden building which had once been the Government Quarantine Station.

That leaking, rotting, unventilated, unlighted, wooden-windowed building was retribution on us Europeans for allowing such a place to exist for the housing of anyone. It had once been used for quarantine of Asiatic arrivals, and in this same building we had imprisoned some of the Japanese internees five months before, when North Borneo was still British. When I entered the building that night I wished that we had never initiated the idea of any human being occupying it.

In the dark we were greeted by women from whom we had been cut off for three and a half months, the wives of the government men who had not been released to work under the Japanese. These women had been interned together in one home in Sandakan, while their husbands had been interned at Government House. Now today, with the sudden order from Japanese headquarters that all Europeans with the exception of doctors were to be placed on Berhala Island in complete isolation and custody, these women and we ourselves had come together again. They had arrived on Berhala in the afternoon.

Here amongst them is Penelope Gray. Here also are Mar-

jorie Colley and Betty Weber, the two American women who escaped from the Philippines, and who were recaptured when the Japanese occupied Sandakan. And here are Mrs. Cho, Edith and Eddie, the Chinese Consul's family.

The sound of men's voices in the distance tells us now that the men are being landed on the island too. They cannot be very far.

Now in the darkness, with every need for calm and accomplishment, that bottle of brandy suddenly takes effect. We have no food or drinking water, for we are afraid to use unboiled water from the tank outside. We have no fire, beds, baths, or lights; the children are exhausted, frightened, crying; they cling to us tightly, making work even more hard. Now is the time when I need cool thought, clear head, and good wind.

Instead I find I am stiff. Only with great concentration can I manage to hang up my mosquito net and lay down the blanket inside. Then in my white sharkskin suit, now mussy and dirty, with rats and cockroaches beside me, George and I lie down together on the floor.

It is our first night of imprisonment. We are soft, weak, foolish, and helpless.

Some days later in the prison compound, behind a thirty-foot wooden boarding, we listen to the first of many addresses by Japanese commanding officers, expressing the following sentiment: "You are a fourth-class nation now. Therefore your treatment will be fourth-class, and you will live and eat as coolies. In the past you have had proudery and arrogance! You will get over it now!"

Throughout three and a half years they did their best to cure us of proudery and arrogance.

3

Strange Nursery

OUR children in captivity were all less than four years old, three of them were only six months. One child was still in the mother's womb when we entered Berhala prison camp.

It was a strange nursery. There was no furniture, and we slept and ate on the floor, which was so rotten that when the children jumped on it they broke through. Centipedes lived under us, and rats lived over us. The rats were so numerous that the noise of their fighting, playing, eating, and copulating kept us awake at night. They were so hungry they ate soap and buttons as well as food, and so aggressive that when we got off our bedding rolls in the dark they bit our bare feet. We tucked our mosquito nets under our blankets to protect ourselves when we were asleep.

As we could leave no food around without the rats eating it, I used to take remnants to bed with me to save them for George the next day. Sometimes the rats would gnaw their way into the net for the food. The first few times that the rat and George and I found ourselves together in the net we all went crazy, including the rat. By and by we got used to it.

The first week on Berhala was mental and physical torture. My muscles were unaccustomed to the work of carrying heavy buckets, of digging holes, of lifting weights and of clearing land, and my stomach was unaccustomed to the food. I suffered inside and out.

But far worse to accept than the physical discomfort was the change in George. I saw that he was badly shocked by the brutal shift in surroundings and manner of living. I was the only thing in that new grim life that meant security and safety, and even I was different. He clung to me doggedly, with a grip that could not be loosened.

He followed me every waking moment, hanging to the edge of my shorts. If I went to the latrine shelter he stood in the grass outside as near as possible, his thumb in his mouth, waiting. If anyone tried to remove him — or take care of him for me — he screamed in terror and rage. I watched his complete unnerving, his loss of confidence, his mystification, his fright, and I saw that he was on the verge of establishing for life nameless complexes and psychological maladjustments. The realization then of his complete dependence on me for mental and emotional stability in his future life, as much as for physical health, forced me to make a tremendous effort to accept difficulties and dangers, if not calmly, at least without hysteria or tears. Weak though I knew myself to be, I wanted *him* to believe me all-powerful, ready to cope with all emergencies.

Fortunately this struggle to establish mental security for him took place before my physical strength was drained by starvation. By the time that I was fighting for the actual food to keep him alive, he believed me all-powerful to do anything, took it for granted that the food would appear, and accepted other incidents of camp life in his stride.

For a while we kept small bowls of oil with wicks floating, which we burned at night to give us light. The oil was coconut oil given as a ration. But soon the Japanese stopped giving us oil, and we got so hungry we ate what we had, and by that time we had burned up all the cloth for wicks. So then we lived in the dark.

The barrack had no glass in the windows, just solid wooden shutters. Although it wasn't the rainy season when we arrived, it rained much of the time on Berhala, the rain and wind driving furiously upon us from the sea side of the island. At such times we had to have the shutters closed tight, leaving no ventilation or light, either by day or by night.

The building itself was made of loose shakes, with cracks between, and the rain drove through. I lived on the side exposed to the ocean wind. It rained almost every night, and for six months I rolled up George's and my sleeping things nightly and moved them to a dry spot, and sat on them until the rain abated. I never could unroll them in a dry spot, because there wasn't room enough. The dry places were full of somebody else. Those nights George slept with Edith and Eddie and Mrs. Cho, the Chinese Consul's family, the four of them lying on her feather mattress which her amah had rescued for her.

There were two cement latrine holes in camp. These had no containers or outlets, and no manner of being emptied, so after a few experiments we stopped using them. Then the Japanese gave us two corrugated tin buckets to use, and these we stood outdoors behind a shelter.

We took turns disposing of their contents. At first we dug holes in the compound, and buried the refuse, but we had no good digging tools, and there was a rock layer just under the topsoil; when it rained we couldn't get the refuse to stay below water level, and excrement floated about the compound. The compound became crowded with refuse holes, and the whole place stank. It was like nothing else I ever smelled. We didn't pass through that smell holding our noses. We simply ate, slept, and lived in it.

In time the Japanese decided to permit us to empty the latrine buckets in the sea, five minutes' walk away, twice a day. The men's camp asked permission to do this work for us, but the Japanese refused, as they believed in equal rights for the sexes when it came to excrement. When it was my turn to empty the bucket, I used to carry George on one side and the

bucket on the other. We carried the buckets out to the end
of the wharf, experimented with the wind, dumped in the
refuse. From thence it was carried back to the shore by the
current, to the beach where we bathed.

It was a rule in camp that the buckets should be used for
faeces only, as otherwise they filled up too fast, so one corner
of the compound was used as a urinal. It did not offer the
seclusion of those in Paris.

A hooded cobra was said to sleep in the latrine shelter at
night, by one of the buckets. Some said they saw it, and all
of us heard it. I never saw it there, but I know that there were
cobras in the grass outside the compound. Whether the cobra
was in the latrine or not, the idea of his being there was
sufficient.

The change in diet for all of us, and a dysentery epidemic among the children, made it necessary to keep one latrine bucket in our sleeping quarters on rainy nights. The sounds of that bucket in use, the odor of it, the thought of it, make war more deadly and unendurable to me now than does the memory of all the bombs dropped over us in 1945.

The first few months on Berhala we had comparatively good food and didn't know it. Looking back later, we envied ourselves.

In our homes we had been used to a balanced diet of fresh vegetables and fruits, milk and butter and eggs, meats and fish, and rice or bread or potatoes.

Now we had rice. It gave us indigestion, but there was plenty of it. It was broken rice with powdered lime throughout to keep the weevils out, which it didn't do. It had to be sieved and shaken and washed many times to get rid of the lime, and hunks of lime still turned up in the finished product. The rice kernels were broken, and it was what the Chinese called Number Three, or Number Four, or "sweepings," meaning rice that had been swept up off the floors when good rice was being packaged. Not even the Chinese coolies would have used it in Sandakan. This was the bulk of our diet.

Once a day we had masses of what we then considered an inedible vegetable. It was in the same category as spinach: green, leafy, with a metallic flavor; but where spinach was capable of being masticated this had to be swallowed in ropes, as the stalks were like green rubber tubes. The local name was *kang kong*. In time we improved our technique with it by chopping it up small before cooking. Then the effect was that of swallowing small rubber washers, instead of lengths of tubing.

Sometimes we had salt fish or dried shrimps. We said we couldn't eat that rotten stuff. Then a few experimented, and got sick. We got hungrier, and more ate it and got sick. We got hungrier still, and everybody ate it, and soon nobody got sick.

For breakfast we had two rolls, then one roll, then after six weeks the flour gave out and we had none. Then we had bananas, in diminishing quantities, until in time we had no bananas.

We always had tea. It was dished up in a bucket similar to the latrine bucket, with the tea floating thickly on top (because the water hadn't boiled) and in the bottom — bugs. A small ration of salt was supplied and a little sugar, about a dessertspoonful a day. Later the salt ration disappeared, and the sugar diminished.

The contract for feeding us on Berhala was let to a Chinese from Sandakan. He supplied the materials and cooked the stuff, and hurled it at us. In time the contractor was discovered in a deal with some prisoners and he lost the contract. Then our men were told to do the cooking for themselves and us. The kitchen was outside the women's compound and we were not allowed near it. The men cooked the food and then stood it outside our barbed-wire barricade in buckets, which we collected and brought inside our camp. Berhala was the only camp in which the women did not do their own cooking.

We learned, by watching through a crack in the fence when the men went by to work, what men were interned on Berhala Island now. His Excellency the Governor and all the government men were present, with the exception of Dr. Taylor and Dr. Wands, and Dr. Laband, the dentist. Most of the commercial men of Sandakan were here, a number of Roman Catholic priests both British and Dutch, and the Church of England priests. The Chinese Consul and his assistants, Mr. Li and Mr. Yang, were also interned.

A thirty-foot solid wooden fence surrounded two sides of our compound, and shut off all view save what we saw through the crack. This high, impenetrable barrier standing close to our living quarters, the first and last thing we saw every morning and night, nearly drove us mad. Once a high wind from the ocean started to blow the thing down: seeing it quiver and lean with the gale, five of us raced outside in the rain and the thunder, and joined our forces to that of the storm. With each gust of the wind we threw ourselves against the fence and pushed mightily, and in the ecstasy and excitement we got it halfway over; it was going, it was really tumbling, and we screamed with the wind and the joy.

But the guard who was hiding from the storm in the sentry box outside looked up in time to see the fence toppling over on him. He raced into camp, came upon our mad behinds, bodies drenched in rain, hair blowing and wild, voices singing and shouting and screaming, women gone mad. He didn't like it a bit.

He called the guards and a lot of our men, and they propped the fence up again from the other side. Then he came in to attend to us. We could see him trying to make up his mind what to do. He was one of the gentler ones that didn't go in for corporal punishment, and that left him at a disadvantage. He said that no one in camp could go for a walk that day, or the next day. As it was pouring rain that day, and the guard was due to change the next day, we didn't care.

The women who hadn't pushed the fence down became very sanctimonious and smug about our irresponsible attitude towards getting the camp into trouble. Mrs. X, who was a born bootlicker, told the guard that we were very naughty, and for this she received an egg from him. But we had the fun, which was even more scarce than eggs. Looking back at this incident, I see that the noteworthy part of it is that we had the energy to push anything.

The other two sides of the compound had a fence made of many strands of heavy barbed wire. Through this we could catch glimpses of the sea. The combination of the towering wall on two sides and the barbed-wire barricade on the other sides was a bad one for claustrophobia victims. The blank wall leaned over us, driving us toward the barbed wire, which, with its vision seaward, gave the illusion of being an escape. Various women at various times threw themselves frantically on the barbed wire in frenzied efforts to get away from the inexorable, down-pressing wall. One woman in particular, time and again, would fling herself upon the sharp barbed wire, clawing at it with her bare hands, leaning on it and tearing at it with her arms and body, weeping and screaming, until she was covered with blood. Try though she did, and we did, it was impossible to keep her away. During these months on Berhala her hands were constantly covered with fresh and festering barbed-wire sores.

There were two Chinese women in camp, Shihping Cho, and Mrs. Li, the wife of the Assistant in the Consulate, both of whom were imprisoned because their husbands had remained loyal to the Republic of China. Whenever Japanese generals shed their occasional passing glory on us, they boggled at the sight of these two Chinese women held captive with us, two Asiatics made literal slaves, in the sphere of vaunted prosperity for the Asiatics.

I sympathized with these two, who not only had our hardships to put up with, but had us to put up with as a race of foreigners. Shihping was attractive, with the peculiarly sleek charm and beautifully made figure of the well-bred modern Chinese woman, who can wear either European or Chinese clothing equally well. She was intelligent and well-educated, with a degree from a Western university in China, spoke perfect idiomatic English, and never missed a joke in any language. She took the long view of captivity, and where I was constantly being astounded by things that happened, Shihping had always expected and prepared for them.

From the day the Japanese landed at Sandakan, Shihping Cho, her children — Edith, three years, and Eddie, four months — and her husband, Henry Cho, were held captive in close imprisonment. From the first, the Japanese tried to force Mr. Cho to renounce his allegiance to the Republic of China and join with the Nanking Government, feeling that such a change would have influence on the local Asiatics.

Don Johnston

While I was still living at my home in Sandakan, I had received a secret message from Mrs. Cho, a prisoner in the Consulate then, asking me to try to get some powdered milk and baby clothes for Eddie. Although the milk supplies had been bought up in Sandakan many months before, I was able by bribery and corruption to obtain some for her secretly through some small shops. The milk and clothing I smuggled to her at the Consulate, under the nose of the Japanese guards.

When we met again on Berhala she thanked me for my help to her, and said that she hoped she could help me, in return. In due time I was to find that throughout all camp life she helped me, returning one hundred to every one, sharing with me food, clothing, and assistance, giving me sympathy when I was distressed, amusement when I was bored, and strengthening my spirit to meet emergencies by the courage of her example.

Mrs. Cho told me the story of the first months of imprisonment in the Consulate. The Consul was warned that the lives of his wife and children would be taken if he did not betray the Republic. She was told that her husband would be killed if he did not go over to the Nanking Government. They were both promised their freedom, and good living conditions for themselves and the children, if they did. Neither one of them wavered; they resisted all forms of physical and mental pressure, and bribery, and remained loyal to the Republic.

When Shihping was imprisoned with us on Berhala, Mr. Cho was locked up with our husbands.

Mrs. Cho was George's first love, for in time he discovered that there were other human beings in the strange world that he could rely on beside me. Mrs. Cho was always courteous and dignified with children, self-controlled in every emergency, excitable over trifles. George would stand and talk with her in Cantonese, which he had learned from Ah Yin, long before he would talk to other women in English.

Violet and Penelope he learned to regard as his own, although Penelope was so popular with all children that each one claimed her as his property. She had a tender heart towards children which caused her to be nice to the nice ones, because they were sweet, and nice to the nasty ones, because they weren't. It was wonderful for the children, but had a denuding effect upon Penelope, because when birthdays and anniversaries came she was always cutting up her clothes and making them into gifts for the children. If the war had lasted much longer Penelope would have swept out of camp in a fringed banana leaf.

Violet had a wonderful game that she played with George — and how I loved that game! It was called the mouse game; he played it by lying down at her side and sucking his thumb, with his big gray eyes on her, while Violet counted quietly out loud to see how long he could lie still, and who would talk first, he or she. The mouse game was only good for a limited time, then Violet would start the alternative game, which George would have played forever; this consisted in having Violet sing to him. This game was conceived as a means of putting George to sleep, but he liked Violet's songs so much that he refused to go to sleep while she sang. The game affected me in the same way, and I used to think that if only she would go on singing the Cradle Song forever I could become a nice person again.

On the island there were no officers in charge, and the eight guards were changed once a week. During the week they had complete power over us. To them island duty was a vacation; the lads relaxed in loincloths most of the time, bathing, doing acrobatics, throwing things at prisoners, picking their noses, beating up people, distributing largesse, or lolling in the women's barrack playing footsy-footsy.

Our barrack was one big room with a loft above it, and no partitions. Each person occupied about five square feet. If the guard wanted to occupy it with you, there wasn't much you could do except roll over. Not that the guards spent all their time lying down near us; a lot of the time they were drunk in the guardhouse.

Some of it was good clean fun, and boys will be boys. But sometimes boys are dirty boys, and one doesn't like being frisked, frolicked, bullied, chased, back-slapped or face-slapped, by a young man with a gun. The gun removes the element of lighthearted gaiety from the game.

Because there were buns, rice, and privileges to be had from tolerating and encouraging the guards, and no means with which to discourage them, the fact that they treated us like tarts was sometimes justified. One good argument against collaborating was the fact that the guards had bedbugs.

They were not sadistic, or masochistic; they were not Oriental, or Occidental; they were just a gang of lowdown young hoodlums who had complete power over a hundred people who could not strike back.

Once a week a worn-out officer arrived in a worn-out motorboat, and both made a loud noise coming. He searched the guards, and us, with equal suspicion. Warned by the motor, the guards could just get their pants on in time to reach the wharf's end and stand at attention. We could just get our forbidden diaries, books, and food hidden in the grass and the latrines. When the officer departed, everybody relaxed.

Life on Berhala was according to the whims of the guards — and they were whimsical. They could be very kind. One guard gave his own buns to the children daily, another distributed loaves of bread to them. They frequently fed us their own surplus, commenting that our food was terrible. Sometimes they let us meet our husbands openly, and sometimes they beat us for smiling at them secretly.

The first guard we had in Berhala made a speech to us after one week, on the eve of their departure. Before making it, they dictated their sentiments to me in broken English and told me to write them out in "literary" style. The result of our effort was this:

GENTLEMEN, LADIES, and WOMEN: Nipponese soldiers are very kindly. We will pray for your health until we meet again. Tomorrow we go back to Sandakan. We are very sorry for you. However, if you get conceited we will knock you down, beat you, kick you, and kill you.

I suggested that the last sentence was a trifle harsh, but they were particularly attached to it.

We lived at high tragedy level because we expected release
to come, the war to end, or ourselves to be dead, quite quickly.
We could not conceive of living in these conditions for years.
So we ate up extra food, used up what drugs we had, spent
our energy lavishly, and took desperate chances, smuggling
through the approachable guards, escaping camp through the
barbed wire at night, and keeping contact with the POWs in
Sandakan. Later we still took desperate chances, but for the
reason a gambler gambles — because it was the only pleasure
we had in life.

We mustered at 7 A.M. and 7 P.M. daily in the compound.
We stood at attention, numbered off in Japanese, bowed, and
were dismissed. Our military style was ragged due to babes in
arms and underfoot. If the guard felt wakeful, they would
muster us several times throughout the night. When they began to suspect that people were going AWOL through the
barbed wire, life was made hideous with surprise musters. But
no culprit was ever caught that way: a system of false answers
was evolved which covered absences.

Sometimes we were ordered to clean the guardhouse, while
guards lay asleep or drunk on their beds. We picked up dirt
and fruit skins and cigarette butts off the floor with our hands,
while the guards threw banana skins and empty bottles at us.
But we could usually steal enough to make it worth while.
Sometimes they ordered us to "massage" them, but this we
avoided by being stupid and misunderstanding.

One guard made us sweep the beach daily with bamboo
brooms. As seaweed and driftwood piled high with each tide,
there was always plenty to do. Several times Mrs. Cho and I
were given the task of dusting the entire length of the wharf
with our handkerchiefs and hands. We did it, and laughed.

We were frequently turned out to cut the long wild grass
in the ground outside the compound. We could choose our
weapons: our own small scissors, or hands. The grass dulled

the scissors, and cut our hands. We cleaned the road leading from camp to the wharf by picking up stones and gravel by hand before the officers' arrival. Thus we learned the joy of manual labor.

If we were good girls while working, and a few fainted, and a few wept, we were rewarded by buns or bananas tossed to us. If we were naughty girls and laughed, or practised dumb insolence, we went hungry to bed.

It was impossible to keep either our surroundings or ourselves clean on Berhala. The compound was a swampy morass from rain, with a few duckboards which sank into the mud, and a lot of children who did. Our Government House babies, smartly clean, with starched amahs, became unrecognizable in the mire of internment. Here, doing very dirty work, chopping our own fuel, mending the broken barrack, working as hired men for the guards, clearing and road mending, we ceased to be the ladies of Sandakan. The mothers with children kept small campfires going to recook their food in the effort to make it more edible for the children; we were always smoke-grimed ourselves, and our clothing was hung out to dry in the campfire smoke.

Washing facilities were limited. The water was piped into a tank three feet by three feet by six feet, which stood inside a small shelter. The tank was used as a reservoir, and from it we dipped out water for bathing and washing, using empty coconut shells as dippers. Drinking water was supposed to be boiled; anyway it was put on the stove and heated until it acquired the dirty bucket flavors.

There was a cement floor in this shelter, on which we scrubbed our clothes, and bathed ourselves, pouring water over ourselves from the coconut shells. There were coconut palms on the island, and the guards sometimes threw coconuts in to us. After eating the coconut meat we cleaned the shells and used them for food receptacles and containers.

A day on Berhala went something like this:

I get out of bed before light, bathe and do my washing in the shelter, before the crowd arrives. This enables me to get a drying space on the clothesline, to hang my wash. Only a few people remembered to bring clotheslines with them when entering imprisonment, and there was always a struggle for drying space; rain sometimes necessitated clothes being hung out for several days before they dried. The barrack itself always had the wet-dog baby-diaper smell of wet clothing. Later we learned to remove barbed wire from the barriers, and use it for clothesline.

After washing, I return to the barrack and waken George, who hates to be awakened. At the children's end the rumpus now begins. Grimy mosquito nets dabble in people's faces, dirty blankets sprawl on the floor, fresh rat dirt and crumblings from the rotten wood above us are over everything.

At seven the tea bucket is left outside the gate, and two women bring it in. Everyone rushes forward to get a mug of tea and as the bucket empties we look to see if it is just cockroaches, or a rat this time.

I go out and start the campfire, or borrow the use of somebody else's, and heat up cold rice I have saved from the day before for breakfast. If I have any dried fish or vegetable I put it in. I borrow Mrs. Cho's frying pan to do this, as she has entered captivity with better equipment than most of us.

After breakfast we clean the barrack and the compound, empty the latrine buckets, and then if the guard is amiable we have half an hour, or an hour, on the beach. Sometimes we can bathe, sometimes collect driftwood for our fires, sometimes the guard puts us to work cleaning the beach or the guardhouse, or the land near by. Then we come back to the compound and keep an ear cocked for the sound of the men going by to the beach, or to work, in the hope that the guard will let them stop, or call to us as they pass.

After lunch of rice and tubular greens the heat settles down, overwhelming, prostrating, stewing heat. George and I bathe again, and I put George inside the net for a nap. Then I brush my hair, powder my face, and settle to read or sew for a few minutes. Now is a favorite time for the guards to come in and (1) enjoy our company, (2) turn us out to take exercises, (3) give us a job of work to do in the sun, as they hate to see us looking comfortable, or at ease.

At three o'clock another bucket of tea comes with another assortment of bugs. Then we chop wood for our fires, or work in the compound, until suppertime, about five o'clock. Supper is again rice and greens, with perhaps a taste of dried fish. After supper, we empty the latrine buckets, and then, according to the guard's whim, we may or may not go to the beach.

Dusk comes now, and we put the children to bed and are glad to lie down ourselves. Part of our overwhelming weariness comes from heavy physical labor in a tropical climate; part from the lack of sanitation and conveniences, which lack makes the mere acts of daily living a struggle; part from the change from a normal diet to one without any protein, and very little sugar; and part of the weariness is from absence of all mental stimulation, variety, or joy.

At first I used to sit in the gloaming and talk with friends at night, but soon I became too tired to bother. Our world had shut down to nothing but ourselves; in talking we were bound by ourselves, and by the tired, hard, untidy people we were fast becoming; in talking we had no escape from each other, or from the distasteful facts of our living. But lying in the dark, inside the semiprivacy of a mosquito net, with George breathing quietly beside me, flat on my back at last, I could return to the world of childhood in which life is not as it is, but as you wish it to be.

At the end of the first month, the children came down with what we called dysentery, although no laboratory examination could be made. They became nauseated, had diarrhea, passed mucus and blood, and lay about the barrack very limply. Most of them were past the diaper age, and we had no provision for stopping the wet ends. The camp became a trail of bloody stools left in the wake of weeping children, who in their turn were followed by creeping infants who crawled through mud and gore. And after the infants would come some childless woman with dainty tread to report to the mother, "Mrs. So-and-So, your child has had an accident. Please clean it up." But we had no waste cloths to clean anything up with.

In addition to dysentery, they had influenza, they had worms, they had impetigo, they had malaria, and always they had colds. We didn't have medicines unless we smuggled, traded, or stole them.

After a few months in camp I developed beriberi, a disease of undernourishment and vitamin deficiency. My legs and face swelled. By evening my legs were so numb that I could not stand on them. The doctor said I must eat all the green stuff I could get hold of. From then on throughout camp life I collected greens, ferns, weeds of any sort, and boiled them and ate them. Now I no longer eat spinach.

My husband also developed beriberi. The Japanese guard gave him some vitamin tablets. Harry asked the guard to take them to me instead, and he did so. In a few months I was better. Then I developed boils. Then I got over those. Then I got malaria, and never got over it. However, I gained perfect confidence in myself. I knew that if I practised long enough I could live on air, with a pinch of salt. But the time came when I didn't have the salt.

Because our compound was very small, we were permitted to have a walk on the beach every day under guard, if the guard saw it that way. Sometimes good guards would allow us an hour in the morning, and another hour at 6 P.M. That was escape from hell into heaven. I believed then that walk was the only thing that kept me sane. In the end I learned that it isn't the outward circumstances which determine what one can endure, but something in oneself which either breaks, or stays intact, under strain. It isn't the difference in strain, it's the difference in tensile strength of people.

One night when I was walking on the beach the old Malay fisherman, Saleh, who lived on the end of the wharf, whispered to me that he had something for me; to wait for him behind the latrines that night. The back of our compound was near the island spring, from which Saleh drew his water. Our latrine was at the end of the compound, near the path which Saleh followed to the spring. I waited behind the latrine in the dark, and when Saleh came by he stopped and pushed a package through the barbed wire to me.

There were eggs in that package. That was the first time I had ever smuggled. The eggs were sent to us by an Asiatic who had been in my husband's service, and with them came a message saying that more food would be smuggled to us, and also, in time, money. Those eggs were more than eggs; they were a pledge of confidence kept, between Oriental and Occidental.

Very soon others began to wait behind the lats in the dark. Those who didn't wait there watched those who did; mistakes were made in smuggled goods, and stuff got hi-jacked. Civil war started.

We had a camp meeting. By this time, summer 1942, we had forty women and thirteen children in camp, as more people had arrived from another part of Borneo. The women who were not engaged in smuggling said we were endangering the safety of the camp by our activities. We smugglers said that getting more food was vital for our children and worth taking a chance for. The anti-smugglers thought that we were paying money for the food, and said that it wasn't fair, as some had money and others didn't. We said we had no money; the food was being sent in as gifts by Asiatics. They answered that they did not believe this; that there wasn't an Asiatic in Sandakan who would do anything for a European, now that we were helpless.

We said that if our friends had already accepted the danger of smuggling food to us, we were going to take the risk of getting it into camp.

We took a camp vote as to whether or not we should smuggle. Only three besides myself voted in favor of smuggling, the other thirty-six said it was too dangerous; they might get slapped, beaten up, shot. The meeting broke up when we smugglers said that we intended to continue doing so regardless of rules.

Three weeks later almost every woman in camp was hanging around the latrines with a hungry look, and an open hand thrust through the barbed wire. From then until release came, we smuggled. We came, in time, to live on the food and excitement of smuggling.

Saleh lived in a little broken-down shack plastered on the end of the wharf. Every time we went for a walk we kept our eyes on Saleh's house for signs of him or his family. If they had anything for us they would signal to us. Then we would dawdle on the edge of the wharf, or lean against his shack until he or his wife or children slipped us the contraband, sometimes passing it through the window into our hands.

After getting it we had to conceal it hastily under our clothes. The test was when we passed the guardhouse on the way home. Sometimes the guard caught us, took the goods away, and punished us; but more often they were half-asleep and didn't bother us.

Some smuggling deals were surprisingly simple. Maureen, mother of David and Derek, had a perambulator with her in camp, taken from Sandakan the day we were imprisoned. She had wheeled Derek and David to the launch in the perambulator, and refused to take them out. The officer, recognizing the same quality in Maureen which kept the rest of us from arguing with her, had let her bring the pram.

The pram proved a perfect vehicle for smuggling. One day

the pram, plus the babies, was loaned to the men's camp, wheeled to the beach by a man; there smuggled eggs were collected from a hiding place and concealed in it; the pram, babies, and eggs were returned to the mother in our camp under the guard's nose. The eggs were later distributed amongst all the children.

Much of the time we could not smuggle. Somebody would get caught, or a guard would be picked up with our goods on him, and we could not do business for months. Then we were very hungry and depressed and quarrelsome, then there was nothing to live for. Then suddenly business would open, and as soon as one person received contraband, everybody wanted it.

The men started a bootleg provision service. A few young men sneaked out regularly at night by way of an unused latrine outlet, went over the hill to the Lepers' Settlement, and got peanuts, sugar, dried fish, eggs from them. These they sold or traded in the camps. The hungrier we got the less we worried over the fact that these things came through the lepers.

When we had been taken from Sandakan into prison camp we were searched, and all money was confiscated. But the people who were brought into Berhala camp from other places on the East Coast did not have their money taken, nor did those interned on the West Coast of Borneo. When we started to do big business in contraband deals money made the difference between being hungry or less hungry.

Then we sold our things inside camp to those who had cash, and sent an S O S for money to Asiatic friends outside, via the Sailor Who Came Down on a Cloud, our "contact." The Asiatics in Sandakan were living on tiny salaries under Japanese surveillance, but they constantly sent money and food to us even at great risk to themselves, and many of them, we learned later, paid with their lives for the food which saved ours.

* * * * *

There were three Roman Catholic Sisters from the Sandakan Convent imprisoned with us on Berhala. They were Mother Rose, Sister Frances Mary, and Sister Clitus. They had one small corner in the loft of the barrack. Here they had an altar, a crucifix hanging, and a Madonna and Child which they decorated with fresh red hibiscus flowers, picked outside the barbed wire with permission of the guard. Here our children were always made welcome in sight of the Madonna and Child; fussy babies and weary mothers found rest and comfort there, and the nearest to peace that existed in prison camp was here in the gentle care of the Sisters, at the foot of the Cross.

On the Fourth of July, 1942, which was also my birthday, I celebrated my first prison-camp party. Penelope, Gwen, and Marjorie North, all Englishwomen; Shihping Cho, Chinese; and Marjorie Colley, Betty Weber, and I, Americans, were guests of the management. We saved our nighttime ration of rice and sweet potato, and added contraband fish, pineapple, and sausage. We poured the last of the oil out of our lamps, and used it to fry with, dumped all the food into Cho's pan and fried it over an open fire which we built in the compound in the evening.

The guard saw our fire and told us to put it out. We misunderstood him, indeed we did, but so politely that he liked it. He sent for Mr. Yang from the men's camp, to interpret for us. Mr. Yang — who was interned as a member of the Republic of China Consulate — spoke Japanese. Mr. Yang said the guard said to put out the fire. We misunderstood him, too. We gave Mr. Yang and the guard some smuggled cigarettes. By then the food was cooked, so then we understood that the guard wanted the fire put out, and we put it out.

We ate well. Then we lit the three altar candles that Mother Rose and the Sisters had given us for a present, and stuck them in the ground. The Sisters came out and sang "God Bless America" with us in the warm darkness, in thin, sweet sopranos, and told us that they said Hail Marys and Ave Marias for America every night.

We drank a toast, in coconut milk from a smuggled coconut: "To America and her Day of Independence, celebrated this year by British and Americans together."

In the first months on Berhala I told myself I could not live without my husband. Two Against the World had been our motto. Then we found ourselves imprisoned separately.

The men could occasionally dally at the women's gate as they went by, if the guard was kind, and exchange words with their wives. During one of these hasty confabs, Harry and I agreed to try meeting secretly at night in the vacant compound between our camps. Another couple was already doing so, and said it was quite simple. We arranged to meet at ten o'clock, and designated a coconut tree, halfway between the two camps, as meeting place.

I put George to bed before dark, and crawled into the mosquito net with him while he went to sleep. I had already warned Violet, who was my neighbor on one side, of what I was going to do, so that if George should awaken and call she would go to him. I pulled on my dark blue slacks, to make me less visible in the dark. I lay in my net until the guard had been changed, then waited for him to come in and make his rounds. When he had gone outside the compound again, I crept out of the net and out of the barrack. By crawling under the barrack I arrived at the far side of the house, listened to hear if the guard was near, then emerged from under the barrack, and ran to the wall.

Here there was a depression under the wooden fence in one place, as the fence was built on uneven ground. I had to lie on my back with my head turned sideways to get through, as the hole was so shallow that my head wouldn't go through it longwise. Like getting born, it was easy after you got the head out; but the head had to emerge first in order to see if the guard was in sight on the other side. After the head found safety, bust and bottom followed; these would just come through; only the thin ones could use this exit. Halfway through I thought how undignified it would be to get caught like that, pinned down by the fence, incapable of hurrying either forward or backward.

I emerged ten yards from the sentry box. There was long grass on this side of the compound and I had been told to crawl through it. I knew there were snakes there, and the thought of them made me stand up and run for the tree, instead of crawling.

I got to the tree, and it was very dark and had started to rain.

In a moment I thought I heard someone creeping through the grass. I whispered "Harry!" I was sure it was someone creeping. I whispered again, in what seemed to me a very loud whisper. Whoever it was disregarded me and went whizzing past in the dark. If only I knew it was Harry, I would whisper louder. But it couldn't be Harry, or he would answer! The unknown creeper vanished from sound.

I lay in the dark and it rained a bit and time went by and I felt miserable. What could have happened?

Then there was a terrific rustling, and grasses waved to right and left, and somebody else went creeping past. Still I waited. There was a third whizzing sound, and again I whispered, and again no answer.

I lay still thinking of every miserable thing which could have happened, and how that whole compound seemed to be full of people, not Harry, and nobody daring to speak and say who. Just as I had decided to go home, somebody bumped into me. It was Marjorie coming to meet George. We lay together and waited. Soon George and Harry turned up together, crashing along like twin tractors through the heavy grass.

Harry wanted to know where I had been. I said, Where had

he been? It turned out that the first noise I heard had been Harry whizzing by. He had not heard me whisper, but with his customary speed and decision had dashed past my tree, to a second one further on, which he thought was the designated one. Not finding me, he had circled the compound speedily, and crashed by me again, then had given me up and gone back into camp. There he met George, who was on his way to meet Marjorie, and Harry had decided to try once more.

We met like this every few nights, with the arrangement that if it rained heavily we wouldn't come. If it rained after we got there we would sneak into the unused barrack and sit there together, with the sentry patrolling near by. If conditions inside our separate compounds proved to be unsuitable, if the guard was too wary, we would stand at the gate and call across some supposedly cryptic utterance such as "No soap!" or "Not tonight." By the time the guard had chased us inside, the signal had been given.

Lying there in the dark and the cool, close together and alone, we would promise each other that the war would be over soon, that the news was good, that we would love each other forever and ever, and at least for that moment we would be happy.

Soon it became an open secret that a few of us were meeting our husbands outside of camp. Some of the women attempted to stop us, suggesting that it was a most lascivious business that we could not live for these few months without a man. This interpretation of the meetings came to me as a shock. That anyone should see only one reason for meeting a man clandestinely in the dark was a revelation to me.

Henrietta, a natural-born Teacher's Pet, with a distorted sense of responsibility for others, and an idea that the Honor Spirit held good in camp, reported the fact of our nightly exits to the Japanese, who were already suspicious. She did not, however, tell who. She liked to be the center of anything, even trouble, so she pointed out to the visiting Japanese officers various places in the barbed wire where strands had obviously been unwoven and separated so bodies could push through, and other apparent emergency exits which we were using. These wires were then rewoven, and the holes closed, and so on. But nobody took seriously that small depression under the wall . . . which we continued to use.

These women were right in so far as what we were doing was too dangerous. When George and I were finally moved to Kuching, although it seemed like the end of the world to me at the time, I felt later that it probably saved our lives by removing the possibility of illegitimate meetings with Harry. But one can only deal with life as it seems at the time, and life on Berhala Island seemed unbearable to me in the first days of captivity, unless I could meet my husband. We were still looking at the war on a short-term basis.

How we women hated each other there on Berhala! Enmities were deeper than ever again. We had no experience of community living, we knew all about each other, and we still had energy with which to hate. The hardships and pangs of captivity were fresh to us, the humiliations were new, and the physical tasks were muscularly almost impossible. And we didn't mind what we said in those early days. One of the Ladies of Sandakan said to me, "I hate your guts, Agnes, and I'm going to tell you so. Although I'd like to be nice to you, just to keep out of that damned book of yours."

The few people whom I knew well before imprisonment, and really liked, I continued to like to the end. But the persons to whom I had been indifferent before, on Berhala Island I came to hate. And they, I observed, felt the same toward me: I was shocked to learn the things they had been thinking of me, perhaps throughout the years. We horrified ourselves with the strength of our antipathies. What criticism I make here of others holds good also of myself; we were not nice people. There was much excuse for us, and I can excuse others more readily than myself.

Malaria

It was in the fall of 1942 that Colonel Suga had paid his first visit to Berhala Island, and talked with me about writing. Shortly after this, in November, when George was two and a half years old, he had his first attack of malaria, and I had a return of the disease. We were probably bitten by the same mosquito, as we were taken sick at the same hour of the same day, and by night both had temperatures of almost 105 degrees.

The second night of illness we reached 105 degrees again, and George was delirious. I was lying by him and feeling very ill myself, when I felt him stiffen: I screamed, someone near by struck a match, and we saw he was having a convulsion. I forced his mouth open and got his tongue from between his teeth, and saw it was bleeding. One of the women ran to the guardhouse to beg the guard's lamp. The guard came back with her, took a look at George and his bloody mouth, and then ran to the men's camp to get Dr. Sternfeld.

Dr. Sternfeld was an elderly Austrian refugee Jew, said to have been a famous Viennese obstetrician, with gentle and elegant foreign ways which prepared us to believe anything. He had come out to Borneo from England to assist Dr. Stookes, who was in private practice in Sandakan, and later he had gone to work for the North Borneo Trading Company as company doctor. He was accepted in Sandakan, and treated with-

out prejudice, but not taken to people's hearts. We who meet
him in the future, we who for three and a half years knew his
work in captivity, will, I hope, give him the warmth we did
not give before.

In Berhala we had no doctor in the women's camp, and no
contact with any Japanese medical officer. The guard accepted
a great responsibility in bringing Dr. Sternfeld over from the
men's camp to us. The doctor verified our temperatures, and
said that he could do little without quinine, if it was malaria,
and could do even less, if it wasn't malaria, with that high temperature. He said we must give George hot and cold sponge
baths, and he told me to lie down again, which I wanted badly
to do, as I was feeling very ill. But I knew that as long as I
could stay on my feet, I must try to help George. The guard
let the women go to the cook shed and start fires to heat water.
Then he brought Harry over from the men's camp.

Dr. Sternfeld returned to the men's camp to look for quinine. Many individuals had private supplies of drugs, and
some were generous in sharing, others sold and traded them at
high prices, which became higher as our needs increased. In a
way this was right: he who had drugs had life; he who begged
for them sought to save his own life, at the cost of the holder.

But we were fortunate, and quinine was quickly donated
in the men's camp for our use. The doctor returned and gave
us both injections.

George was still unconscious, wrapped in wet towels. While
I was holding him, and shaking with fever and weakness, I
became unconscious. I remember thinking as I started to pass
out, "Perhaps God will save him now. I can't."

Throughout the night various women took turns sponging
us, a difficult job without lights, running water, towels, beds,
or changes of clothing. Everybody donated nightgowns, wrappings, draperies. The next morning our temperatures were
down and George was conscious. In camp there were always
a few who gave of their strength and spirit, as well as their

possessions. To four women, Tess Houston, who nursed us, and Betty Weber, Violet, and Penelope, who helped, George and I owe our lives.

Malaria is misleading to strangers, but reliable to those who know it. When the bugs are hatching in your blood and the fever is rising you are so ill you don't care; when the bugs are dying the fever drops for twenty-four hours, or whatever life cycle your bug has, and you feel almost well. But after a series of rebirths on the bugs' part you become very weak.

At nine o'clock the ration launch came from the mainland with a Japanese officer to inspect camp, and Dr. Sternfeld risked a beating to ask him to take us to the Sandakan hospital. The officer was amiable, but afraid to take the responsibility of removing us. He promised to return the next day for us, if permitted by the military police.

Next day the officer returned with permission to take us to the hospital. George and I were placed on the stretcher together, covered with sheets, and carried to the launch in the rain. The cabin was small and the stretcher was not, so we were left outside on the deck. The Japanese officer stood by us trying to shield us with his army cape. At intervals he raised the corner of the dripping sheet, and asked, "Are mother and child safe?"

Two hours later we were deposited in the second-class Asiatic ward of the Sandakan Civil Hospital. This was the hospital where I had produced George, in the elegance and luxury of a European birth — not in the second-class ward!

We were unveiled by an old friend of mine, Eurasian Nurse Mary, who deluged our dampness with tears. Mary was the adopted daughter of a Filipino ex-Forestry man who had been a clerk in my husband's department for twenty years. Hysteria, of mirth or grief, was her chosen state, and she played on her state of unstrung nerves as a pianist plays on her keyboard. In Mary's mind it was bad luck for us to be ill, underfed and unclothed, helpless in the hands of the enemy — but it was high tragedy for us to be in the second-class Asiatic ward of the Civil Hospital! That we, who had been accustomed to better than money could buy, to that which only pull, position, and purity of race entitle you in the Orient, should be reduced to second-class Asiatic category was overwhelming, for no one is so snobbish about Asiatics as a Eurasian.

Mary wept for us, but I did not. I rolled off the stretcher and into a hospital bed and dry blankets, and thanked God for being there. My ambition was to get as much quinine inside me, and as much hidden about me, as might be necessary for the duration of the war.

Here in the hospital we remained for six weeks. Hospital fare was badly served but nourishing, and we had plenty of eggs and milk. Every Asiatic who came to visit friends in the second-class ward secretly left gifts on George's bed, of eggs, bananas, biscuits, sweets, papayas, or money. We ate everything that came to hand; I have never eaten so much in my life. I ate for the years to come, with a lean future in view, and I believe those weeks of good food helped to carry me through the years to follow.

The hospital was in nominal charge of Dr. Taylor, an Australian by birth, the British Principal Medical Officer before the Japanese came, and of Dr. Wands, a Scotsman, both of whom were working under the Japanese military regime. They had been taken from internment by the order of the Japanese, with the concurrence of the deposed British Civil Government. In working under the Japanese they were following the principle that the doctor's first duty is to the sick of a country, regardless of the race or politics of its administrators.

These were men of determination and spirit, but it was impossible for them to accomplish anything under the Japanese.

They received blame for all that went wrong, yet were without authority to right it. Under the slogan of Asia for the Asiatics, doctoring and nursing became a farce, for the Asiatics.

The only cases treated promptly were venereal diseases among Japanese officers and soldiers. These cases, oft repeated, took priority over all else. During my hospitalization I learned the medical histories of all the Japanese dignitaries of Sandakan. Unfortunately I was not in a position to blackmail them.

Working under the Japanese offered one inducement to our medical men. They had access to the hospital drug and powdered milk supply, the only supply on the East Coast. Some of these supplies the doctors were trying to smuggle to us on Berhala, and to the Australian POWs at their camp in Sandakan. By the time I returned to Berhala Island a small amount of milk and drugs was being smuggled in regularly. This continued until we were sent away from Berhala.

During this period in hospital I talked a great deal with Dr. Laband, a refugee German Jew, dentist by profession, who had been employed by our government when the Japanese came in, and was now trying to work under them in the hospital. He did his best to discourage me from false optimism, telling me that peace could not come in less than a year at least. A year was to me an unendurable length of time. He, with his past experience of war, had learned that it is false to believe that because conditions are unendurable one cannot endure them.

Dr. Laband was an angel to George and me, bringing extra food, extra clothes, getting me a thermos, doing anything he could think of to do. I was nervous for his sake, as he had something still to lose. I had not. But he would not be warned. He said, "If they imprison me, I do not mind. Until then I will help you all."

And he did so fearlessly for months, until finally with the

other doctors he was accused of conspiracy, and sentenced to jail.

I talked also with Dr. Stookes, who was being interned and externed every few weeks, at the will of the Japanese. Just now he was in Sandakan, free — to do what the Japs told him to do. His plane was an inducement to them to keep him outside prison camp. I don't think anybody but Dr. Stookes had ever had the temerity to fly it. For years he had been flying to inaccessible Borneo places, landing on all the rivers in all kinds of weather, without weather reports or landing aids, in order to care for the sick.

Since the European war commenced he had been unable to get any new parts or servicing for the plane, and now when I heard it in the sky it made such a noise I expected to see a shower of nuts and bolts shooting down.

He told me his sister, Dr. Alison Stookes, was still working under the Japanese at Lahad Datu. He looked well, thin and brown and wiry and ageless as ever. I always wondered if he was as nonchalant as he let on. Harry had described him to me before we were married, and I came to Sandakan. Harry had said, "You'll like him. He tries to be tough, but he isn't."

The Sandakan lottery was the day's excitement in the hospital. Numbers were drawn in Sandakan at 3 P.M., and at 3.05 the hospital corridors rang with the shouts of nurses, either rejoicing or bewailing. All day they looked for signs to guide them in their choice.

While in child labor, Mrs. G. Takino was called upon to draw a number to decide what number the nurses should play. She did so, and drew Number Three. When the baby was slow in arriving, the nurses decided that the drawing had been too preliminary for luck, so just as the baby's head was appearing, the cards were again thrust under Mrs. Takino's nose. This time she drew Number Twenty-eight. The nurses all placed on it, and lost. Number Three came up.

I thought the nurses would strangle Mrs. Takino and the

baby. Instead they neither lost faith nor held malice. "Well," they said, "the cards knew all right, but we didn't trust them, and they got mad."

These nurses nursed for money, fun, friendship, or spite, but they did nothing for duty's sake. Fortunately they happened to feel kindly towards George and me. I accepted what help they offered, but never asked for anything. I knew I was there on sufferance. I often felt guilty in overlooking their neglect of others without censure or attempt to change, but I knew that I was helpless.

The nurses were very good to George. As he recuperated they played with him, took him for walks, brought sweets and biscuits, and sometimes even bathed him. But throughout all of our illness, although I myself was ill, I emptied his pot, nursed him, washed his clothes, fed him, and put him to bed.

There were a number of Japanese soldiers who were hospitalized in other parts of the hospital. They wandered about the hospital grounds in kimonos, and breeches and stocking feet. As soon as George was out of bed they made friends with him. They would sit on the grass outside the ward and play with him for hours, or until some officer appeared in the distance, when they would vanish hastily. They brought him sweets and bananas, games, and postal cards of Japanese film actors, and sent cigarettes to me. Most of them thought they spoke English, and wrote long dedications on the postal cards to "Mister Groge." They asked me why George didn't wear shoes. I said he didn't have any. They said they would buy him some, and tried to do so. There were none to be had in Sandakan. They were more upset about this than I was.

When I told them George and I were going back to prison camp on Berhala Island in a day or so, they told me they were sorry we were imprisoned there and said that Mister Groge was a very good friend, that they would never forget him. Every soldier we met in hospital was kind to him.

*　　*　　*　　*　　*

Mrs. Cohen, an old friend of mine, a Palestine Jewess who kept a cloth shop in the bazaar in Sandakan, was a patient in the hospital when George and I were. She was gorgeous in being and soul, with an Oriental splendor of face, hair, and hands. Her eyes were melting, her features fine, her expressions dramatic, her tears quick, and her emotions real. She loved bright colors, especially the varying reds of hibiscus blooms, and she wore gowns in these shades cut Mother Hubbard style, fitted to her bosoms and flowing from thence downward. From her handsome head flowed chins and bosoms, from bosoms flowed draperies, from draperies flowed bare feet, and when she moved she flowed along the floor.

Her heart, like her body, was large and soft and lovable. No one ever asked her for anything and was refused: time, sympathy, money, or help. They all came to her for help, Eurasians, Chinese, Malays, housekeepers, kept women, nurses, coolies, myself. Her pocketbook was under her pillow and she had constant recourse to it. The first thing she did when she found me in the hospital was to press ten dollars into my hand.

She was a force in Sandakan Asiatic life; she was the core of Eurasian society, business, and commerce. No wedding or funeral or birth was complete without her.

Daily her Arab boys came from the shop to bring her delicious Kosher cooking which she shared with all of us. She and George sat cross-legged on the floor together eating, she rolling the rice into balls, native-style, and popping these into his mouth with her fingers. George would eat until he was in pain; then she rubbed his stomach, massaged him, sang to him until he went to sleep. When he awakened they began eating again.

If he was naughty and I scolded him, I was the one she rebuked. She then would engulf him in the folds of her bosom, kiss him, tell him stories, and mesmerize him into passivity.

She was having injections in the hospital for skin trouble, and was expecting to remain a week longer. One afternoon

Mr. Cohen arrived, begging her to come back to the shop, to save him from the Japanese soldiers. He was older than Mrs. Cohen, a small man badly crippled from diabetes and systemic poisoning, and Mrs. Cohen stood like a mountain between him and the world.

Mr. Cohen said the Japanese soldiers were demanding goods at half price in the store, and when he refused to sell they stole the stuff and beat him up. Mrs. Cohen had her own system in dealing with the soldiers. She combined collaboration, coercion, bribery, and betrayal. She hid all the better store goods, sold inconsequential gifts to them for what they would pay, donated worthless souvenirs, gave them coffee, and let them confide in her. Meanwhile, she gained friends amongst them to help her smuggle to the European prisoners.

She didn't want to leave the hospital and go back to the shop, principally I believe because she hated to leave George. But Mr. Cohen was as helpless as George, so she folded up her Mother Hubbard dresses, her several chins and bosoms, and went back to the shop. She left, throwing kisses to George, calling advice to the nurses, waving at me, and weeping. With her departure all ribald gaiety was gone. After she left I found under my pillow fifty dollars, to be delivered by me to her friends on Berhala.

She came several times after that to visit us, against the orders and warnings of Japanese military police, bringing sweets, biscuits, and clothes for George. I told her I was frightened for her. She said, "You are my friends. I am sad to see you need things, I must help you. I am not worried for myself; I am not afraid of these Japanese. But the old man is sick and he cannot take care of himself. Also he must have brown wheat for his diabetes, and Kosher food. If I get put in jail he will die."

I never saw her again. Sometime later she was accused of conspiracy in connection with the escape of some Australian

POWs. She was imprisoned for a long time, but finally released. Later she was taken back into custody, and she was
executed by the Japanese shortly before the Armistice came.
Her husband fortunately died some time before.

One afternoon when I had been in hospital two weeks,
Major Takakua, our Sandakan Japanese Commandant, arrived.
He was very angry and very drunk. He swaggered through
our ward, where there were five Berhala prisoners beside
myself and George. Shouting at them that they should be out
working, instead of lying in bed, he ordered them to leave
the hospital immediately for Berhala. Then turning to me and
George he said, "What disease?"

"Malaria," I said weakly, closing my eyes and expecting to
feel a crack on the knuckles or the head.

"Baby what disease?"

"Malaria, also."

"You stay," he said. I never discovered why.

An hour later the others left under guard. One was an old
man of seventy-five years, bedridden for a dozen reasons;
one was the American dentist, Dr. Laidlaw, who had broken
his foot and was scarcely able to drag his leg in the cast. One
woman had stomach ulcers and gallstones. The other woman
was Mrs. Li, wife of the Assistant in the Chinese Consulate,
with her ten-day-old baby. Mrs. Li had milk fever and a temperature of 103 degrees at the time she was ordered to leave,
carrying her baby and her luggage. These people had to walk
down a steep hill for a mile to the wharf, and carry their belongings with them.

I learned later that Takakua had contracted a bad case of
venereal disease, and had come to the hospital for treatment
that day.

Nurse Mary and every Asiatic whom I saw, one day in the
hospital, told me sadly of the Day of Humiliation for the pris-

oners on Berhala. It seemed that all Berhala prisoners, both men and women, who were judged physically fit to leave camp were brought to Sandakan by launches. The men were set to work on the roads, mending and grading, and clearing weeds, and other public work jobs. When they finished their work they were stood in the public square as Exhibit A in the collapse of the British Empire.

The women were taken to the back quarters of the former Sandakan Hotel, where in the old days we had held our dances, and which was now the Japanese soldiers' barracks. Here they were told to wash and mend for the soldiers. The

Japanese soldiers came to them, stripped off their uniforms before them, and threw them down, and told them to mend and wash them. The soldiers sat down naked or with loincloths only, and waited while the women did as they were ordered. Many of the soldiers remained naked in the kitchen with the women throughout the day.

One woman said to me later, "I don't mind seeing men naked, but it throws me off to have them sitting about the kitchen."

The day was given much publicity among the local inhabitants by the Japanese. "Come and see your British Administrators now! Here are your masters!"

But the natives sympathized with the old masters; a lot of smuggling took place that day.

Nurse Mary in the hospital gave me her eyewitness account: "It was terrible! I weep for them! They were beaten, tortured, kicked. I saw Mr. Keith. He lay swooning and moaning on the square, he lay wounded and bruised. Oh, these Japanese! I feel very sad for you!"

I said, "Are you sure it was Mr. Keith swooning and moaning?"

"Oh, yes, madam. He said, 'Tell my wife I will endure to the end!' "

"I don't believe a word you say, Mary." But I did.

I learned later that Harry was ill on the Day of Humiliation, and never left Berhala Island.

At the end of the day the prisoners were returned to Berhala. They were glad to get there. It was a hard day to laugh off.

While in hospital we were warned by our doctor to have no contact with outside persons, as we were under the same rules of imprisonment as when on the island, and under military supervision. Knowing that the doctor would suffer if we were caught breaking the rules, I attempted to obey him.

But Ah Yin, our old amah, learned immediately that we were in hospital, and smuggled money, food, and possessions to us, and George's enamel pot which she knew I had forgotten. After three days the military police learned of this and warned her, on pain of death, to stay away. I was frightened for her and begged her to stop, but Ah Yin was indefatigable and things kept creeping in.

All our old Asiatic friends, Chinese, natives, Filipinos, in due time established contact with me. The proper time for doing so was between two and four in the afternoon. This was hospital rest hour and smuggler's hour. The nurses either went to sleep, or went into town to play Bingo, or listened on the telephone for lottery results. The patients slept, died, or made their beds. But no official was ever afoot with legitimate business at this hour in the hospital.

I would be awakened from my nap in the afternoon by some old Asiatic friend seated on my bed, with a fistful of Japanese money and a basket of food. Generally I would not take the money, for I knew they were making very little themselves, and could not spare it.

I spent the last evening before I expected to return to Berhala sewing $350 in Japanese currency into the hems of my trousers. This was sent by various Asiatics to be delivered by me to their friends in camp. Our return was unexpectedly delayed twenty-four hours when George developed a boil. Thanks to this delay, the following afternoon at rest hour a young Chinese arrived, sat on my bed, pulled out from under his coat a stack of one-dollar notes, requested me to deliver them in stated sums to the people whose names he had on a list. He said that he had brought it in one-dollar bills thinking these would be more easily disposed of by us. There were $325 in all. This, with the other cash I had, made $675. This was a fortune in the first days of the war, with moderate prices.

I was horrified. My clothes were already stiff with money, I had no place to conceal more, and I did not dare to take a list of the people to whom it was to go. I might be called on to leave at any moment, but I could not refuse to take what meant food and health to the prisoners of Berhala. I asked the Chinese to change his money into ten- and twenty-dollar bills and bring it back to me, saying I would do my best to get it in. In twenty minutes he was back with the change in the bills I had requested, and with the physical dimensions of the cash considerably decreased.

I sewed busily that night. I made an inner belt for my trousers and lined it with bills, and then sewed two brassières together with the money between them. None of this concealment would stand up against an exhaustive search, but I hoped that the Nips would continue to be stupid about searching. I then memorized the list of people to whom the money was to go.

I did not sleep easily that night. In addition to the money I was hoping to get into camp ten pounds of sugar, two tins of butter, two tins of powdered milk. This was "concealed" in a moderate-sized suitcase; that is, it was bundled inside clothing. If the Japanese questioned my having it, I would say that the nurses had given it to me, and hope that nothing happened.

None of this contraband compared in hazard to the delivery of the letter from the Australian officer at the Australian POW camp in Sandakan to a civilian prisoner on Berhala. This was concealed in George's panda bear, and George carried the bear.

During all internment, George's toys and other possessions concealed my secrets. I could not take him into my confidence for he had the habit of confiding our secrets trustingly to everyone he met. Instead I put my trust in his toys and possessions, which he treated with a casualness that gave me heart failure.

We left the hospital at 9 A.M. By 10.30 we were back on Berhala. The same officer who had brought us from Berhala when we were ill escorted us back. The guard searched our luggage, and made no comment on the food; he felt me all over carefully, turned my pockets inside out and pinched the thick places in my garments, and passed me in.

We re-entered prison camp. The blank wooden fence again bore down on me. The barbed-wire barricade closed to behind. I was met at the gate by a friend. "Is there any news? Is it true that Singapore has been retaken by the Allies?"

"No."

"Will it be much longer do you think?"

"A year anyway."

"Oh, don't be a pessimist!"

This was December 1942.

George was met by a pal of his. They instantly engaged in a struggle over Panda. The pal grabbed the bear and threw it over the barricade outside camp. It fell ten feet away at the feet of the Japanese guard. In it was the news letter from the Australian POW. I felt sick.

"George, ask the guard to throw in your bear." The guards would do things for the children that they wouldn't do for adults.

George, becoming coy: "The guard will be angry."

"But you want your bear, darling."

"I don't care; the guard can have it."

"Don't be stupid. Ask him for your bear."

"It's my bear, and I don't want it."

"GET THAT BEAR!"

George recognized the tone; he got the bear. The Berhala prisoner got the letter. And the next time I concealed secrets in Panda, I told George that Panda had an operation and had to rest in hospital. Then I sewed up the incision and laid Panda to rest in the suitcase, until release came.

I sent word to Harry to meet me that night at ten at the usual place. I hadn't seen him since the night George and I were delirious with fever and the sympathetic guard brought him over to us.

Harry was waiting for me under the coconut palm. I passed over a wad of money to him, for the men in his camp. He had a nice little hollow scooped out in the grass for us. It was good to be with him again, even here, even back in prison.

We looked up at the sky and the stars. Not the moon, for if there was a moon we didn't meet. We listened to the men singing in his camp.

"My God, how can they do it? What keeps them cheerful?" I said. "It's no use kidding ourselves — we won't be out of here for a year. None of that dope about Hong Kong and

Singapore being retaken is true. The U. S. hasn't even been heard of yet! The doctors in Sandakan told me that the war is just where it was six months ago. My God! I just can't stand it for a year more. I'll be dead by then!"

"There's a lot of talk in camp about repatriation," said Harry. "Perhaps the women and children will be sent home."

"But what about you? I don't want to go home without you."

"If you get a chance to go, you go!"

"But Harry, I can't believe that we may be here for months and years more! It isn't possible. Why, we can't stand it six months longer on this food, in this climate, and in this filth."

5

Happy New Year

HERE on Berhala I r net a family of four Europeans from Sandakan, who had g ne up the Kinabatangan River to escape the Japanese before the occupation. The mother and two children had been staying on Dr. Stookes's farm up the river for some time before, and when news came that the Japanese were on their way to Sandakan the husband joined them, and they went hastily up the Kinabatangan in a small boat, for many miles.

Here they hid for some months, establishing a small homestead well away from traffic. If they had been self-supporting they might have remained undiscovered for some time longer, but they had to rely on the nearest native shop on the river for tinned milk and certain foods. When a price was placed on the heads of escapees by the Japanese, someone who knew of the whereabouts of this family betrayed them for a reward. The Japanese came up the river, surprised and made them prisoners, brought them back by boat, and imprisoned them on Berhala Island with us. There I found them when I returned from the hospital in Sandakan. They told us that they had not been mistreated by the Japanese when taken prisoners.

Here now were two more of the Sandakan Junior Leaguers, lovely, elusive, redheaded Fenella, who was George's age, and solid, big-eyed, stubborn little Fiona, two years younger, born the same month as Eddie Cho.

This family had brought news that Hong Kong and Singapore had been retaken by the British; the victory had been duly celebrated in camp. And then I returned from the hospital!

Some three months after Colonel Suga's visit on Berhala Island, some military personages of superior importance and inferior size, surrounded by a swarm of civilian Japanese yes-men and two interpreters, arrived. From the bustle and the interpreters accompanying them we knew something unpleasant was coming.

We were mustered, and sunned, and taught patience, and in time we were told: the women were to leave Berhala prison camp for an unknown destination. The men were to remain behind for an unknown fate. This was to happen at 5 P.M. two days later, January 12, 1943, at Colonel Suga's command. We were meanwhile to be happy, cheerful, keep up our morals, keep clean and healthy, and get ready to depart.

The evening was spent listening to the rumors of the guards; we were going to Kuching (1) to a new camp, with electric lights, beds, and furniture, (2) to be repatriated, (3) to work for the Japanese soldiers in a brothel.

The men were to stay behind on Berhala to be (unfortunately there was little disagreement on this) executed.

The next morning some Japanese officials arrived at the men's camp with armloads of European clothing, which had been collected at random from the houses in Sandakan in which we had lived. Some clothes were bundled like dirty laundry into sheets, some were loose, some in suitcases; a number of suitcases and trunks arrived empty. There seemed no reason behind the choice of goods. Everything was dumped in the men's compound.

Having delivered this mass wardrobe, the Japanese demanded that we sign documents saying that we had received from them all of our possessions. This we refused to do, although I felt it made no difference what we signed in the war, as whoever won the war would scrap the papers.

The women were told to identify their things. I found an assortment of dinner dresses, tweeds, silk scarves, sheer silk stockings, fancy pocketbooks, but very little that I could use in prison camp except a tweed coat, and my box of "scraps" from old dresses.

When I looked at my clothes dumped on the ground at Berhala, it made me ill to see them lying there, the remnants of glory passed. It didn't bear thinking on. I abandoned most of them, saying that anybody could have them who would carry them away. Women with more foresight than I picked up a few, but many felt as I, that they did not have the heart for finery. Nor did we have receptacles to hold them, nor strength to move them. The box of scraps, however, I took for mending.

The next day my empty trunk was thrown into the compound by the Japs. Now it was the men's turn to salvage from the clothing heaps. Harry fell upon my trunk and filled it with what was left of my wardrobe, hoping that some day, if he wasn't executed first, he could get it to me.

The day came. We packed up our miserable belongings, and ate our miserable meal at four o'clock. We looked around our barrack which had been so dreary to us, which we had hated so. Now, compared to the unknown it was almost home. We climbed down the broken steps, and walked out of the prison compound. I carried two suitcases and the blanket roll, and George dragged behind him a little bag and his stool.

Our husbands were lined up outside in the rain, on the far side of the drainage ditch. We had five minutes to tell each other good-bye, they standing on one side of the ditch, we on the other.

Harry was there. I stood and looked at him. He had smuggled a letter to me the night before, enclosing a farewell gift of five handkerchiefs. When I read the letter I had cried and cried.

The letter said:

Take care of our little son. I love him because he is you. He is ours, he is you and I that will live. Although our bodies may die, I know there is something between us that will never die.

The letter said everything in this world that I wanted the man I loved to say — and it said good-bye.

I looked at this man across the ditch who was my husband. I could not see him clearly because the tears were pouring down my face. I felt that nothing could ever happen to me again that would hurt like this, because if I lived through this, my heart would be broken.

We had five minutes to say good-bye. I reached across the ditch and took his hand. Our hands clung. It seemed that I could not let his go.

George pulled at me and said, "Don't cry, Mum." Now George was the one to comfort me. The rain poured down and washed away my tears. I let go of Harry's hand; loneliness began.

Something very hard and cold formed inside my chest, where I had used to feel a heart. This something said: I am alone, I, in all this world, stand between my child and destruction. I only. There are certain things which have gone out of me now forever: softness, love, dependency. Those are back there with Harry. I am no longer a woman. I am hard, I must fight, I am alone.

The rain poured down, and mixed with my tears. Without one word I turned away from Harry, and started towards the wharf, George following and sobbing.

When we were on the deck of the launch I looked back. The husbands had followed to the beach and stood on the shore; they didn't wave. The open windows of the men's barracks were blocked with men's gray faces, with men's gray smoke-stained handkerchiefs extended towards us in good-bye — they didn't even flutter in the rain. There was no sound at all, except the noise of the launch and the slapping of the waves, and a little sound of women crying.

At the Sandakan wharf we transferred from the launch to a small steamer. There was no gangway, and as it was high tide, in order to get on board we had to straddle a strip of water, and climb up the side. The Japanese officers watched and laughed. We could not lift our luggage on board ourselves, and we asked for help. They shook their heads and laughed. In the end we found we could lift our luggage on board, sooner than leave it behind.

It was a small steamer with only one cabin, which was occupied by three Japanese officers, and three Japanese women with the ugliest legs that I have ever seen detached from pianos. One officer was Takakua, former Commandant of the Sandakan Civilian Internees, who hadn't thrown me out of the hospital once. He was being transferred, we learned. He was known as a hot lover and a cold master. He was gross and greasy-looking, had venereal disease, was a woman chaser and a rump rubber. We laughed at most Japanese officers, but Takakua we hated.

There were forty-seven women and fifteen children on board. We squatted on the open deck of the boat for ten days and nights, traveling without lights at night, eating little. There was not space enough to open out our blanket roll or to lie down. We slept in the clothes we wore. There were neither life belts nor lifeboats. It rained most of the time, and the deck was awash with rain, sea, urine, and vomit.

At first Takakua came out of his cabin in his kimono, and stood on the fringe of his captives — guffawed, leered at, and patted them. By and by we stank, and he stayed away.

There was one water closet without water on board. This soon filled up with excrement, which then poured over, ran under the door, and leaked out on the deck. Then we used the children's pots and emptied them overboard.

We had the last meal on Berhala Island at 4 P.M. on Monday. We had our next meal at 5 P.M. on Thursday. For drinking water we got water out of the boilers, climbing over the coal pile to the engine room.

The crew of the boat was Chinese, Malay, Javanese. Never have I received so much care, courtesy, politeness, and help on any ship. And there were no tips. The journey was hell, but we lived through it; without the help of these men I do not think we could have done so.

They hung and draped our wet blankets and the children's wet clothes over the boilers and around the engines in an effort to dry them, until the engine room looked like a steam laundry. They placed a bucket by the pump for us to bathe, and looked the other way when we did so. They helped us cook in the galley and boiled water for us. By every look and deed they showed us kindness and sympathy.

The Japanese had tried to eradicate the use of honorific "Mem" and "Tuan" in address to Europeans. But on this boat I never heard a woman addressed other than "Mem," and I heard no Japanese addressed as "Tuan."

One thing the trip did for us. I had felt broken on leaving my husband. We mothers particularly felt the weight of our children. Each one now, like myself, knew that she must go it alone; the very aloneness drew us together.

On that boat, shivering on the deck, lying with our children in the rain and the spray and the vomit, we sealed a pact of unity. From then on we mothers stuck together. Our children were all that was left to us of our men. We were the preservers of our children now, against every other human being, and against overweening fate. Never again did we think in terms of one child alone: from then on we fought for The Children.

We were seasick much of the time because of the heavy swell. Between spells of sickness the children were famished. They would rear up their heads from being sick into a pot, and demand food. The food given us was limed rice and Japanese tinned fishballs. The children would eat it, and be sick again.

There were a number of Japanese soldiers on board who shared the deck with us. One of these, a young man with a thin face, large glasses, and hesitant English, told me that he had read *Land Below the Wind* in the Japanese translations and liked it. He said he was sorry to see me there, and I said I was sorry to be there.

At every port native peddlers came to the side of the boat with fruits, sweets, and eggs, which they sold to the soldiers, and sometimes, through the soldiers, to any prisoner who had money. When the children saw this, they begged for fruit. I asked my soldier friend if he would request the Japanese authorities in charge of us to get us some fruit for the children, who were all ill from traveling. He said that he would ask, but did not think that they would do it, and I could see he was nervous about asking.

He came to me that night and told me that the officers had refused his request. Then with a finger on his lips, and a whispered, "Do not tell," he handed me an envelope. The envelope enclosed ten dollars, and a letter which said:

I present to you $10 which is my salary. That is a few money. I am regretable not to be able to give you enough money because I am only soldier. Please don't fear. Take this money. I don't need money because I may die in battle and have no wife, no child, no father, only mother.

That gift went far to make the journey bearable, not only from the material aspect of food, but from the warmth its kindness brought to my very cold heart.

At Jesselton a smartly dressed Japanese officer in military cape, with a sleek head and a svelte figure, came on board asking for Keith. It was 8 A.M., it had rained all night, I was wet, dirty, sick, miserable. I stood up and bowed as slightly as I dared, with a grim, dead-pan expression.

This was Lieutenant Nagai. He brought a letter from his wife in Yokohama, who had read my book in Japanese. She had asked him to help me, if he ever met me as a prisoner, and to give me her regards. He had heard that the women prisoners were being moved from Berhala by this boat, and had come to give me the message, and ask if he could do anything for me.

I thanked him, and told him that the food was very bad — would he ask the authorities to give us fruit or milk for the children? He said he could not effect any change over our conditions as he had no authority over us, but he would try to bring me some eggs for George. I guessed that I had put him on the spot: he was neither big enough to help me openly, nor small enough to be able to do so secretly. I didn't think that I would see him again, nor did I, until one year later.

At Labuan we were allowed on the wharf for a walk. One of the military police came up to me, and said he had read my book and would like to do something for me. Again I said we needed food. He disappeared. Shortly afterward he returned, and with some display of guile and legerdemain, he slipped me some cake and fruit, without the other military policemen seeing. Later on, my soldier with the glasses brought a tin of milk for George. He had with him a soldier friend, to whom he introduced me as "My friend Keith, who writes."

We laid alongside a captured Philippine Island ship. There were Filipino prisoners below decks. We whispered to them in the dark, but we were more willing to communicate than they.

Nine days after we left Berhala Island, we arrived at the mouth of the Sarawak River. In the gloom of the dawn we poked silently up the dark slow-moving stream between the mud banks and the nipa palms. Crouched on the deck in the rain I thought of James Brooke, the first White Rajah, who had blended in Sarawak and in his person the romance of East and West. Had he seen Sarawak as I did now, I wondered, wet, nauseated, with diarrhea, a cold in the head, and fever, from the deck of a prison ship, would he have seen any possibilities in it? I certainly didn't.

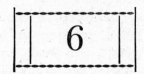

6

Imprisoned Sisters

Kuching, the capital of Sarawak, lies two degrees above the equator, on the West Coast of Borneo.

Here in the jungle aboriginal, just over one hundred years ago, James Brooke, a young English officer, captured his dream of a white-owned, native-benefiting state to be his very, very own. Here he purchased his kingdom by fighting for it, here he worked and sweated and prayed, and almost lost his life. Here he earned his knighthood, while building a tradition of White Rajahdom which lives, while soldiers die.

He was followed by two Rajah Brookes — Charles Johnson and Charles Vyner — who wed, and bred, and lived in the *Astana* there — sometimes gayly, sometimes sadly, but always regally. These handsome Westerners ruled an Oriental kingdom where scenery, costumes, and temperament met in exotic design, where monkeys and race horses, jungles and pianos, mixed harmoniously. Here the white man assumed the highest title, and the native retained the say. Here the Rajah and Ranee of Sarawak made headlines, when Borneo never did.

Under the Rajahs and Ranees of the Brooke family, Kuching became famous for its night life. Asiatics were welcome to shine, Oriental women in bizarre costumes stole the show from drab ladies from home, beauty was its own reward, and dullness was not confused with virtue. People who went to the *Astana,* the Rajah's palace, had fun; were amused; stayed awake; a shocking condition of affairs for Far East social life!

In 1940, Kuching celebrated a centenary of progress. Vacuum cleaners, radios, refrigerators, loud-speakers, clean politics, cigarette lighters, jazz bands, free speech, and suffrage became as common there as any place, and prosperity came right around the corner and sat down with native princes, Ranees, and Residents.

Into the bosom of this happy family scene came the Japs, in December 1941.

And here, as prisoners of the Japs on January 20, 1943, came the women and children of Sandakan, wet, sick and miserable, on a murky morning at dawn.

Came here to Kuching, which lies on the equator, sweats and swelters on the equator, pours with rain and shakes with thunder on the equator, and which, so far as my money goes, can continue to do so forever without me again.

Kuching is about twenty-two miles up the Sarawak River from the sea, and our prison camps were located three miles outside of Kuching. Here was the headquarters in Borneo for all Allied prisoners of war and internees. Here Colonel Suga, Commander of all Prisoners of War and Internees, whom I had first met on Berhala, had his headquarters, and acted *in loco parentis* to the camps.

We remet on my second day in Kuching, when I asked Colonel Suga to return to me a portable typewriter which had been confiscated from a friend by the Japanese office. I said the typewriter was mine, hoping to get it back under heading of "Patronage to Art." Suga didn't release it, then, but I got it in the end.

Lieutenant Nekata was the local boss, under Suga, of our camps, and never failed to assert himself as such. We soon learned that these two were constantly at variance; both had favorites, but never the same favorites. To be a friend of Suga was to be singled out by Nekata for trouble, though it did not work inversely. Nekata had a long, thin, drab, blank face, trained to hide all human intelligence, although I believe he had some.

Our camp, known as Batu Lintang, was composed of eight separate camps. Four of these prison camps, and the Japanese offices, were grouped about a square. From this square radiated the roads that led to the other camps, and in it stood the sentry who controlled the roads; across it drove Colonel Suga's motor car, through it passed the Japanese soldiers, and in it the prisoners worked. This square was the place for speeches, celebrations, commemoration of Japanese victories and holidays, place of punishment and pillory. This square was the core of prison camp life; the best and the most beastly of captivity took place there.

Each of the eight camps in Kuching was as completely segregated from each of the others as the Nipponese could make it. But — armed guards, barbed wire, rules and punishments, to the contrary — they could not stop secret contact between camps, and this the Japanese officers always feared. At times there were very few Nipponese soldiers under arms in Kuching, and they were anxious to avoid trouble from our camps.

Sometimes various hotheads tried to incite rebellion amongst the men, but we knew that this could only end in murder for all of us. In the beginning the Nipponese had come victoriously into Borneo because they controlled the air and the sea, and so long as they continued to control the air and the sea they would stay there. Any hostile move the prisoners in Borneo made would probably be suicide.

The aggregate population of the eight Kuching camps, both prisoners of war and internees, was at this time over 3000 persons. The divisions and personnel of the various camps were as follows: Australian officers and N.C.O.s,

Sentry box by prison square

British officers, Dutch officers, British soldiers, Indonesians, civilian men, Roman Catholic priests, and the women and children.

In the women's camp in Kuching we joined women and children from other parts of Borneo, to form an aggregate population of 242 persons. Although in one camp, we lived in three community groups: 120 Dutch Roman Catholic nuns, 20 English Roman Catholic nuns, 73 women, and 29 children. Some months later we were joined by 12 more British and Dutch women, 20 Sisters, and 6 children. Malay was the common language in camp between Dutch and English people.

Here we were housed in five very small barracks, with an approximate living space for each person of four feet by six feet, without partitions or privacy. We had three sets of latrines, built over pits, emptied sometimes by ourselves, sometimes by British soldiers.

The best thing that happened to me in captivity happened here in Kuching: I was thrown into close contact with a community of Roman Catholic nuns. Before this I really knew nothing about them, except through the three on Berhala Island, Mother Rose, Sister Clitus, and Sister Frances Mary. They were white-robed, soft-spoken, touched by divinity, apart from us — but they scarcely seemed human.

Now in Kuching I met nuns as women, and sisters, and mothers, hard workers, and my friends. Here I met them as people who sang, and laughed, and made jokes and had fun. As people who prayed and fasted as a privilege and joy, not as a duty. As women who had chosen a way of life, not had it thrust on them, and who loved it. As women who never, never refused to give help. As women who were sorry for *us*, merciful to *us*, tried to help *us*, because *they* had the Way and the Life; while we, poor fleshly creatures of this world and now cut off from this world, had nothing.

We secular women living with our own sex had already

tested ourselves, and found ourselves wanting. We could not get on without men, their stimulation, comfort, companionship. I say companionship, because very soon, with poor food, hard work, and nervous strain, that was all we had the sexual strength to long for, or to offer.

But the Sisters were different, they were complete. They were wedded to Christ and the Church, and for the first time in my life in Kuching, I saw that this was so. Then for the first time it became credible to me that they were Holy Brides. They formed in general a background of prayer and peace, for the rest of our world which was mad.

The thing that struck me first of all was that the Sisters were happy; next, resourceful; third, they were holy; and finally they, like ourselves, could sometimes be hysterical.

The English Sisters were from convents at Sandakan, Jesselton, and Kuching, twenty of them to begin with, and forty when some months later the Japanese interned the nursing Sisters who had been working in the Kuching hospital for the Japanese.

The English Sisters wore white robes with white veils. When they were cooking or working they tucked these veils behind their ears like little dust caps, rolled up their sleeves, and folded up their skirts to keep them out of the dirt; then the Sisters looked like white napkins folded into fancy shapes.

The Dutch Sisters were working missionaries, and they

lived in three groups in camp, and came from different parts of Dutch Borneo. They wore gray robes, and black and white pin-striped ones like pillow ticking. Another small group of about ten Dutch Sisters were the Slot Sisters, the Holiest of the Holy: they were contemplatives, and only prayed and thought. In peacetime their only contact with the world was through a slot in the gate. They were of the order of Poor Clares, possessing nothing, wishing nothing, and prison camp was the ideal place for them. They wore heavy brownish robes like sacking.

All these costumes, except those of the Poor Clares, were the tropical-climate workday costumes. On special feast days the Sisters brought out their rusty, black, home habits, dusted them off, put them on, and looked at each other with satisfaction — the same satisfaction that we showed when we got dressed up and went to meet our husbands.

As our clothes wore out we made shorts out of trousers, play dresses out of skirts, short dresses out of long ones, and finally left large open spaces, becoming gradually more and more visible ourselves. But as the Sisters' habits wore out they had to remain invisible, so as the material of the habit disappeared, it was replaced by a hand-sewn patchwork of pieces — sometimes not all white.

Finally when they had no gowns left for sickness, or emergency use, or bed, they were forced to acquire some of the colored clothes from the secular women, and I think they thoroughly enjoyed the excuse to use color. I held a lottery once for a royal blue dinner dress, and it was won by a Dutch Sister who made it into a handsome gardening frock which she wore while distributing manure. She told me she enjoyed wearing it immensely because it was such a nice color.

The first thing I did when I got to Kuching was to sell my three sheets for five dollars each to the Sisters for habits.

The smart thing for each mother to do was to get herself adopted by a Sister, as the Sisters were unfailingly kindhearted, and hard workers. The Sister was then referred to as "your" Sister, and came around on feast days with extras of food for your child, helped you to do sewing, helped you to plant a garden, helped you to work, and helped you to worry.

My Sister was Sister Claudia, a Dutch Sister, ten years older than I, with snapping black eyes which held both peace and challenge, and beautiful chiseled features. Sister Claudia was always ready to give me practical help, but the best thing she did for me really was to exist as a lovely and lovable person.

Here in this first Kuching camp we now had twenty-nine children. The eight eldest children, then six to nine years old, were being taught lessons for two hours a day by Sister Dominica, an Irish Free State Sister and a gifted teacher.

The Sandakan children were younger, and we mothers longed to have them join the ranks of pupils, but Sister Dominica could not take any more, nor could she teach widely assorted ages. There were other British Sister teachers in camp, but the community work was too heavy for them to be spared for teaching.

The Sisters were great on singing and fun. Usually I loved the feast days: the singing of high, sweet, reedy voices, the deeper-toned murmur of prayer; the clatter of dishes and party food (where they got it, God only knew, but they got it!), the laughter and dancing and mellowness that spread to the people around. Usually I loved the feast days.

But some days, as life grew grimmer, I found myself wishing that they'd quit singing, with nothing to sing for, from my point of view.

They prayed for peace, believed it would come; set dates, and hours and deadlines for it — and when it didn't come they said "Thy will be done," and prayed again. They reconciled themselves, either by strong faith, or by delusion. They were happy, either because they didn't know any better, or because what we knew better, and what kept us from being happy, was wrong. Anyway, they were happy, when the rest of us beat vainly against the bars of our prison.

I couldn't be Roman Catholic myself because I ask Why too frequently. I can't be anything, but sometimes I'd like to be. It is so restful to give up the struggle and relax in belief in The Word.

All through camp life I studied the Sisters and loved them, and I tried very hard to learn. I learned one thing: that it isn't any particular sect or religion that gives one strength. It is putting your mind on something outside of yourself, that you believe is good. We wives had put our minds and our hearts on our husbands, which is what a good marriage is, and we now were without them, and lost. The Sisters had put their minds and hearts on God only, and they had Him, and they only were whole.

Mother Bernardine, a fragile, other-world-looking English Sister from the Kuching convent, was the camp master for the entire women's community. The Japanese at this time refused to deal with any representative of the secular community. The Sisters were well organized and disciplined, and outwardly accepted Japanese edict with better grace and more obedience than we, who were never reconciled.

The Sisters were deferential to the lawgivers, and acted as if they took the Japanese seriously, but they perpetrated the biggest and best smuggling deals in camp. The Sisters were commanded to supply a sewing party to sew for the Japanese officers and soldiers, working daily in a barrack near the Japanese office. They did this, not unhappily, often with a gossipy amusement, and always philosophically. All men were alike in the eyes of God, either enemy or friend, they said.

But some days soldiers came into the room, stripped their clothes off, told the Sisters to mend them, and sat about unclad. Then one day the sergeant major came in, took off his trousers, told the nuns to mend them, and went to the corner of the room and urinated.

Now no one could like that, the Sisters said. Still, he did go to the corner, they agreed.

In conversation with me, Colonel Suga frequently referred to the Roman Catholics as being without race prejudice, which belief I am sure prejudiced him in their favor. A Roman Catholic priest from the near-by camp was permitted daily to come into our camp at 7 A.M., to hold mass. A Church of England priest and a Dutch Protestant priest were sometimes allowed to hold service in the women's camp on Sundays, but never regularly.

When we arrived at Kuching Mother Bernardine and the camp doctor were the only two females permitted to have contact with the Japanese authorities. Mother Bernardine was a delicate creature whose starched robes, made stiff and shiny with rice-water and ironed with the heavy charcoal-burning iron which the sisters owned, looked as if they had more body than she. Her delicate, lined face grew from the throat of her habit, and her reed-like wrists with the thin, blue-veined hands drooped from her full white sleeves. That she could do the job of camp representative, which required many interviews with the Japanese, seemed unbelievable.

When our presence enlarged the camp community, a representative was elected by the secular women, to work with Mother Bernardine, though she was not supposed to deal with the Japanese. This representative was Dorie Adams, from Jesselton, the wife of the British Commandant of Armed Constabulary, Borneo's only armed force.

She was a slender, shy, medium-sized, medium-aged woman with short, wavy brown hair with a gray streak, and green eyes, a woman who never sought notice. How she happened to be elected I do not remember. She was not the leader type. I decided afterward that it was certainly fate guiding us. I am sure no other woman in camp would ever have had the patience to put up with us, and the Japanese, both.

Soon after our arrival in Kuching Mother Bernardine's ill-health required her to turn over active management of camp life to Dorie; and, as her assistant, Dorie was permitted by the Japanese to deal with them as a temporary measure only. But when they knew her, even the Japanese could not but like and admire her. Mother Bernardine was never able to resume active management of camp, and Dorie from then on was camp master.

Some months later, as food became poorer in camp, and Mother Bernardine's health became worse, a great concession was made for her: Mother Bernardine was permitted by Colonel Suga to leave the prison camp and return to her Kuching convent, there to live with the Chinese Sisters, in the hope that better food would strengthen her.

It was a remarkable concession for a military man to make, and a tribute to the light in which Mother Bernardine was regarded in camp by all — as almost a saint. When she left some said good-bye, others restrained themselves from speaking, simply from the feeling that she was so frail, so nearly out of this world, that even an extra good-bye would waft her over. No one expected ever to see her again.

But we were wrong. On the Feast of the Assumption, Colonel Suga himself, in his motor car, brought her back. She celebrated her feast with her Sisters, they sang and laughed and prayed — and again she said good-bye. And Colonel Suga took her home.

In time, Dorie Adams assumed complete responsibility for explaining us and our actions to the Japanese, and vice versa. Poor Dorie! What a horrible job! But she, I believe, felt sympathy for both of us, and equally annoyance with both of us. She was a great humanitarian. I believe she was the only woman in camp whom *all* the Japanese respected. She was tireless, selfless, fearless, and was ruled completely by her own conscience. I could look at her and know that imprisonment had strengthened her fiber without hardening her heart.

The other woman who dealt officially with the Japs was

Dr. Gibson, our camp doctor. She was taken prisoner on
Christmas Day, 1942. She had been appointed by the Japanese
to act as camp doctor, and was permitted at intervals to have
contact with Dr. Yamamoto, the Japanese medical officer in
charge of prison camps, and to ask him for drugs, which he
did not produce.

Here for the first time I met Bonita and Barbara, who
brought me friendship and help.

Bonita was the wife of the West Coast Resident, the one
who didn't get shot when the Japanese launches carried him
in their leading prow to Sandakan. Bonita was tall, blond,
beautiful, and racy, country gentleman style. She had blue
eyes and a skin like a baby, and we called her "the Wonder
Child." She could be lovely and charming and gracious. She
had a clear-thinking, quick, critical mind which made her
exciting company, but made it hard for her to be patient with
bumbling ideas or people.

She was an ardent garbage collector throughout camp
years, and a marvelous cook. Somehow she wangled scraps
away from pigs, poultry, and Japs; grew a few greens and
leeks herself; raised a few giant African snails; and then tossed
them all together over an open fire with a culinarious hand,
and out came a meal.

Night after night, after dark, after the children were asleep,
Bonita would come to me quietly, speak my name, then pass
a bowl of glorified garbage inside my net and whisper, "Here,
eat it yourself! It won't keep!" She came late at night after
dark so that George would not be awake, hungry, to look
longingly at it; so that I would succumb to my hunger and
eat it myself. The garbage was her food and her strength, and
she shared it.

Barbara was the widow of a government man who died of
illness when the Japanese were occupying Jesselton. Barbara
was tall, and looked like Gertrude Lawrence, as everybody

remarked. She was the only one in camp that nobody ever said anything mean about. She was never touched by the greed, bitterness, sharpness, that many of us felt. She could always smile, respond politely, and be kind. "Get Barbara to do it" was a motto.

Jo and Co.

Here in camp we all picked bare the bones of nationalism, and gnawed ragged the phrases, "All Englishmen are . . . All Dutchmen . . ." and so on. Here, when hungry, empty, and tired, we retreated into thoughtless, witless, and truthless, but comforting, generalities about each other and the meanness of each other's race. The British are dumb and stupid. The Dutch are greedy and ruthless. The Chinese are brutal and stolid. The Americans are crude and selfish. The Japanese are worst of all.

In camp we had two Chinese women, each the antithesis of the other; four Americans — Marjorie, Mary Dixon, Betty, and me — with only one common quality, American slang; we had ten Eurasian Dutch, and four Javanese Dutch, whose only common quality seemed to be that they could put up with the life we were leading better than most of us. We had three secular European Dutchwomen and three Dutch children, as different as dark and light, except for the Dutch songs they sang. The two groups of Dutch and English nuns were more alike, because of common ideals and way of living, than either group was like its own secular nationals. The bulk of the secular community, one hundred and seventy British women, had ceased long ago to seem to me British, or English, or anything except individuals, with perhaps one thing in common, less freedom of expression than we four Americans had.

The children were British, Dutch, two Chinese, two Borneo aborigines, one half-American, George, and in time two Javanese, Mitey and Kusha. These all had more in common with each other than they had with their parents, for all children have their youth, the loveliest, most endearing, most coveted quality which any being has — the one thing we are all born with in common, which we all must lose, and which as it goes from us leaves in its place something perhaps worth while, perhaps to be admired, but never so lovely as youth.

In due time, our men were also moved from Berhala to Kuching, where they were placed in the civilian men's camp, which was in sight of our camp. The morning they came we were informed, through Mother Bernardine, that they were about to arrive in Kuching, and we were ordered not to go near the front of our camp for fear of seeing them.

An hour later we heard lorries arriving. We were ordered to continue work as usual, and stay behind the barrack out of sight. By noon several women disregarded the order, and peeked around the end of the Sisters' barrack. Husbands could be seen in the distance, unloading the lorries. By 3 P.M. somebody saw Harry in the distance, and passed the word along to me.

At 6 P.M. I saw him myself standing behind the barbed wire in the men's camp. Thank God, I thought.

If we met by accident, while on working parties on the road, we were not allowed to speak to or look at each other. At this first camp in Kuching we used to look at our husbands across the distance, through barbed wire. The Japanese commanded us not to do so, they said it annoyed them. Temptation was too great. So the Japanese moved our camp a half-mile further down the road, to where we couldn't see our husbands.

In time I discovered that our women's camp was the healthiest of all the camps and the best-treated. And after more time I learned that all we had to complain of was semistarvation, weakness, occasional blows, and hard work. Hard work did not hurt us, as long as we could stand on our feet on the food to which the Japanese in time reduced us — five tablespoons of rice per day, and greens — and do it. But we scarcely could.

Our death rate was never spectacular. Being women we hoarded our strength, eked out that one kilogram of energy, and lingered on. We could probably have lain on the flat of our backs and just continued to exist for some time. But we mothers could not spend much time on the flat of our backs.

Once a month, sex got in our way. Having been limited by the Japs to one suitcase each, we couldn't bring in much sanitary goods, and by the end of the first year, rags and cloths were at a premium, and absorbent cotton precious. By the end of the second year we requested the Japanese to supply towels for menstruation. The Japanese instituted a personal poll of camp needs, as a result of which they supplied one towel for every three persons. Lieutenant Nekata, who was in charge of us then, acted as expert on such matters, took measurements, dictated the specifications, requirements, and so on; and they were very poor towels. By the end of the third year, nature solved our problems, and most women ceased to menstruate as a result of malnutrition.

I use the term "prisoner" and "prison" camp, instead of "internee" and "internment," because throughout the Nipponese conducted the camp on Berhala Island, and all the camps in Kuching, including the civilian ones, under the prisoner-of-war rules.

When we first realized that we were prisoners and our camp a prison, instead of internees with civilian rights, we thought we would point this out to the Nipponese. We mentioned international law. The matter was discussed very delicately with Colonel Suga. Colonel Suga agreed with us that there was such a thing as international law. He was it.

We had hated each other on Berhala, but in Kuching we began a new life, and were all glad of the chance to do so. Here with a larger group of people, many of them Sisters, or strangers to us, we forgot old grudges. We had more outdoor space to exercise in, the camp life was better organized, and the guards did not overrun our sleeping quarters. In time we gained a pseudo-privacy, because we ceased to see each other when we looked at each other. Nudity and public exposure lost their novelty and passed unnoticed. And we learned to leave each other alone. On Berhala Island we had let ourselves go; in Kuching we learned the need for restraint of word and deed, if not of thought.

A common enemy did not bind us together, hunger and danger did not do so, persecution did not, our sex did not. One thing only bound us to comparative peace: the lesson that life was hideous if we surrendered to our hatreds; more livable only when we tried to be decent.

Greatest and most intolerable enemy of all was the despair of hope deferred. From the day of internment to the day of liberation, we fed on false rumors. Throughout three and a half years our release was always three to six months ahead — or tomorrow. Perhaps we could not have lived without these false hopes, but we lived miserably with them.

In camp we had all of the sins. Some were greedy. I have seen a woman stand in the kitchen and fry five smuggled eggs for herself at one time, while hungry prison mates stood near with saliva almost dripping from their mouths. Some people ate in corners, stuffing themselves secretly, while others starved. There was one thing I learned then: no meal on earth was worth losing self-respect for.

This smuggling business sounds lavish but it wasn't — except in comparison to starvation. Fifty per cent of the time we were 50 per cent underfed, lived on rations only, and were desperately hungry. So hungry we could not sleep at night, and thought only of food by day. Then we would get an egg or a teaspoon of sugar or a taste of coconut oil, the results of smuggling, and it seemed like luxury. But what we ate even in a heyday of smuggling was still way below body needs. Everyone lost weight.

For a while the Japanese weighed us every month, according to Red Cross regulations, they said. Then they found us losing weight so rapidly that they added several kilos with each weight entry. When we still continued to lose weight, they discontinued weighing us. Some women lost as much as one hundred pounds during imprisonment, but they had been heavy to begin with. I was always thin, and only lost about thirty pounds. My husband, who is six feet tall, weighed only eighty pounds just before release.

The amount of contraband one person could obtain was limited. A mother smuggled for two, but could seldom get more than enough for one. In two and a half years of imprisonment in Kuching I ate five eggs, but I got a lot for George. Sometimes I was so hungry that I had literally to keep my eyes off his food when he was eating. But that extra food and my hidden haliveroil and calcium tablets are the reasons why he is well today. The fact that our children lived through captivity was not due to the Japanese rations.

The children were different from the adults: they were always generous with each other, sharing any delicacy, if their mothers would let them. Their greatest joy in having was giving.

We mothers, knowing the value of extra food, and the struggle we had to get it, felt that each child should eat his own. But confronted with the generosity of children, in contrast to adult greed, we hesitated to discourage them. In the end the children won; in every case they shared.

We saw in ourselves the toll of the struggle for self-preservation, but in our children we saw the generosity of nature when removed from the threat of fear. Psychologically we had always tried to take the rap for them, we did the fearing and fighting. They did not see ahead as we did, that an egg today meant life tomorrow. But we saw also that an egg shared with another child today meant life in our children of the qualities which made them lovely.

One day I had two eggs that Colonel Suga had given me. I hard-boiled them in the community soup caldron, then waited eagerly to show them to George at noon.

George saw them; excitement and joy came to his face. "Hey, chilrens! George having egg! Chilrens! Egg! Egg!"

"*Sssh!* George, we haven't enough for the others, so don't make them feel badly. Here, dear, sit down."

"Who gave, Mum? Who gave?"

"Colonel Suga gave them to me for you."

"Oh, isn't he kind! Say Mum, can I give one to Eddie? Can I, Mum? Can I?"

George needed the eggs. Eddie needed the eggs. I needed the eggs. But there was that impulse in George which I could not discourage.

"All right, George. Give one to Eddie. Tell him to come

here and eat it with you." I hoped that the gain to his moral nature would offset the loss to his constitution.

Eddie came. Eddie and George sat together over their eggs in conspiratorial glee. Over those tiny Borneo eggs bent two heads, one soft, blond, silky head, one black, black one. Two small dirty faces glow and grin, while four dirty hands pick eggshell off eggs, flick eggshell at each other and at me, two wide-open mouths are just about to be crammed full of hard-boiled egg, when suddenly Eddie remembers, and shouts, "Oh, save some for Edith!" (His sister.)

I, firmly then (this thing has gone far enough): "No, Eddie, not this time. You eat all that egg yourself. Next time we'll give the egg to Edith."

And so at last two wide-open mouths are crammed full of one egg each. Oh joy! Oh glee! Oh Happiness beyond the power of eggs to bring to the rest of us — and yet these two were eager to share that happiness, and the rest of us were not.

Here in Kuching we got in the Japanese military spotlight, and were visited frequently by majors, colonels, and generals. I found it was much like the zoo, and I was Exhibit A: "Author in captivity, with young. Note unusual height, lack of breadth, length of hands. Bites occasionally. Beware. May be fed bananas and biscuits."

I was called to the office at noontime one day by Suga, and presented to Lieutenant Colonel Maeda, a medium-sized, austere-faced Japanese, his unnamed aide, and his military interpreter. Lieutenant Nekata of our camp was also present. I had George with me to establish proper maternal atmosphere, and in hope of biscuits or bananas. George and I were both given chairs, and I a cigarette.

Maeda first asked me my age, which occasioned the laughter which ages always do with the Japanese — I hope sometime to find out why. Then:

Maeda: "How do you like life as internee?"

I: "I do not like it."

Maeda: "What do you think about war?"

I: "I think that I want it to finish, so I can go home to my husband with my child."

Maeda: "War cannot finish until British are completely beaten! They will be beaten. You know that, do you? Do you think the British will be beaten?"

I: "I know nothing at all about the war. We have no news. I have been interned over a year. We have no papers or magazines. *You* should tell *me* about the war."

Maeda: "Before the war the British always talk about humanity. They say they are humane people! All other people, no. Always talk humanity! All that stuff. Now, they are not humane people! They act like Japanese people would never not do — Japanese people very humane! *Only* humane people. Very humane — act very humane and good. Now British people see. British not good! All talk!" These sentiments are reiterated by all. Throughout, Maeda and Nekata are gesticulating for emphasis, and the interpreter is translating.

I continue silent, and gaze vacantly out of window. Maeda and Nekata now look proudly, challengingly to me, for answer. I remain silent, and smiling.

Interpreter: "Do you understand, Mrs. Keith?"

I: "I understand. I am listening."

They wait hopefully for a further answer which I do not give. After a time of silence and tooth-sucking on their part, Maeda speaks again.

"Do you think the camp life is difficult?"

I: "Yes. I am not lazy, I have always worked, but I am used to working with my head, not my hands. Also we do not have enough food."

Maeda: "All Japanese internees all over world made to work very much harder than here! All Japanese very little food. This camp very easy — not hard!"

I: "I do not complain. I understand that in wartime life is hard. It is hard for soldiers, for men, for women and children too. No one is happy in war. I do not like it — but I do not complain."

Nods of (for the first time) approval, acquiescence, from all.

Maeda: "What is most difficult here?"

I: "Beside the fact that we are hungry, the most difficult thing is to have no contact with my husband, and for him that he cannot see his child. For me, it is not so bad, because I have my child."

Maeda: "That is so. I understand. But it must be so."

Then Interpreter says Maeda has visited my house in Sandakan, and has read my book. Officer looks at his watch. Nekata signifies that interview is ended.

I arise and bow. Officers remain seated, nodding heads and saying, "Haaah! Haaaaaah!" George and I exit — without a banana.

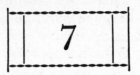

7

Working My Way

THE day that we were dumped out of the lorry into Kuching prison camp in the rain, the first thing that caught my eye was the fact that many of the women were comfortably covered with British soldiers' waterproof rain capes, and the more superior ladies sported elegantly cut officers' capes. This fact appealed to me instantly, as I had been wearing a bath towel on rainy days. I had a tweed coat, but I knew if I once got it wet I could not get it dry until the weather changed.

I asked the "Old Girls" how one acquired these miraculous garments, wondering if perhaps here in Kuching, where Colonel Suga had promised us the internees were all happy, there was some open market for exchanging goods. But I was told that this must all be done secretly by the route known as Over the Fence — via the civilian men's camp, and the men's vegetable garden. As the men's camp adjoined the soldiers' camps, the men were able to make contacts with the soldiers, who, I learned, would sell almost anything in order to get money to buy tobacco.

A number of civilian prisoners worked as gardeners in the plot of land which adjoined our camp, a job which was popular with the men who had wives in camp. The men would shout messages back and forth to each other at the tops of their voices, for their wives to hear. If a husband had anything he was anxious to give to his wife he would bury it in a hole or hide it in a tree, making some signal to his wife of its whereabouts. That night, after the men had left the garden, and the guards there had gone and the dark had come, the woman would crawl through the barbed wire and unearth the hidden article.

Three women worked together on this, one going through the wire, one standing close to the wire to warn her if a guard approached, and the third stationed further away in a position to see an approaching guard at some distance. The best time was five in the morning. Then the guards were always dopey, and they liked to sit at the kitchen fire which was just being built by the Bubor Queen, as we called the woman who cooked the breakfast *bubor*, or rice gruel.

My first step in getting a rain cape was to sell a pair of slacks, which I found were not practical in camp life because of all the mud. Shorts were easier to wash, and took less soap.

I sold my slacks for the price the soldiers were asking for their capes, ten dollars. That afternoon I tied the ten-dollar bill to a stone, and as my husband was not then in Kuching, I threw it into the garden near Don Tuxford, whom I knew to be softhearted. I then discussed loudly with Julie, his daughter, inside our camp, my need to have a rain cape immediately, and the fact that I was prepared to come out into the garden any night and look for one.

Don picked up the stone, and called out to a friend near by that he reckoned those soldiers had more capes than they needed anyway! And that he'd sure like to see one hanging over that dead tree branch near our fence tomorrow night!

The next afternoon I saw that Don had something over his arm. As many of the men wore capes also, this did not arouse suspicion from the guard — although how the Japanese thought we acquired soldiers' clothes without coming into contact with the soldiers, I do not know.

That evening before dark Julie and I went out and looked through the barbed wire, and there sure enough was the soldier's cape hanging over the dead tree branch. When dark came we returned to get it. It was so close to our line that we didn't have to go through the wire ourselves, we just fished it in with a pole. I never felt better dressed in my life than when I put that cape on.

In Kuching we had a canteen service which sometimes offered fruit, biscuits, peanuts, and tobacco. With this food innovation, money again redoubled in value. The canteen functioned weekly, or monthly, or yearly — according to whim rather than need. A Chinese contractor sold the stuff to the Japanese who sold us what they didn't want themselves.

By the time we needed food most, the canteen had ceased to offer it, but it never failed to supply tobacco. They called it tobacco; I called it banana and papaya leaves. Sometimes we had to roll the dried leaves and cut them ourselves, sometimes they would be cut like plug, but always we rolled our own cigarettes.

Wrappings for cigarettes were a problem. Paper was invaluable: first because the Japs confiscated all they found; second because we needed it for writing, for children's books, for toilet paper, and for cigarette wrappings. Even old newspapers (two- and three-year-old ones were sent in by the Japanese for t.p.) became rare, then newspaper-rolled cigarettes became classics. I found that the cigarette tasted according to the paper it was wrapped in, rather than the tobacco. Often we rolled the tobacco in its own leaf. The less food we had, the more dependent we became upon smoking.

One day "The Mothers" received secretly, smuggled in to them by a Roman Catholic priest, a gift of fifty dollars. The gift came from the Australian soldiers in the camp down the road, and was a gift from them for the use of the children.

We were overwhelmed. The soldiers were worse-treated than we, they had less, they were thinner, worse clad, and sick. Beside them, our children seemed husky.

We talked of sending back the money. But we couldn't

do this: to take from the men the gift of giving was to take from them what strength they had. Anyway, we craved that money for our children.

So we wrote and smuggled to them a letter, without salutation, without signatures, in case it should fall into Nipponese hands:

On behalf of the children behind the barbed wire, we, their mothers, thank you with all of our hearts for your generous gift to them.

We are thinking with gratitude of the extra food which this gift will buy for them: a gratitude which is especially deep because we know that you must do without food yourselves for their sakes.

Words are too weak for times like these. But when we say Thank you, we mean, God bless you, and keep you.

FROM THE MOTHERS OF THE CHILDREN BEHIND THE BARBED WIRE

Shortly after this, those soldiers were sent away from Kuching on a forced march, from which they never returned.

In packing for internment I had determined not to be caught without cosmetics. But when first I experienced the brutality of imprisonment on Berhala, I stopped using make-up completely. I was too tired to put it on! And what was the use? Why look like a woman, and live like a dog? I gave away three boxes of face powder, two lipsticks, several cakes of rouge, two jars of cold cream, and a very nice hand mirror.

I soon found I had been wrong. It was more necessary than ever in our circumstances to make an effort to look attractive, for the sake of our own morale. By then it was too late, and I could only hoard what little I had left. In time, face powder sold for ten dollars a teaspoonful — if you could get it; lipstick became priceless, cold cream could be had only by a trade for some necessary article.

When the Japanese had dumped my clothing in the compound at Berhala, I had been dismayed. They were not dresses I could use in prison camp, and I had not yet discovered the possibilities of trading and selling. If I needed a thing myself, no price would get it from me, and if I didn't need it, I gave it away. Most of these clothes I left behind me in the prison yard.

But when my trunk was dumped, empty, the next day in the prison compound, my cautious, determined Harry packed those things into the trunk for me, although I had left Berhala. When the men were moved to Kuching he himself carried the trunk onto the boat, and after he arrived at Kuching he finally obtained permission from the Japanese to send it to me in camp.

On the contents of this trunk and a little jewelry George and I sold and traded our way through captivity, living on the proceeds of my weakness for nice clothes.

In time all material possessions came to mean three things to me: (1) food and drugs for George, (2) food and tobacco and one presentable dress for me, (3) tobacco for Harry. In the women's camp we could always get tobacco of some sort, but the men couldn't. At intervals we were permitted to send it to them through the office, and sometimes when meeting our husbands we could smuggle the tobacco to them by wadding it up in a handkerchief. The men would not accept food from us.

Those clothes were worth nothing to me in camp, because I had George's health to compare them to; but fortunately they were worth something to others. Women without children could at least eat their own rations, and did not feel the press of necessity as grimly as did we mothers. For a few people in camp beautiful clothes, just for beauty's sake, still had a value, and to possess them they would sacrifice a necessity.

Values were established by needs. I traded a very exotic rose-taffeta negligee for some soda-bicarbonate tablets. I traded one dinner dress, long, full, heavy black crepe, price U. S. ninety-eight dollars, for six aspirin tablets, when George had a toothache. I would have traded it for one aspirin, if necessary. I traded a black velvet dinner dress for a white cotton sheet, because the sheet was a commodity which I could trade with the Chinese outside camp, for food.

During the first six months in Kuching I accumulated a furniture suite. When we arrived it was January and the rainy season, and water stood on the ground under the low-standing barrack in which we were housed, and there were inch-wide cracks in the floor on which we, without beds or mattresses, slept. George and I shivered through each night with chills and fever.

After a week of this I got up one morning, desperate and determined. I went to the bath shed, removed a wooden door from its hinges, and a wooden shutter, and took them home and placed them on our floor, raising them slightly with old chunks of rotten wood which I found. The door was for me and the shutter for George to sleep on. These formed an extra layer of wood between us and the ground, and cut off some of the chill and the wind. That night we slept.

The idea achieved such popularity that soon there were no doors and shutters left hanging. As there were not enough to go around, those who didn't get them protested our lack of community spirit, and a few, still wedded to modesty, complained.

Then I wanted legs for our beds, so I removed planks from the latrines. I wanted nails, so I removed as many as I could from the barrack supports, and stole some from the Indonesians who worked in camp. Literally the nails of our beds were numbered. In this manner I made two beds, two tables, two stools, and a number of shelves.

Sometimes the Nipponese officers inspected our quarters, found that beams were collapsing for lack of nails, and supports had disappeared. They questioned, but nobody could answer: they threatened, but nobody understood. They looked at our growing furniture, and their dwindling housing, and asked "Who did it?" Nobody answered.

One day I was lying on my bed looking up at nothing, when my eyes suddenly registered the four-ply partitions in the roof of the barrack above me. I called Mary's attention to them. Mary Bewsher, my neighbor, was a young Australian missionary who was full of bright ideas. We agreed that the four-ply was necessary for table tops and unnecessary for partitions. We and all our neighbors got busy.

That very afternoon the Japanese sergeant major decided to inspect camp. He had very bright black eyes, which he used to good purpose; they lit on the absence of four-ply partitions and the presence of table tops. We watched him, and we saw that very glance. He pinched his lips together and said nothing; he was that rare article, the Impassive Oriental.

That night we received notice that the canteen would be discontinued as punishment. It was some weeks before it appeared again.

The table tops were not worth the loss of food, but because we got by with so much so often, we were always ready to take a chance. And so many punishments descended on us for things we did not do, or did from ignorance, that living a law-abiding life was no promise of security.

Mary was a great person, I'm not sure how great a missionary. Before food got too short she had a lovely figure which she told me that she had acquired on the Japanese dieting system, as she had been too plump before. By 1943 the result was perfection, made doubly so by shapely legs, which no one could ignore.

The glance of her deep blue eyes was almost uncomfortably direct, her nose was surprised and inquisitive, and her hair was silky mouse-beige cut into an Eton crop which became her extremely, but was disastrous to others in camp who tried to copy it. Mary Bewsher was an Australian who was proud of so being, and Australia might well be proud of her.

Mary had two adopted children in camp, Danis and Dandi, as black as little Sambos. These children were true natives of Borneo, from the Bisaiya tribe, from the interior of Borneo. Mary and her husband, who was also a missionary, had adopted the twins at birth in order to save them from death, as the Bisaiyas consider the arrival of twins an ill omen, and do away with such infants immediately. As the mother of the twins had died with their birth, they were considered doubly bad luck, and only the fact that Mary and her husband took them away from the Bisaiyas immediately had saved their lives.

The twins were one month older than George, and had been imprisoned with their adopted mother since they were two years old. At time of internment they could not speak a word in any language, but communicated their desires by sounds and actions which Mary understood. In camp under the Sister's schooling they were slowly learning to speak English — at least we thought it was English.

They were quick in their reactions, but slow in getting out the responses. Their physical agility was in excess of that of the other children, and also their maturity of body.

They were naturally intelligent, but slow in their mental processes. Our children showed that they came of races which had for generations worked with their minds; the twins showed that they did not. The intelligence was there, but not the habit of mind.

Mary planned to take them to Australia when peace should come, and she hoped to educate them as medical missionaries, with the idea that they would go back and help their own people. I often visioned Danis and Dandi, with their naked brown bodies covered with Australian schoolboy clothes, with their books on their arms, with bright eyes shining,

white teeth flashing, defying learning together in some Australian school. I wondered if they would be as recalcitrant
as most offspring are in following their parents' ambitions
for them.

In keeping my record of imprisonment in Kuching I
always tried to write my notes secretly, sometimes after dark
at night, by starlight, moonlight, or no light at all, just by
sense of feel. I did not write daily, but every few weeks,
looking back and trying to judge what was important. Conversations of interest I tried to record as soon as possible, for
I wanted facts, not conclusions. Everything was written in
the smallest possible form, because of lack of paper, and
limited hiding space.

There were many things I did not dare to put on paper,
even for myself. Diaries had been discovered in the men's
camp and the authors — and others involved — spent months in
the cells, or were executed, on the guilt proved therein. If my
notes had been uncovered, the Japanese could have shot me
and others on the strength of them. And even if they did not, I
feared the words of people in camp as much as Japanese
bullets. *What a fool she was to keep such notes!*

Often Japanese searching was desultory, and superficial,
and the searchers did not keep their minds on what they were
after, if they knew. But with me they knew; they were constantly looking for my papers, written-on or otherwise, docu-
mentary or personal. Often the person who searched could
not read English, and read my papers upside down. Bit by
bit I fed them various documents to placate them, letting
them uncover something with every search. Often they were
stupid, but I could not rely on this.

The most incriminating evidence I kept in empty tins
which I wrapped in scraps of soldier's waterproofing, and
buried under my barrack. I tried never to reopen an article
after I had once concealed notes in it. Frequently I shifted

the hiding place of the article, however. Sometimes I got up in the middle of the night on a hunch, dug new holes to bury my tins, and moved them in the dark. I felt that if I was out-witted I could not help it, but I had a horror of being caught through carelessness.

As well as filling George's toys with notes, I rolled them inside a half-roll of toilet paper, and I stuffed them into a medicine bottle covered with labels, and I sewed them be-tween the layers of his grass sleeping mat. George had a false-bottomed stool, made by Harry for the purpose, which I filled with notes, and then nailed up. These were obvious places for hiding if suspicion of "conspiracy" ever fell on me, and if the Japanese decided to do a thorough job of searching. In fact they did go through and feel this stuff, but they never ripped it open.

Any camp upset always brought officers inside camp for a search. During searches George sat outside the barrack on his little false-bottomed stool with my secrets in it. I never ceased to be afraid, while searches were going on, or to think with envy of the joy of a clear conscience.

One time they proclaimed that all pictures, photographs, snapshots, illustrations must be stamped with a Japanese censorship stamp, within five days, or they would be con-fiscated. Some women had books full of snapshots in camp, representing every stage in their own and their families' progress. Some had their barrack wall lined with photos of families at home. For the next five days our camp master and volunteer assistants spent their lives carrying armloads of pictures up the hill to the Japanese offices for stamping.

There in the Japanese office they sat, officers, sentries, underlings, office boys, having the time of their lives looking into our past, studying snapshots of English country life, dogs, horses, infants, grandmothers, Henley, Ascot, gradua-tions, weddings, groom and bride, Poppa and Momma and baby. Great hissing and sucking of teeth, great *ttuuuutt-ing*,

great laughter, much fun. And every single snapshot had to
be stamped on the back with a stamp one inch by two inches
long, and many were stamped on the front.

Then when they felt really familiar with Western life at
home, they said, Never mind! Take it all away! We're tired
of it. . . . So then everybody got back the wrong snapshots.

I had only one picture, a photograph of Harry. This was
thoroughly stamped, at my written request, on the back. I
kept it straight through prison.

Throughout prison life I constantly marveled at two things:
(*a*) the fury of the Japanese in dealing with us, and (*b*) their
restraint. One never knew which it would be.

A chair, a table, a bed, a shelf, an egg, an aspirin tablet,
things like this were luxury. We might be shot, kicked, slapped
— or rewarded, in acquiring them. The element of gamble
made life difficult, but at the same time it was the breath of
life. Many a night I have lain awake promising myself never
to smuggle again, sick with anxiety because of the apprehension of a Nip guard through whom I was smuggling, who
had identifiable goods of mine. But always, I did it again.

Most of the Japanese officers who came into our camp
were overwhelmingly self-conscious when dealing with us.
We were women and we were inferiors: we could either be
kicked, or slept with. But their orders were to do neither.
That eliminated all method of possible contact.

Officer baiting was our one weapon. They knew we were
laughing at them, and when we were not, they thought we
were. They could shoot us, but they couldn't shut us up.
Why they didn't shoot us I don't know. They were either
kinder or less enterprising than we credited them with being.

I have watched a Japanese officer walk away from a group
of female internees. At a certain distance he hesitates, knowing what is going on behind him, questioning himself as to
what to do. Turn back and catch them laughing? Shout at
them and lecture them in Japanese upon the superiority of

the Japanese over the white man? Make them stand at attention in the sun? Smack them? Or go quietly away and try to forget those abominable creatures?

Indecision and indignity is in every inch of him: whatever he does, he's licked. He can shoot us, but he cannot shut us up.

Sometimes he turns back and vindicates his manhood. But more frequently, as his knowledge of white women increases, he pulls himself together, and heads down the road towards the British soldiers' camp. There he can feel himself a man while slapping the face of a British soldier twice his size — with the guard's gun in the small of the British soldier's back.

George had his third birthday, and his first one in captivity, shortly after our arrival at Kuching. On the strength of its being his birthday, I obtained an unusual concession from Lieutenant Nekata, who permitted me to purchase thirty-four eggs through the canteen, one egg for each child now in camp. I sold a dress to get the money, and paid twenty-five cents per egg. On his birthday morning George distributed an egg to every child with birthday greetings.

At nine o'clock we were sent for and told to come to the Japanese offices. Here we found Harry waiting in the next room. Lieutenant Nekata told me to my surprise that we were permitted to have an interview.

Harry and I had not met since leaving Berhala. We looked at each other, and again we were speechless. This time we could not even touch hands. Then Harry held out his arms for George, and when he had his arms around him it seemed he could not let him go.

I asked Harry if he had asked for the interview. He said no, that he had been working in the fields when he was called to the office. When he arrived Nekata said, "Today is your son's birthday. You may see wife and child." Evidently my request to Nekata to buy eggs for George's birthday had

been noted. I did not know how to account for this kindness, especially to me, except that sometimes the Japanese were kind. We had half an hour to talk, then said good-bye.

George liked my presents least of all, they being necessities. I made him two pairs of pants, cut from the bottom of the old blue gingham counterpane that I had used to bundle our

George

blanket roll in, and a *baju* and sarong to sleep in, cut from the bottom of my rose kimono. The Oriental effect was more to his taste than were the blue gingham pants.

Penelope made him a Tom Sawyer rag doll out of scraps from her clothing, stuffed with cotton from her pillow. Tom had a fishing rod and line with a fish attached. Marjorie North made him a small pillow covered with a piece of her dress and stuffed with rags, also two tiny wool golliwoggs riding in a newspaper boat. Tony gave him pictures cut out of an old newspaper, Pete and Frankie gave him two lumps of sugar, the last of the supply their mother brought into camp. Alastair and David and Derek gave sago-flour biscuits, and Edith and Eddie Cho gave three rusks, the last of Mrs. Cho's tinful that she brought in a year ago. Susan gave a blue elephant that Babs Hill had made out of the end of Susie's blanket. The greatest luxury was a tiny cake of soap from "Auntie May," as there was no more soap to be had in camp.

George went to bed very happy. He would not have liked his presents any more if they had cost a lot of money. He was so good that he wasn't spanked all day, a fact worthy of mention. I went to bed happy, having seen Harry.

One morning in June 1943 there was a crashing and banging of lorries down the road, a great running and shouting of Nips, and the message was sent in to us to stay away from the front of the camp — men were passing!

We soon learned by the grapevine news service that fifteen hundred Australian soldiers from Singapore, on their way to the POW camp in Sandakan, were stopping for a few nights in Kuching. We were all excitement, in the hope of war news, and Mary was particularly thrilled at the thought of her countrymen near by.

The men were established in a shelter on the far side of the men's vegetable garden, about a quarter of a mile from the women's camp, but in plain view of us.

The first thing that happened was that an Australian stumbled across an electric wire which was lying on the ground in the vegetable garden, and was electrocuted. The wire had been there for some time unprotected, our men had passed it daily without knowing it, our children had occasionally been allowed in that field for recreation, and had missed it.

The next thing was that the Australians started visiting the women's camp at night. They crept across the vegetable garden to our barbed-wire barricade, then lay there and made noises to attract attention until somebody came out. It was a toss-up if a woman got there first or a Jap guard.

Mary and I lived in the end section of the end barrack, and our window looked out on the wire. The first night we heard hoarse whispers, and stones came rocketing in the window and dropped at our feet. When the barrage became too thick we sneaked out to the wire and whispered equally hoarsely: "Cut it out! Shut up! You'll get us into trouble with the guard. He's just around the corner of the other barrack right now!"

"Aw, no, lady. We're coming in to see you. We ain't seen

a lady for a long time. Look, we've got lipstick and cigarettes that we brought from Singapore for you."

"*Sssh!* We've got our children here with us, and whenever the Nips get angry with us they cut the food ration. We don't want to get into trouble. Now go away before you get caught."

"Get caught! Say, lady, getting caught don't mean nothing to us. Me and my pal here have been sentenced to death twice and escaped. We ain't scared."

I could see this wasn't my pace. "Please go away. I'm scared, if you're not."

"Say, we ain't scared of no guard. We can do him in!"

Worse and worse!

Then the other soldier spoke. "Now look, when we get to this place we're going to, called Sandakan, we are going to escape. Can you tell us anything about the country?"

"You can't escape from Borneo while the Nips control sea and air, and if you try to escape into Borneo, you'll be betrayed by somebody for a price. Now go home like good boys. A guard is coming."

"O.K. But we're coming back in an hour after the guard changes, and come inside your wire and talk to you some more. Say, we like to see a lady again!"

"We won't come out if you come back!"

We went in. Mary and I talked over what to do. They were her countrymen, and naturally she trusted them and wanted to help them, and talk to them. I was cautious; I said the only good advice we could give them about escaping was Don't. If we were caught talking with them not only would the Nips be furious, but our own camp would be, and it would end up in camp as a scandalous episode described as "Lying out there in the dark in the field with the Aussies!"

Soon the whistles, catcalls, hoarse whispers, hissings, began again and the stones started landing inside the window. We had to go out to quiet them.

We crawled to our fence in the dark. They heard us.

"Is everything clear on your side, gals? We're coming in."

"Now listen," I said in my most forbidding tones, "I'm tough and old, and I wouldn't interest you. If you hang around here you'll get us in trouble and yourselves too. The guard's due to come along in just a few minutes. Please go away and leave us alone."

"Aw — lady! . . . Say, what about that other gal with you? Wouldn't she like to see us? We got that lipstick and cigarettes to give to somebody."

I to Mary: "I'm going in."

Mary: "What part of Australia are you from?"

"We're from Sydney."

"Do you know So-and-So . . . ?"

"Come on, Mary! Quit being a missionary to them, and save yourself."

Mary: "You boys had better go away."

I: "Here's the guard; I can hear him talking to Dorie! Get going, soldiers, quick!"

"Don't hurry, gals, we're just going to give you that lipstick, and cigarettes. Catch . . ." And through the air they came whizzing.

We caught the cigarettes, lost the lipstick in the grass, then crawled for the barrack, got there just before the guard, and crawled inside our mosquito nets, panting.

In the distance we heard rustlings of grass, then further in the distance we heard a whistled tune: "Waltzing Matilda, Waltzing Matilda, I'll go a waltzing Matilda with you!"

The next day we found the lipstick in the grass. The next night a guard patrolled up and down outside our wire between the Australian camp and ours. Three days later the Australians left.

Some months later we heard that a party of Australians had been successful in escaping from Sandakan POW camp, and that Dr. Taylor had been accused of helping in the escape, and made prisoner. Later again the escape was in some way connected with Harry, by a letter and description of terrain which Harry was said to have given to one of the Australians, when they were in Kuching. I always imagined that our visitors were among those escapees.

We learned in time that those Australians who escaped were probably the only ones to survive, as almost the entire Sandakan POW camp was wiped out in a forced march.

In Kuching we began organized labor. This work was done in addition to our community jobs of camp cooking, keeping the road and grounds clean, and cleansing of baths, latrines, and sleeping quarters.

Our first job was clearing a strip of secondary jungle growth which had once been planted with rubber trees, then abandoned to jungle again. The largest trees had been cut down, and our job was to fell the smaller ones, remove the rubber tree roots, clear the land of all growth, and then plant it.

Our introduction to forced labor was a speech by Lieutenant Nekata, as follows:

"This work is to be done by voluntary labor. You are commanded to turn out a working party of volunteers every day, to work four hours in the morning and one hour in the afternoon. This will help you to while away the time, so it is to your advantage to volunteer. This labor is voluntary and must be done by volunteers. I command you to volunteer."

We reasoned with him as follows: "We are too weak — or too ill — or too old — or have too many children to care for — to do this work. The diet is too poor to do heavy work on. The implements are too heavy for women to use."

Nekata replied: "In Japan poor diet also; women work. You will become accustomed. Mothers take children with them. This is my command."

At first we did not have a guard. Nekata said that, as we

were doing this work voluntarily, we need not have a guard. But we did not work hard enough to suit him. He stationed guards then, saying that if we did not volunteer to work harder, the guards would volunteer to slap our faces.

The work was very fatiguing. At the end of an hour I was exhausted, by the end of four hours I could scarcely walk back to my barrack. I would be so filthy that I could not sit down inside, and so tired I could scarcely stand up to bathe. Later on I learned better how not to work, while seeming to work. But later I was also weaker.

About this time there was a lot of face-slapping for which we could not account. We asked to know the reasons for which we were being slapped, and requested instructions which we might follow, in order to avoid being slapped.

Instructions were then written out by Nekata, and translated to us by the interpreter as follows:

"To avoid punishments or beatings the ladies should presume themselves to endeavor, with passive behavior not negative."

Nekata would come and visit our clearing, and stand and watch us work. He said we did not work hard enough. He ordered extra work hours for us because he saw some women playing cards one afternoon, and others resting on their beds.

One day he told our gardener-overseer that a Japanese lieutenant general was coming to inspect camp, and that our clearing must be full of growing vegetables in time for his visit. The tree roots were not then out of the land, nor was anything planted. Our overseer asked Nekata when the lieutenant general was coming. Nekata said, "Tomorrow, because it is the Emperor's birthday. It is my command that the vegetables be growing."

We worked hard and long that night, digging small holes and sticking in sweet potato cuttings. The result was quite effective.

Next day the lieutenant general visited, the garden grew;

Nekata flourished, was commended and promoted. The following day the potato cuttings died.

In Kuching we learned to bow seriously. We had printed instructions, demonstrations, and practice. The Nipponese orders for bowing were: Incline the body from the waist to a fifteen-degree angle, with head uncovered, hands at the side, and feet together: remain thus to the count of five (silent); then recover. (If not knocked down.)

The first time we were instructed in bowing in the Kuching camp, we were being trained to present a good appearance for the visiting lieutenant general for whom we had planted potatoes.

The day came, we were all assembled in ranks, the Sisters in front, the women and children behind, where it was hoped we could do the least harm by our frivolous ways. The order was given to bow. The Sisters had wonderful behinds, the bow made the behinds spring into sudden prominence; by standing too close and bowing too swiftly we managed to meet the behinds with our heads. Confusion and concussion reigned, and order was not restored. The lieutenant general was hastened away to review the pigs, who had more respect for lieutenant generals than we did, or else did not understand the meaning of the phrase "dumb insolence," as we did. We were never again assembled together in one group to bow to a visiting general.

The Japanese order demanded that a prisoner bow when an officer or soldier "came into sight." This was an equivocal phrase: some of us saw far, and some near, and some turned their backs to avoid seeing, and some saw and bowed before the officer saw them. The answer was that the officer was "in sight" when *he* saw *you*. To bow one was supposed to put everything on the ground, remove hat, hair band, scarf, sunglasses, eyeglasses (if the guard so wished), throw away the inevitable stinking, newspaper-wrapped cigarette, and arrive at the fifteen-degree angle swiftly enough to escape a slap for not bowing.

Sometimes we were ordered to "volunteer" for concert singing, or some other performance, in order to entertain either our captors or ourselves on some Japanese holiday to be celebrated in the camp square. If performers did not volunteer, individuals were singled out and ordered to perform.

At these entertainments, there were two or three thousand prisoners present. The Japanese officers sat in the front rows waiting for honorable insult, while the prisoners spread out behind them in the dark — either standing, squatting, or sitting on some stool contraption they had made. The husbands were always placed at one side of the audience, and wives at the extreme other side, with several fireproof layers of Roman Catholic Sisters and British and Dutch soldiers between them to prevent connubial contact. Japanese guards moved busily about the outer edges of the crowd, and inseminated warily throughout the audience with guns and bayonets; not to prevent escape, which was almost impossible from Kuching, but to prevent contact between married couples.

Husbands and wives went to concerts for one purpose, to catch a glimpse of each other, or to smuggle a note or message. Occasionally a very daring husband would crawl along the ground to where his wife sat, and stay near her in the dark. Then suddenly would sound the roar of a wounded bull in the dark: this would mean the guard had discovered the atrocity. It was not the prisoner who was roaring, but the guard, at the heinousness of his discovery. Then the prisoner would be flicked out of the audience at the end of a bayonet and chased to the guardhouse.

Harry never came to me in the audience; the indignity of the mode of arrival and the publicity of disgrace if caught were discouraging. But he did send me aspirin and notes through those asbestos layers of Sisters.

The British soldiers' camp put on some very amusing programs, with female impersonations, and some remarkable costumes were created out of old clothes from the women's camp, by two British Tommies, "Fifi" and "Annie." The women adored these programs because of the costumes, and the men adored them because of the jokes, the costumes being well done, and the jokes rare.

Other camps put on programs of varied ability. Throughout the evening the strain was great: which would the Japanese officers do first, take insult at some joke or song which they misunderstood — or take insult at some joke which they understood?

I usually arranged to be ill at concert times in order to enjoy the pleasure of staying behind in the deserted camp, and because I was too tired to exert myself to go. On three occasions I was sent for by the Japanese officers, and escorted by guards from my "sickbed" to the "voluntary" holiday celebrations. It seemed that they wanted me to commemorate these gala nights in writing, as a lasting memorial to Japanese kindliness, and this I was ordered to do.

But Lieutenant Nekata wrote the best story himself. Fifteen of our women, of which I was not one, put on a concert program of home songs, wearing their best dresses and make-up. At the end of the program Lieutenant Nekata was asked by one of the women what he thought of their singing. He refused to comment. The next day he sent the women this note: "I admire the ladies' lipstick and gowns more than their singing."

Shortly after this a Japanese general made a visit to Kuching. The camp was held to a high pitch of exhibitionism, during which we were not allowed to hang out any washing for three days, in order to keep the camp "neat and clean." Our Concert Ladies were ordered to sing at a lunch party given in the general's honor, being ordered to "dress neatly and wear make-up."

This had an early Roman Empire flavor, and the singers

were not pleased, but the order could not be disobeyed. It was decided that the eight eldest singers would be sacrificed, either to whet or to take the appetite of the general. The seven younger women would be kept safely at home.

The day came. The hoary-headed hostages were oiled and anointed to appear before their captors. Lieutenant Nekata was handed a list of the singers. He looked at the list and looked at the singers, and saw what had happened; the virgins had been sent to the rear! He tore up the list, and commanded that *all* the Concert Ladies should appear.

Tears on the part of a mother or so, but the virgins had to go forward. The lunch took place, the ladies sang, Nekata leered, the general smiled and relaxed. The ladies were given biscuits and bananas and returned to their camp in the same complete condition in which they had left it, only less hungry.

News came that a barricade would be erected between ourselves and the Sisters, who lived in the front part of the camp, from whose territory we could see our husbands. The object of the barricade was to prevent us from seeing our husbands, and from "misbehaving," as the Nips termed our habit of gazing longingly at each other.

Lieutenant Nekata ordered the erection of the barricade, and work was begun. We were dismayed. Dorie Adams, now the camp master, went to Nekata to plead. She promised no more "misbehavior" on our part, if only the fence was not erected. Nekata refused to listen. Dorie requested an interview with Colonel Suga; Nekata refused it.

She came home and reported, and the camp seethed with unhappy women, dismayed at the idea of more barbed wire and less husbands. We decided that the only hope for a reversal of decision was to picket Colonel Suga unofficially and make a personal plea, if he should visit camp, as he frequently did in the evenings. As Nekata had expressly forbidden Dorie to speak to Suga, I was chosen to make the plea. Suga had just recently commanded me to write for him, and it was thought that I might have influence with him.

Fate was with us. While we were discussing this matter, Colonel Suga's motor car drove up to the men's camp, and he entered. We waited hopefully inside our barbed-wire gate, praying that he would visit us, too.

Waited an hour . . . then our dinner gong went, and I had to go for George's dinner. I had just gone for it when Violet ran to my barrack to tell me that Suga was now leaving the men's camp. I ran to the front, George racing after me.

Suga was standing outside our camp near his motor car, talking to Nekata and other officers. I prayed that Nekata should not accompany him inside our camp.

Henrietta, uninvited, joined George and me.

Suga came towards us and entered the compound. We all bowed.

Suga: "How are you?"

"Well, thank you. How are you?"

Suga: "I am well. How is George? And how are you, Mrs. Keith?"

I: "I am well, but very unhappy."

Suga: "Very unhappy?"

I: "Yes, we are *all* very unhappy because you are going to build a barricade and separate us from the Sisters. We love the Sisters: they are good and kind, they teach our children, and play with them. Also, this space in front of camp is the only playground for the children. If this is fenced off, they will have no place for exercise. We beg you, do not build a barricade between the Sisters and us."

Colonel Suga, somewhat floored: "But Sisters live life of seclusion! Not nice to have men staring at them! Wives occasion husbands to stare at women's camp now! Also, we Japanese think not nice for husbands and wives to stand and stare at each other. We think this misbehaving — not nice. Must stop."

I: "We promise if you so instruct us that we will not wave, or try to communicate with our husbands. But please, do not build a barricade. You are always kind to us and our children. Please be kind about this."

Henrietta (determined to be practical): "And if you divide us and the Sisters with a barricade, the Sisters will have no toilets. Their toilets are in the back of camp. Anyway, you could put up a nice big barricade in front of the men's camp, instead of our camp, to hide the husbands. Now I can show you just how to do it. . . ."

I: "Colonel Suga, we all beg you to reconsider the erection of the barricade because you are kind to us. You say you wish us to be happy; you told us before we left Berhala that the ladies here were happy. We beg you not to cut us off from our friends, the Sisters, and to shut up our children in a more limited space. Remember our health! Remember our happiness! We all beg you for this kindness."

Henrietta: "And you can make a nice barricade in front of the men! I will show you how! And still the Sisters will have their toilets!"

The next day we were told that the barricade would not be built. We relaxed. But in time we relaxed too much: we could not resist the temptation of looking across at our husbands. It seemed such an innocent pleasure!

But not innocent from the point of view of the Japanese. Or else it was only an excuse they gave, when they told us a few weeks later that we must move to a new camp.

Getting Rid of Proudery
and Arrogance

THE new camp site was to be over the excrement pits of the soldiers' camps, where the ground was full of hookworm, and the air was full of mosquitoes. It was the third time we had moved in fourteen months, and with each change we lost strength, and gained new diseases. This time we were exchanging our newly planted vegetable garden for an offal pit.

We begged Colonel Suga not to move us, pleading that the children would die of hookworm, as they had no shoes; the adults would die of malaria, as they had no medicines; we would both die of starvation if we had no garden; we would all die of the move anyway, as we were overworked and underfed.

Colonel Suga answered that it was too bad and he was very sorry because he liked us to be happy, but we must be removed from the sight of our husbands.

He could not move our husbands to the new camp, he said, because it was half a mile further down the road and he did not trust them so far from the Japanese officers. Thus isolated, husbands might smuggle — might even escape! But not so ladies . . . ladies he trusted!

So we trusted ladies were to move camp at nine o'clock

in the morning. George and I had been ill in our barrack for three days and nights with malaria, which was always with us. George had a high temperature, and I had had no sleep, fearing convulsions for him again — and I was dopey with fever and fatigue.

Now moving day came, muster was called, and I was not there. Had I been executed for it, I could not have been ready at nine that day.

I arrived at the camp square ten minutes late, dragging two suitcases, and George; he feverish, but uncomplaining, with an unchildlike submission now to pain — which hurt me more than his tears. In the square there were eight other women and five children standing at attention, under arrest for being late. The rest of the camp personnel had already left for the new camp.

The Nipponese officer was furious with us. We ladies had no sense of discipline! (Bang! Bang!) We were not standing at attention even now! (Bang, bang.) If the Japanese were not so kind they would beat us! (Three bangs.) For kindness was wasted on us! (Bang, bang.)

We had insulted him, and the entire Japanese Army, by being late! Therefore we would spend the day standing in the public square, and the night in the guardhouse, and not proceed to the new camp until tomorrow, in order to wipe out the insult we had paid the Japanese Army by being late! (Bang! Bang! And a Bronx cheer!)

The way I felt about the Japanese Army at that moment, the insult could not have been wiped out by a lifetime spent in a brothel.

So we stood at attention in the sun, while our husbands, who had arrived at the old camp in a group, to help with the moving, were allowed inside with guards. I saw Harry, but couldn't wave; when he saw me he looked worried. It was an unusual concession on the part of the Japanese to let the husbands help us move.

Fourteen months before we had been imprisoned with one suitcase each. Since then we had acquired furniture. Inside the barrack our homemade acquisitions of stolen timber had been comparatively inconspicuous, lost under the seething mass of women, children, dirty clothes, falling mosquito nets, and reclaimed garbage. But when our husbands came to remove the furnishings from the old barracks, one wall of the place fell in, and when they carried the furniture down the road to the new camp the Japanese officers were confronted with the fact that 50 per cent of the old housing system had been converted into furniture.

Faced with the evidence of our wholesale disobedience, they were put to it what to do. The ladies had been naughty again! But what could one do? One could not shoot them all, one could not beat them all, one could not shame them, for they had no shame. One could not even successfully ignore them.

Meanwhile Lieutenant Nekata rested in the shade of the trees near by, watching the movers at work. His polished army boots were off, his stocking-clad feet propped upon a tree trunk, his trousers undone and open, with cotton underpants visible underneath. If the Britons had built their Empire in dress suits, the Japs were equally determined to tear it to pieces in their underpants.

The movers themselves matched the goods that they handled: they, like our material belongings, were broken-down, ragged, pathetic; they, like our beds, chairs, stools, and tables, were inelegant, but invaluable. Shirtless, shoeless, stockingless, hatless, each one bandaged, with a septic leg or arm, a cough, a limp, a droop — in the past these men had suffered with excess punctilio; today they scarcely had pants. Yet when one looked from them to Nekata, one could appreciate the fact that even so one distinguished them from apes.

Our husbands soon finished their moving work, and I saw Harry look anxiously over at me in the punishment party, before he disappeared into his own camp. We had been told to stand at attention for punishment: soon we just stood, and then we sat.

It was twelve o'clock now and very hot, and we were in the sun, and George became sick at his stomach. I carried him over to the side of the road and placed him in the shade of a tree, and stayed with him. Soon we all moved under the trees, opened our baskets, and took out the bottles of boiled water and tea without which we never left camp. Lieutenant Nekata watched us without comment from his seat near by. All I could think of as I looked at him was, "The little army-adjective so-and-so!" — which was a quote from Harry that used to comfort me greatly.

After a while Teresa, another one of the late mothers, who was always 101 per cent Mother Love, came to me and said, "You should tell Nekata that George is ill. Tell him we are all very sorry we were late, and ask him to let us go on to the new camp now. Perhaps he'd do it."

"No, I'm not going to. He's just sitting there waiting for us to plead with him. Look at him, with his pants half off! I'm sick of these Nips! No. We were late, and they can punish us."

"For George's sake, you ought to," she urged. I knew that I ought to, but I wasn't going to.

"You go over yourself and tell him about Alastair's sore toes!" I said rudely.

However, I did go over to Nekata and say, "It is lunchtime, and we have no food. Will you send rations for the children?"

He nodded "Yes," and I returned to tell the others. We made a little fire with twigs, and started boiling water for tea. Then Teresa could stand it no longer, she had the courage of a hundred convictions where the kids were concerned. She went to Nekata and spoke as always — volubly, dramatically, hysterically, as if demonstrating complete, utter, abject misery. In answer to her story of pain, Nekata's face remained as blank as a piece of paper. She returned, and we drooped in the heat.

Then "Wilfred," the Japanese civilian who interpreted for the military, came over to me. Wilfred was almost invisible owing to negative personality plus anemia, but the Japanese had awarded him a position of contentious importance, which perpetually involved him in breaking bad news to people, conveying insults and epithets, telling people unpleasant things about each other, witnessing violent scenes. All this had made poor Wilfred into a nervous wreck.

He came over to me, sent by Nekata, and asked if George was ill. I said yes, he had malaria; yes, that was why I was late to muster. Several voices around me spoke up and said the children were not well, it was too hot for them, we all felt ill, and could we go on to the new camp now?

Wilfred returned to Nekata and reported. Then after some time he came back and ordered us to go over to the lieutenant. We did so, and stood at attention before Nekata, who still lolled at ease with trousers agape. Nekata spoke, and Wilfred interpreted:

"The lieutenant says you are very bad ladies because you were late, and you have thus offended the Japanese officers. This is a great crime. If you were soldiers he would put you in the guardhouse for five days, without food, or beat you, or shoot you.

"But you are ladies — and the guardhouse is not big enough for you all. Also Nekata is very kind, like all Japanese, and very kind to ladies and children, like all Japanese. So he will forgive you this time, and you may now pick up your luggage and proceed to the new camp."

So then like good ladies we proceeded down the road to our new camp, swinging three and four suitcases on long poles between every two women, and dragging our children

behind us, while the Japanese, like very kind Japanese, permitted us to do so.

At the new camp I found that my "flat" was a good one, near a doorway, which meant opportunity for air and expansion: here in my allotted space I found our beds already delivered by Harry. The locating of a claim in a new camp was done by alphabetical arrangement, gambling, or fighting, and as I was late in arriving I would have been out of luck had not Shihping Cho staked my claim for me, by her side.

In this camp I found we had five long palm-leaf barracks, but only four were to be used for sleeping in, as the Japanese had ordered one kept free. This one, they said proudly, was to be our chapel.

This meant that we were painfully overcrowded still, and again George and I had only four feet by six feet in which to exist. Again there were no partitions or privacy. The mothers and children settled together in one end of the first barrack.

George continued to be ill all afternoon with a high temperature and vomiting. I washed our flat and unpacked the belongings, and stole some nails out of the beams for shelves, prying them up with a table knife, and knocking them cockeyed with a stone, and extracting them by wiggling. There was little to eat all day as the new kitchen fires wouldn't burn, the chimneys wouldn't draw, the water wouldn't boil; no wonder, as the firewood consisted of the branches of green rubber trees we had cut down that day.

I was awake all night with George, but towards morning his fever broke, and he slept. I got up at six o'clock, as I liked to arise early and dress quietly before the pandemonium of the children broke loose, to be ready for my morning job. Although I was writing for Suga I was doing camp work also. It was six by arbitrary prison time, but 4.30 by sun time, and pitch black outside the barrack and in. The stars scarce showed, the dawn still hung far in the distance, and the only other people awake in camp were the Sisters, who got up early to say their prayers.

I sat on my doorstep in slacks, for I was chilly with the aftermath of fever, and brushed my hair, and thought. Thinking was sometimes the way to wisdom, when bitter realities could be left behind in the foretasting of dreams and ambitions; but sometimes it was the way to destruction, when one was overwhelmed in an agony of despair. This morning, with me, it was despair.

Daily I saw myself becoming hard, bitter, and mean, disgracing the picture I had painted for myself in happier days. My disposition and nerves were becoming unbearable. I was speaking to George with a hysterical violence which I hated, but could not control. I did not have the food to give him when he asked for it; if I did I was so hungry I could not sit with him when he ate it; for this he was not to blame — and yet he must suffer.

I wept in despair for what I could not give to him. Not for material things alone, food, playthings, comforts, but for the gentle, loving mother that I could not be to him. I was the only living thing that stood between George and destruction. I was not a mother, I was the whole force of circumstances in his world. My body was worn, my nerves torn, my energies flagging; because of this I could only show him a stern woman struggling grimly to get his food.

As I sat grinding the teeth of despair I became conscious that somebody was watching me. Glancing over my shoulder I saw the dim outline of a Japanese soldier in the doorway on the other side of the barrack.

He shuffled across, stepped through my doorway, descended two steps, and stood very close to me, while I continued to brush my hair. He mumbled to me in a combination of Japanese, Malay, and English, and offered me cigarettes. I shook my head, wanting nothing from them that day. Some days, yes, but this day, damn it, no! He continued to proffer the cigarettes, pressing against me on the steps. I shook my head, but when he persisted, I morosely jerked my head backward, meaning that he could toss the cigarettes on the floor behind me, if he were fool enough to give them. He leaned his rifle against the door, fumbled with the cigarette pack, bent over me, and put them on the table.

The thought came to me, I should say Thank you. I should get up and bow. Or I should say Get away, you're too close! Or I should move away myself. What is he? A jailer, or a Sweetie-Pie?

The guard hesitated, giggled, and shuffled his feet — and then bent quickly over me, ran his two hands roughly down my breasts, over my thighs, and forced them violently up between my legs. The gesture so astounded me that I was paralyzed. I could think of nothing but, Well, it's fortunate I have on slacks.

What followed then was unpleasant, a kind of unpleasantness that a woman resents more than any other, and which hurts her as much psychologically as physically. The soldier was strong and rough and crude and nasty, and he enjoyed humiliating me; his ideas of pleasure were new ones to me; had they been familiar I still could not have liked them. I hated everything that he represented; but that was superfluous, for that was endowing him with human faculties, when all that he represented at the moment was an animal.

I was not strong enough to combat him, and did not have the power to escape him, but circumstances were with me. To debauch a captive thoroughly even the jailer needs time and quiet; he should have chosen the latrine or the bathhouse for his assault. The scuffling, the pawing and groveling, that we made, plus shouting on my part, began to arouse my neighbors. They were worn-out and sleep-sodden, and they had long ago learned to mind their own business where soldiers were concerned; still, the noise and struggle aroused them, and they began to stir and call out. The soldier relaxed his em-

braces for a moment, and I swung on him, taking advantage of
his distraction and an unprotected stomach area, and almost
knocked him down. He stumbled backwards down the stairs,
and there he hesitated as to what to do: whether to kiss, or to
kill, or to pull up his pants and go.

Keith

I was on my feet and shouting, "Get out! Get the hell out!"
and a lamp was approaching us from the Sisters' barrack across
the way, and our barrack was awakening, and I guess he'd
lost the primary urge. He picked up his fallen rifle, and went
sourly down the path.

I stood wearily in the doorway in the darkness: the stars
were still dim, the dawn not yet come, the Sisters still praying;
I had not even seen my assailant's face.

My neighbors slowly aroused themselves. Shihping Cho
crawled out of her mosquito net and asked me what the trouble
was, Maureen called across to me and said "What's up?" — and

Mary said sleepily, "I thought I heard a noise." I told them that a guard had been unpleasant to me, and they accepted my reply without discussion. We had learned in camp to ask no questions, and give no answers; each person's trouble was her own affair; she must bear it, or otherwise, as best she could.

We were captives, we were helpless, our life was unbearable, and we had to bear it. We cried out "I can't stand it!" — and we stood it.

A captive has no rights: I knew that one. I felt now that there was no further way for me to demonstrate it. But I was wrong.

I got my morning mug of tea, and even took some sugar in it: I needed something to stimulate me, and sugar, when one is unaccustomed to it, will do almost as much as whiskey.

As I drank tea, and thought about the happening of the morning, I became apprehensive. Only yesterday we had been moved to the new camp, last night the guards had sat on women's beds, laughing and talking until late, today I had been attacked. Would the new camp, because of its isolation from the Japanese officers' supervision, repeat the same conditions of unwelcome intimacy under which we had suffered on Berhala Island? I felt that, at this stage of fatigue and strain, it would be unbearable to put up again with the intimate antics and unwelcome familiarities of guards. The thought made me desperate.

Since we had been moved to Kuching we were under constant supervision, and regulations were numerous, but the life had been one of reason and consistency compared to Berhala. Within the boundary of our camp we had comparative security, and persecution was official, rather than personal. The contrast in our treatment in the two camps convinced me that it was not the intention of the Japanese Command that women prisoners as a sex should be subjected to indignities by the guards.

While still drinking my tea, and worrying about the future in our new camp, I heard a commotion near by, the order *"Kutski!"* was shouted, and the people about me struggled to their feet. The toy-soldier figure of Colonel Suga, very immaculate, fresh-shaven, clean-shirted, appeared down our aisle between children and pots. He was alone, had come apparently to inspect the new camp quarters, and as usual had come to the children's barrack first. It was easy, I thought to myself, to smile benignly upon us, with a stomach well-filled, and a body well-soaped, and the odor of Shanghai perfume seeping out of every pore.

I bowed as he came to my place, and on the impulse of anger and worry I said, "Colonel Suga, I wish to complain."

He stopped in surprise, and said politely, "Yes, Mrs. Keith?"

I told him then that a soldier had behaved indecently to me. I described the incident in unequivocal terms, and ended by saying, "Although I am a prisoner, I believe I have the right to live decently, even in prison. I believe that you intend us to do so. For this reason I report this occurrence to you, and as your prisoner I ask you for protection. This barrack is the only place we women have to live. I request you to forbid the guards to enter our quarters."

His reaction to my words was unmistakable: he was shocked. He looked at me in blank amazement, and said, "Perhaps I do not understand you. Please repeat."

I repeated my words, while he listened carefully, and then answered, "If another person had told me this, I would not believe it. But I know you, and I believe that you are an honest woman. Come to my office at ten o'clock, and I will talk with you. I am sorry that this has happened."

Since we had been moved to Kuching, Colonel Suga and I had had many conversations. He had recently ordered me to write for him, and had read the first chapters of "Captivity." I believe that each of us had become convinced of the desire in the other for sincerity — but each knew also that he was dealing with the enemy, and must be wary in order to save himself. Still, we wished that it might have been otherwise. It was this effort for mutual respect which had made him say, "I believe you are an honest woman."

I went up the hill to his office at ten o'clock, and repeated my story, telling him that I feared a repetition of Berhala Island conditions, from which so far we had been free in Kuching. He requested me to describe these conditions. I did so, and ended by saying, "The Japanese accuse European women of immodesty, but such conditions do not allow us to live with modesty, decency, or honor."

He then surprised me by saying, "My soldiers have orders never to enter the women's barracks, unless there is a disturbance inside. I am shocked! Japanese soldiers are honorable. . . . If I did not know you myself, and believe you to be an honest woman — I would not believe what you tell me."

I answered, "I am not a girl, I am not flirtatious, I have done nothing to attract this soldier — in fact he could not see me in the dark. If he could, I am sure he would not have chosen me. He came to me because he wanted a woman, and I was helpless and a prisoner. I know that Japanese men are not attracted by Western women — but they enjoy humiliating us."

He looked at me silently for some minutes, pressing his clean delicate finger tips carefully against each other; then he said again, "I believe what you tell me, Mrs. Keith. I am very sorry that this has happened. I apologize to you on behalf of a Japanese soldier."

He asked me then to identify my assailant, but I said that I could not do so because of the darkness. He called for Lieutenant Nekata, and asked me to repeat my story to him. Nekata listened, obviously did not believe me, became obviously very angry with me. He said that if the soldier had embraced me as I described I must know who it was. Then he said, how did I know that it was a Japanese soldier? Said it might have been a Chinese loiterer from outside, or a POW.

I replied that in all Kuching only a Japanese soldier had a rifle, boots, and a uniform, and all these my assailant had.

I remembered then that Nekata was always jealous of Suga's power, and jealous of his own position in the Kuching camps, and that they never liked the same people. In appealing to Suga I had made the mistake of passing over Nekata. But had I appealed to Nekata first I believed he would not have allowed the appeal. Because Suga liked me, Nekata disliked me, and disbelieved me. In telling Nekata of the affair it became not only an unpleasant episode but a nasty, dirty, grubby piece of lechery — on my part.

The interview ended with Suga repeating his apology to me for the incident. At that, I could feel Nekata squirm.

The next morning at ten, Nekata sent for me to come to his office, some distance from Colonel Suga's. At my request, Dorie Adams accompanied me, and Wilfred was present.

Nekata first told me to repeat my story, which Wilfred wrote down. He then said, "You are lying."

"I am telling the truth."

"I say that you are lying! I say that you accuse this Japanese soldier of attacking you, in order to revenge yourself upon the Japanese for the humiliation which I inflicted upon you three days ago."

I looked at him with surprise, and asked, "What humiliation did you inflict on me?"

"I punished you for being late, on the day that you moved to the new camp. I made you stand in the square in the sun, where your husband and others could see. You were angry with me that day, I could see that. Now you tell me a lie about a Japanese soldier in order to revenge yourself on the Japanese!"

As Nekata raged, I recalled my mood of exhaustion and

perversity that day in the square, and I saw that coincidence was against me. From his point of view Nekata had a case against me, perhaps even believed himself that I was lying, especially as I could not identify my assailant.

I answered him, "You punished me because I was late; that was your duty as a soldier. But my duty was to my child, who was ill, and whose illness made me late. Therefore your punishment did not humiliate me: it was just, it gave me no cause to revenge myself on you."

Nekata listened, unconvinced. He ordered Wilfred to type out a copy of my statement, and have me sign it, saying, "If this story proves to be false, it is serious. It is a death offense to conspire against a Nipponese soldier." We then went through it all again, he demanding that I identify my assailant, and saying that I was lying, and I reiterating that I was telling the truth. He demanded that I produce witnesses to my story, and I assured him that the women in the barrack near by heard my shouts and the struggle, and I gave him their names. He dismissed me, and Dorie and I returned to camp.

That evening, Poker Face, the sergeant major, brought in the soldiers of the guard, one after the other, demanding that I should identify someone as my assailant. There were approximately twenty who had been on duty amongst the camps, and it might have been any one of them. They had all been beaten by their officers for slackness now, and they were determined to make me name a culprit. Time and again I repeated my statement that it was impossible for me to identify the soldier because of the dark. In fact, even in the daylight and after several years of association, most Nipponese soldiers still looked a good deal alike to me.

Meanwhile, I learned from an Indonesian prisoner that Colonel Suga had departed suddenly from Kuching that evening, to be absent for an unknown period. My only hope was gone.

* * * * *

The next day at ten o'clock Wilfred comes for me again, and orders me to the office, telling me to come alone, without the camp master. At the office, I find Sergeant Major Poker Face, a guard, and Nekata. Wilfred is dismissed, and I am seated in a chair in front of Nekata's desk, and a typewritten document is placed before me, which I am ordered to sign. I read this through and find that it purports to be a statement made by me, in which I admit that I have falsely accused a Japanese soldier of attacking me, in order to revenge myself upon Lieutenant Nekata and the Japanese for the humiliation which recent punishment by them has caused me. I "confess" to having lied about the whole matter, and say that I am sorry.

Nekata orders me to sign this. I reply that it is impossible for me to sign it because it is not true, reminding him that I have given him the names of several women who can witness to the truth of what I say. Nekata says never mind about witnesses, sign that. Again I refuse.

He turns to the sergeant major, and speaks rapidly in Japanese; and then he, Nekata, leaves the room. I think to myself, "Can it be over this easily?"

The sergeant major looks at me with the coldest eyes that I have ever seen, and his tight lips fold over like a creased brown paper. I feel there hatred, contempt, dislike; behind that cold face I see subconscious memory of the years when we and our race have shown contempt for him and his race, when our power and strength have humiliated him. I see years of resentment resolving themselves now in his complete power over me. If he hates me as much as he seems to do, I admire his self-control in not murdering me.

He speaks to the guard in Japanese, and walks to the furthest doorway in the room, and turns his back on me. The guard comes close to me as I sit before Nekata's desk, and I look up at him in surprise. He takes hold of my left arm, and twists it backwards so violently that I cry out with pain.

He pulls it back further, and twists it time and again, letting it relax and then jerking it again, and the pain becomes sickening.

I call out to the sergeant major, I cry out again and again; but he remains standing at the door with his back to me. Subconsciously I know that he will not help, that this is going to happen to me, that I can do nothing — but I cannot stop calling to someone for help. The guard proceeds with his treatment.

Many times in my mind, since imprisonment, I have lived through such scenes vicariously; I have almost expected something like this to happen today — still, the surprise and the shock are great, now that it happens. It is the sort of thing which occurs to other people, but not to oneself.

Bearing pain before people who hate you is not like bearing it before those who admire you and expect you to be brave; there is no stimulus here, no standard for you to live up to. When the enemy hates you and hurts you and you cry out, it is what he wishes you to do, and he likes it; and if you don't, he just hurts you more. Nothing is any avail then. You become too weak to be shamed by your weakness, or to attempt to be bold. It takes great courage, or much phlegm, to stand torture, and I have neither. I can behave like a heroine for a moment, but I can't just sit and take it.

The guard continues his work on me, and I think that I must be making too much noise, for the sergeant major says something suddenly in Japanese, and the guard lets go of my arm. When he releases me I am so faint that I slide forward out of the chair onto my knees. He shouts at me in English to get up, and as I try to do so he pushes me back on my knees again, then kicks my knees, and I fall flat on the floor, and lie there.

Now another surprise comes, although I have seen this happen often enough to soldiers. The guard kicks me heavily with his boot in the left side in the ribs a number of times, and then in my shoulder several times, and very hard. I cover my breasts with my hands to protect them, and roll onto my stomach. He kicks me then again and again, muttering to himself while I cower under him. Then he stops kicking, and just stands and mutters. I cannot tell if the scene is just beginning, or ending, but I am too frightened to move.

Then the guard walks away from me, and nothing else happens. I turn over and look cautiously up. The sergeant major has disappeared completely, and the guard is looking out of the window as if none of this were any concern of his.

I lie still for a few minutes, there is an acute pain in my ribs, my left arm and shoulder ache badly, and I am sore all over, and worse than the pain is the shock.

In time, as nothing else happens, I pick myself slowly up from the floor, and sit in the chair again. I try to straighten my clothing and hair, but am trembling too much to do so. The guard pays no attention. The thought in my mind is, Just a minute, wait a minute, before you do anything more!

The sergeant major comes into the room again, and he looks at me. If he wanted revenge for old humiliations, he has it now; he should be satisfied now, but he shows nothing on his face, and says something to the guard which might equally well be "That's enough!" or "Give her the works!"

Then Nekata comes back and sits down, pretending to be busy, and not looking at me. The thought goes through my mind that I should protest to him at the guard's beating, followed by the thought that I have done too much protesting. Well, perhaps in time I will learn about these people, but not soon enough.

Nekata leans over and pushes his version of the "confession" towards me on the desk, and for the first time looks at me, and says, "It is a very serious matter to accuse a Japanese soldier. It is better for you to confess the truth."

My instinctive reaction is to agree to anything in order to escape. I understand now why people confess to crimes they are guiltless of, and I know that I can never again criticize anyone who does anything under physical stress. But I have thought this matter out beforehand, and, distraught though my body is, my mind still tells me, How can it help you to say that you have lied? Be careful. Keep your wits. The truth may still save.

I reply to Nekata, "I cannot sign this. It is not true. I have told you the truth." But my voice trembles, and I do not present a convincing picture. Nekata busies himself again at his desk. I have the feeling that the situation has gotten the best of all of us. I imagine Nekata thinking to himself, "Damn the woman, why couldn't she let herself get raped, and keep still about it!" I mentally agree with him.

But the feeling that Nekata is also at a loss what to do gives me courage. I reach out and push the confession away from me, and say, steadily this time: "I have told you the truth. I am a decent and self-respecting woman, and it is very bad that I should be insulted by your soldier. You are a Japanese officer and a gentleman, and you know yourself that this action is very bad. I tell you this story in order to ask for your protection. This is all I can say."

Nekata shows a definite reaction to this, breaking into a rash of embarrassment at my appeal to his chivalry as an officer and a gentleman: it seems to me that I have broken the impasse. He speaks to the sergeant major, then turns back to me and says, "You may return to your camp. You are not to speak of this to anyone, do you understand? That is my command. To disobey is very bad. Do not speak to anyone."

I pull myself together and leave the room with more relief than I have ever left any place in my life. Oh God, just let me get back safely again to the boredom, drudgery, and dirt of that which I have hated, I pray, and I won't complain. Miserable though prison life is, I know that I don't yet want to die.

The air braces me, but I still feel so ill that if anyone had been around to help or sympathize, I would have collapsed. As it is, I walk home the half-mile to our camp as if nothing had happened.

Arrived at camp I had a bath, and put on the remnants of my make-up which I had saved for the special occasions of meeting my husband. Today was a special occasion of another sort — and I needed make-up.

There was little temptation to tell my story in camp; probably half of the people there had been suppressing the desire to kick me. And I could not risk going to Dr. Gibson for medical aid in my present condition, for that would have meant being questioned, and I dared not confide. Nekata meant business when he said "Keep quiet."

I was particularly anxious that the truth should not reach Harry. Rumors could not be avoided, but we no longer believed rumors. He need not know the truth if I refused to give factual evidence of it. He could be of no help to me now, and in anger or indignation at my trouble he might endanger himself.

I went to Violet, however. I told her that I was being questioned in the office, and that I did not think I would get out of camp alive, and I asked her to take care of George if anything happened to me. I told her also where my diaries were hidden, and asked her to try to save them when the end came. She promised me she would do what I asked. I gave her no details of my trouble, not wishing to involve her more than was necessary.

At last night came, and George and I went to bed, and I thanked God for the dark. Nothing in this war, I thought, could be so hideous as having to do everything before people — having to eat, sleep, bathe, dress, function physically and emotionally in public; having one's private sentiments washed in the public bathhouse, and hung up to dry on latrine walls.

If I ever get out of this camp, I thought, dear God, just give me privacy — take everybody away, and let me die alone. I wept then secretly, painfully, in the dark.

George was very good to me that night. For his sake I usually didn't cry; I was his world, and the world collapsed, if I did. But he knew that tonight was something different; he was only three and a half then, but he had maturity in matters of suffering. So George said to me, as we lay together on our beds, that he was going to do my camp work for me tomorrow, if I was ill. I thanked him. He said then that he would stroke my head until I went to sleep, for we both loved being stroked. So he sat by me cross-legged, stroking gently with one soft hand, sucking the other thumb, until his eyes were glassy with slumber, and he fell over asleep on my breast. He lay there then with his fair, hard head on my stomach, his lips just open, snoring and sucking.

But I could not sleep. The pain in my ribs was acute, my left shoulder was swollen and aching, I could scarcely move my arm, and I was bruised and sore. I felt my breasts anxiously, for like most women I feared bruises there, and in addition to physical discomforts, I was sick with the dread of what might happen tomorrow.

I saw that I had been incredibly stupid not to foresee the course of these events. There was an almost routine procedure in such cases. A prisoner comes accidentally into Japanese notice, either because he is accused of something, or he asks for something, or he is unwilling witness to something. He is taken to the office and questioned, and if they cannot force a confession, he is freed. Shortly after, he is taken, and requestioned, and freed. Shortly after that, he is removed from Kuching, for further questioning. In time his removal is followed by the report to Kuching that he has died of dysentery or malaria, these being the equivalent diseases to knowing too much.

I had become a thorn in Nipponese flesh. They knew that

I was a writer, they constantly searched my belongings for notes, they believed that if I got out of camp I was going to write what had happened there. The threat was not strong enough to alter conditions, but it was strong enough to be an annoyance to them. My presence reminded them that the things they were doing would not look well in print, and they did like to be thought nice people! And now I had committed the crime of becoming myself the victim of assault and brutality.

I believed that Colonel Suga had left Kuching in order to avoid an unpleasant situation, for to interfere between Nekata and myself, Suga would have had to run the risk of being labeled "Pro-British." And why should he risk himself to save me?

Next morning came. At ten o'clock Wilfred again ordered me to Nekata's office, alone. I sent George to Violet, and told myself that this was the finish. I put on my neatest dress and make-up, to meet the end.

At the office there are Nekata, the sergeant major, and a guard. Nekata's typed "confession" is again offered to me to sign, and I refuse. My own statement is then read through to me, and I affirm that it is the truth.

Then we proceed as we did the day before: Nekata speaks to the sergeant major and the guard in Japanese, and Nekata leaves the room. The sergeant major speaks to the guard, and the sergeant major leaves the room. The guard lounges over to the window, and leans against it. I sit and wait: nothing to come can be more terrifying than this sitting and waiting for something to come. Dressed for slaughter, hair carefully combed and braided, lipstick on colorless lips, rouge on malaria-yellowed cheeks, in neatest white dress, good sharkskin, once very smart — this is how the Well-Dressed Internee will dress to be beaten up, I tell myself.

Through the window I see Nekata walking slowly up the hill towards the Japanese officers' quarters. He disappears.

Nothing happens. After ten minutes he comes into sight again, descends the hill road, and re-enters the office. He has in his hands a newspaper-wrapped bundle, which he places on the desk.

About that bundle my mind jumps instantly to a conclusion: it contains some of the articles which I have traded to the Japanese guards in exchange for contraband food, articles which, now that the heat is on, have been identified and brought in to make more trouble for me. Oh, for a clean conscience! That white hand-knit wool sweater that somebody made for Harry — they can't prove that's mine, can they? Still, I wish they didn't have it. And Harry's wool socks, and his gray flannel trousers with Wm. Powell's Hong Kong label in them! And my gold thimble with "Agnes Newton on her sixteenth birthday from Mom and Dad." Oh, what a fool I've been!

Nekata dismisses the guard, and we are alone. He motions towards the newspaper-wrapped package and says to me, "You do not look well. You are very thin. Here are six eggs for you. Take these eggs and eat them. This affair is finished. But remember, I order you not to speak of this. Also remember, if your statement is not true, that it is a death offense. You may return to your camp now."

With difficulty, I arise, bow and say "Thank you," pick up the eggs, and leave.

What an incredible people, I think. An omelet for my honor! Six eggs for broken ribs! Well, an egg is still an egg! This time I intend to eat some myself. Three for George, and three for me. I really do need something. . . .

I walk down the road towards home in a state of semi-hysteria; the eggs have brought the situation down to earth; surely Nekata can't swing it back to the high tragedy level after this!

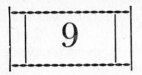

9

Suga Babies at Play

SOME three days after Nekata had released me, I noticed a guard in camp with a working party of Roman Catholic priests; I felt him almost before I saw him, because of the hatred behind his stare. He hung around my doorway outside the barrack all morning, and when I had to go outside to the latrine he followed me, and entered the latrine after me.

He shook his fist and spat at me, and shouted in bad Malay and English: "You are a wicked woman! You tell Colonel Suga bad things about me! I come to you as your friend, I give you cigarettes, I try to make friend of you, but you tell Colonel Suga I am bad. *You* very bad woman. You tell! There is much trouble now, all our soldiers beaten. The soldiers hate you. We make trouble for *you* now. Pah!" And he spat again.

I looked at him in astonishment at his foolishness in revealing himself as my assailant. But astonishment that lasted only a moment — then I saw that he was right, and always had been — he was safe whatever happened. He was the man with the gun. That I reported him at all had been my error in conception of conditions, not his.

His venom made me shiver. I walked away from him, while he was still shouting.

Two weeks later the pain in my ribs was no better. My shoulder was improving, and the bruises had disappeared, but my arm was weak and almost useless — and I still had camp work to do.

I went to Dr. Gibson, and asked her to bandage my ribs with elastoplast, saying that I had broken them some years before, and they were paining me again, perhaps as a result of heavy work.

She had only a small amount of elastoplast, and said she could not use it all on one patient. I suggested that she ask Dr. Yamamoto, the Japanese surgeon, for more, but she said it would be useless to ask him. However, she bandaged me from armpit to waist with a bandage made from spliced strips of old silk underwear. I returned to my work, and after a few minutes of movement, the silk bandage slid down to my waist.

I went and bargained with a fellow prisoner for a roll of new muslin bandage. I took this to the doctor, and she bandaged me again, under the armpits, and over the shoulder and down to the waist. This gave me support, but the inelasticity allowed no leeway for breathing. By midnight the tension was unbearable, and I removed the bandage.

I arose the next morning, feeling desperate. Taking French leave of camp, I walked out of the gate and up the road to Dr. Yamamoto's office. I expected to be caught and stopped by the camp sentry or the road sentry; I did not care. But luck was with me, and neither was in sight.

Dr. Yamamoto, the Japanese medical officer responsible for the welfare, or otherwise, of the Kuching prison camps, commanded the drug supplies. I disliked going to him, as the Japanese accused us of lack of fortitude, inability to bear suffering, and physical cowardice. Pride made me at first dislike to ask for anything, and give them further excuse for their contempt. However, I got over this as my needs increased.

We were forbidden, both by our community rules and by Japanese POW rules, to go to Dr. Yamamoto. We had orders to deal only with our individual camp doctor, who was appointed by the Japanese, and had authority to approach Dr.

Yamamoto at specified times to ask for medical supplies, and to present requests concerning the health of the camp.

The Japanese rule was made in order to save Yamamoto from annoyance. The camp community rule was based on the theory that the camp doctor would make requests for the good of the community as a whole, whereas the individual would think of herself only, and she alone would benefit. As the supply of drugs and Dr. Yamamoto's patience were equally limited, the theory was wise. But throughout camp life, the way to get a thing was to disregard all rules, both British and Japanese, and go after it. This was antipathetic to the law of community living, but sympathetic to the primary law of survival of the fittest.

Dr. Yamamoto was a man of extremes — either delightful, or devilish. He had a violent, uncontrolled temper, which sent him literally insane when he was annoyed, and a sense of humor from whose scope he excepted himself. He was the one officer in the Kuching group that we did not dare to ridicule. When he was not hurling swords and kicking people, he was gentle in his ways and manner, entertaining and kind.

A private feud existed between our doctor and Yamamoto. She thought him a twirp, charlatan, medical fake, brute, and stupid. But stupid he was not; he knew that she thought him all this, and the knowledge resulted in constant strife — our doctor got the last word, but Yamamoto took the last kick. Before the war was finished, he had struck her on the head, struck her in the face, knocked her down, and kicked her shins until the blood ran.

This morning, fortunately, I found Yamamoto in a good humor. He was a good-looking, spotlessly neat man, fairly tall for a Japanese, with a long straight face, a definite jaw, very bright alive eyes, and well-shaped, well-cared-for hands. We bowed to each other, and he told me to sit down and gave me a cigarette. He commented that I was extremely thin, and did not look well, and asked me if I still had malaria, as I had gone to him once for quinine.

I said Yes, but it was not about malaria I had come; I believed I had some broken ribs. I described my pains and symptoms, and asked him to give me a roll of elastoplast to use for bandaging purposes. He listened to my diagnosis sympathetically, and agreed with the probability of its correctness, but did not offer to examine me. I was reminded of the fact that he never examined a female patient, when he came into camp, unless our doctor was present. She said that this was because Yamamoto did not know enough medically to examine a patient alone; but we always suspected that it was because he knew too much psychologically to do so.

He asked how I had received the injury, and I told him it was an old one from some years before. He sucked in his breath at that and said, "I am surprised!" Then he said, "I hear that you have some trouble with a Japanese soldier?"

I made no reply, and we looked at each other silently. Then he said, "We Japanese either kill, or get killed, in war. It is better so. I think it is not pleasant to be a prisoner."

I said, "Well, it's not too late to kill us all still!"

"Ha! I think not. Very awkward now." We both laughed, and I knew I was going to get the elastoplast. He left the office and went into the storeroom, and returned in a minute with a new tin of Red Cross elastic adhesive tape. He handed this to me, saying, with a laugh, "Don't tell the doctor!"

He asked me if I needed anything else. I said that I would like a narcotic, as the pain kept me awake at night, also I would like a piece of soap for George's bath. He gave me some small white tablets out of a Parke-Davis bottle, one of the barbiturates, I think; then reached into his desk drawer and, with his penknife, cut in half a large piece of soap; then reached into another drawer and produced four ripe bananas, and said, "For George."

I said, "Thank you very much. You are kind to us."

He left the room for a moment, and returned with two eggs, which he handed to me, saying, "For you, not George."

I thanked him again, assured him he was kind, and stood up to go, but he told me to sit down. He asked me then my age, and laughed at the answer, assured me that the war was going to last for at least ten years more, said that the Nipponese were going to win it in the end, but that it didn't make any difference to him as he would either get killed, or kill himself, warned me again not to tell the doctor that he had given me anything, told me to take care of myself, handed me a packet of Saigon cigarettes, and motioned me to depart.

Just as I was leaving I remembered soda bicarbonate; this I always needed for George, who suffered with bladder irritation from the starch diet. I said, "I do not like to ask you for anything more, Dr. Yamamoto, but you are so kind, so very kind, that I do. Could you give me some soda bicarbonate for George?"

He looked a bit annoyed first, tutt-tutt-ed, then laughed, and said, "Haah, Keif, I am very kind! Haah! O.K. Keif! I give you soda bicarb." And he did.

I bowed good-bye, and walked home, reflecting that the quality of brutality was not isolated in the Japanese, nor was the quality of mercy unknown to them.

Mary helped me to apply the bandage immediately. The elastic support brought relief, and with the help of the pain-killer, I had a real night's sleep. The next day I swallowed my pride and asked Dr. Gibson to take me off the camp work schedule temporarily. She agreed, and put me on sick list for two weeks. I said nothing about my visit to Yamamoto.

The following day a bottle of Red Cross multiple vitamin tablets arrived for me from Dr. Yamamoto, with the sole instruction: "Do not tell the doctor!" These I put away for the greater emergency, the expectation of which always overshadowed prison life.

* * * * *

Meanwhile we learned that before the sudden departure of Colonel Suga from Kuching, he had ordered that all of the guards should be disciplined, as a punishment for their recently discovered slackness in their relations with prisoners. "Discipline" in the Japanese military vocabulary meant beating up. Consequently our sentries were suffering from bruises which they blamed on me. We also learned that Suga had ordered guards not to "touch" us, which explained why they were now striking us with sticks instead of their hands.

They would slap our faces, or make us hold out our hands to be caned in schoolboy fashion; it was unpleasant and humiliating, but the pain was not severe. The feeling of the hatred of the guards, and the knowledge that they were waiting to get us and we were helpless, brought a nervous reaction far beyond the physical effect of their blows.

They were particularly unpleasant to me. But before long I realized that what I was suffering might be stern punishment to a European woman, but was not very serious from the point of view of an Oriental soldier. I came to see that the guards were like silly children; only they were big and powerful ones. The hissing, spitting, smacking, was relieving them, and in time they would be laughing instead.

Meanwhile we had to stay as far from the barbed wire as possible, and inside the barracks, in order to avoid the guards. All this added to the misery of camp life, and especially to mine, because I had involved others in trouble. The ethics of my action had been right, but ethics made little difference to people in our condition; whatever added to the distress of daily living was the greatest evil now.

The reign of terror extended against the men's camps also, and all along the road the prisoners were struck, bullied, and abused. We women were slapped and smacked, but the men had bones broken, skulls cracked, and received blows from which they did not recover.

There were so many Nipponese regulations governing

camp behavior that we could not pursue the round of daily living without infringing them, if the guards wished to hold us to the letter of the law.

Sometimes the officers complained to the camp master that we were not bowing in good style, and if our bowing form did not improve, rations would be cut. Then when officers appeared on our furthest horizon, all the unemployed women in camp sneaked into barracks, kitchen, or latrines, out of view. The officer entered a deserted compound. For a Japanese officer to review an empty chicken run, and closed latrine doors, is a disappointment. At the next camp meeting the camp master would be informed that the officers did not like the attitude of the ladies, who disappeared from sight when the officers were kind enough to visit them. This was not polite; hereafter the ladies were to emerge from their quarters and welcome the officers — or rations would be cut.

We could avoid the perimeter guards by staying away from wire, gate, and sentry box, but there was no escaping from those who entered camp looking for trouble. A favorite place for a belligerent guard to stand was between the mothers' barrack and one of the necessity stops — kitchen, bathhouse, or latrine. Going to and from the kitchen for food we were caught regularly, as we couldn't put down our dishes quickly enough to please. Going to and from the bathhouse and carrying a child, we couldn't deposit child, soap, towel, clothing, on the ground in time.

Going to the latrines was equally difficult. Most people had diarrhea most of the time now due to a diet of rice, weeds, and germs; a guard between us and the lats was the height of discomfort. In addition to delay we had to throw away our cigarettes, and the loss of a cigarette was important, and equally so the loss of a light, as we had no matches but had to go to the fire in the kitchen, which was never allowed to go out. The alternative to throwing away a cigarette was to hold it in closed hand or mouth until it burned you.

Minor persecutions now made life almost unbearable. The Nipponese accused us of not being serious, and we maddened them because we laughed, when they wanted us to weep — but had we not laughed, we must have killed ourselves, or each other. Laughter was our only outlet, our only relief for emotion. Our laughter was pain, passion, love, hate, occasionally humor; it was horrible, high, hysterical, grim — because the joke was grim — but it was better than tears.

There were four weeks of petty persecution after the guard became enraged at us for the discipline which my complaint had brought on them. Then the peak came.

It is Sunday afternoon, five women are in the community kitchen preparing Sunday dinner of potato greens and rice sweepings. Mrs. B has a bright scarf wound around her head to stop the sweat which otherwise would drip into the food. She bends over the large iron caldron and stirs the rice with a long-handled wooden paddle. To move the heavy mass of rice which she is preparing for one hundred and twenty persons, she must exert all her strength, and bear down with all her weight upon the paddle.

A guard, known to us as the Wife Beater because he was the kind of man who would, comes tearing into camp. His hoarse shouts are heard on the road, even before he enters the gate, and it is evident that he is looking for a victim. The warning goes swiftly around, and those who do not have business in the compound retreat silently inside latrine, bath shed, or barrack.

The Wife Beater heads for the kitchen and calls the women to attention. Mrs. B, stooped over the rice caldron, is slow in coming to attention and bowing, and when she does so, has not removed her headband. Although the wearing of a headband has been permitted by office regulation, individual guards take umbrage, if feeling unpleasant.

The Wife Beater shouts at Mrs. B to take off her scarf,

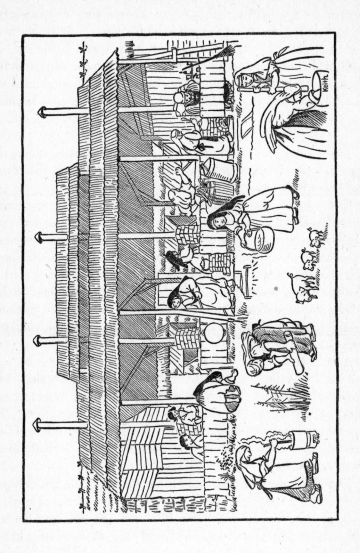

striking her heavily in the face as he does so, and then continuing to slap and strike her while she struggles to remove the scarf. Mrs. B tries to protect herself with raised hand and arm; and then, reacting instinctively to the attack, she strikes back at him. At this sign of resistance, the guard's hysteria increases; shouting and bellowing, he strikes and slaps her on face and head until she falls to the kitchen floor, insensible.

The other occupants of the kitchen stand silent, helpless. This is an armed guard on official duty, and for us to strike or resist him is a death offense. He is so crazed now that to offer further annoyance or resistance will only expose more of us to his violence. At one time we could not have remained passive; now we have learned.

As Mrs. B falls to the floor, Dr. Gibson enters the kitchen. Fearlessly she goes through the ranks of motionless women, and takes her stand over Mrs. B. She points to her Red Cross emblem, and orders the soldier, in the name of the Red Cross, to leave Mrs. B alone. The Wife Beater hesitates, surprised by her daring. Faced with the Red Cross emblem, one of the few symbols which seem to mean anything to the Japanese soldiers, he allows Mrs. B to be carried away by friends to the hospital ward.

Then he dashes from camp, to report a brutal attack made upon himself by a female prisoner. Soon he is back again, bringing with him another guard and an order from the office to arrest his assailant, and bring her to the office immediately.

Meanwhile Mrs. B has revived to a state of semihysteria in the hospital ward. As the office order cannot be disregarded, she is placed on a hospital stretcher, and six women prepare to carry her up the road to the office.

I was not one of those women; but Bonita, my friend, whose brisk words always tried to deny the humanity of her actions, was one of them. She told me what followed.

As they move up the road the Wife Beater trots by the

litter, panting and shouting. The women who carry the stretcher move grimly forward with inscrutable faces; their mouths, when they open them, speak almost inaudible words which they did not use before captivity.

On the way to the office, the procession must pass four other camps — those of the British soldiers, the Dutch officers, the civilian men, and the priests. The litter and its escort are noted in these camps, and anxious glances follow.

At the office, the officer in charge looks rather abashedly at this small-boned, delicate-looking, middle-aged woman lying on a stretcher before him, accused of attacking an armed Nipponese soldier on duty. However, he recites the charge against her, and listens to a storm of Japanese from the guard. Then he says to Mrs. B that this is a very serious charge brought against her; to attack a guard on duty is an offense punishable with death. What excuse has she?

Mrs. B's answer has been practised all the way up the road. Mrs. B says that she was not resisting the guard, did not strike the guard, only raised her arm instinctively to protect her face, while he was striking her. This gesture was mistakenly interpreted by the guard as one of attack; Mrs. B had no idea of striking him, would not think of such insubordination, and the whole occurrence is a misunderstanding. The six women with Mrs. B bear witness with her.

The officer and guard then shout at each other in Japanese. The guard declares that the prisoners are lying, as of course they are, but the six women stick to their story, and the victim's condition is a mute plea for mercy. The officer rules that Mrs. B is to apologize to the guard for her action which occasioned a misunderstanding, and to be careful in future to avoid misunderstandings. Mrs. B apologizes, the guard mutters angrily, and the female bodyguard bows its way out of the office — defeated but victorious — and proceeds back to camp. The British soldiers are waiting close to their barbed wire as the procession passes down the road again. Obviously they are anxious to learn what the trouble is, and impatient at being powerless to help.

The following day the weekly liaison meeting was held between the Nipponese representatives and the Allied camp masters from the eight prison camps. The representative for the British officers lodged a protest against the physical abuse of the women by the Japanese guards, stating that the officers could not be responsible for maintaining discipline amongst the Allied prisoners if such mistreatment continued. The British sergeant major, camp master of the British soldiers' camp, warned the Japanese that the soldiers could not be restrained further if the guards continued to strike the women. The civilian men internees' representative lodged a similar protest against our mistreatment.

The next day the camp masters asked for an interview with Colonel Suga, who had by then returned to Kuching, and the protests were made to him in person. He was apologetic in his attitude to the prisoners' representatives, and said that the guards would be forbidden to strike the women in future. "But," he said, "if the women disobey orders — the soldiers must of course *enforce discipline!*" He did not say how. It sounded to us as if the man with the gun was still right.

But the protests had their effect, for the Japanese officials in Kuching were still afraid of the potential power of their underfed, unarmed, naked, ill-treated, half-starved prisoners, if some final outrage should drive them, against judgment, to rebel. But one of the tortures of our situation was its inescapability; escape into Borneo was useless, and escape from it, almost impossible.

Many hotheads in the men's camps constantly urged large-scale rebellion. Had they rebelled they could have killed some Japanese soldiers, and a large number of local Asiatic non-combatants, but they would have been massacred themselves almost immediately. And for the two hundred and eighty women and children, the fate would have been certain. Life was not sweet in prison, but it was sweeter than meeting death by mutilation and torture, which was the Japanese answer to women and children who resisted captivity.

The first time I saw Colonel Suga after my trouble with Nekata was at a propaganda newsreel appearance. News films were being made of a Japanese general who was visiting Kuching Camp and inspecting our prison unit, and of the camps.

A few chosen prisoners were again ordered to "Dress neatly and be clean," and come to the Colonel's office, there to be photographed against a picturesque background of flowers, trees, shrubs, and the pig pond. Then they were taken to the city of Kuching to the onetime White Rajah's garden, where they were photographed standing smiling and picking flowers. The newsreel photographers were never allowed inside our prison grounds.

This afternoon, dressed in clean dresses at Japanese command, instead of our old ragged camp shorts, Dorie Adams and I went up the hill to Suga's office. Our dresses were seldom worn inside the camp as they were too fragile for our life, but they were requested by the Japanese for office visits. Arrived at the office we found there about a dozen representatives from the men's camps, all looking unnaturally respectable in whatever "neat and clean" dress they could acquire in their communities, for to appear in habitual camp nakedness would have been to precipitate punishment. As we had to wait an hour before the general was ready to reveal himself, the guard allowed us to sit in the shade of the near-by garage, in order to maintain our neat and clean appearance until the newsreel could record it.

In the garage under temporarily relaxed discipline I was able to talk quietly with Le Gros Clarke, former Government Under Secretary for Sarawak, now head of the civilian men's camp. He asked me if I knew the reason for the period of persecution we were going through, for he had heard rumors connecting me with it, and he said that Harry was worried. I told him I had been the unwitting cause, because I had complained of the misbehavior of a soldier to me, and this had precipitated punishment upon the guards, who had in turn retaliated against all of us. I said that I believed I was right in reporting the incident, but would not do so again — right or wrong — for every day I was learning more surely that a captive had no rights.

Le Gros was too kind to be quite honest with me in what he said, but I was sure from the fact that he did not say, "Oh no, you were right to report such conduct!" that he agreed with my second judgment that I might better have kept still. Sex made little difference now; misery, danger, and death had neutralized us.

It was good to talk with a man again, an intelligent, gentle, courteous one. Harry was in the group in the garage too, but because the guard knew he was my husband, he was not allowed near me, while Le Gros and I were permitted to talk undisturbed. Le Gros promised to tell Harry all I said, and that all was well with me now, and the trouble finished.

I never talked with him again. Some months later he was removed from the men's camp with Henry Cho, the Chinese Consul; was accused of conspiracy, and was taken away from Kuching.

Now the prisoners line up on the road at attention, Colonel Suga takes the Conquering Hero stance on the office veranda, cameramen pant expectantly at their reels, the motor car clanks up the drive, and the general is revealed. Is it a big one, or a little one? It must be a big one, by the noises of the guard. But a captive never sees a Japanese general; a captive is always bowing, and a general is lost in his uniform and motor car, which are always too big for him.

The cameras wind, the prisoners bow, Colonel Suga smacks

his sword, the general ascends the steps, the military party enters the office, and the veranda trembles under the footsteps of patriots. The bamboos outside sway humbly over the Nipponese memorial to the dead, and the Red Poached Egg flies proudly and eggily overhead. Inside the office, the military party sits down to tea, coffee, saki, tapioca chips, sago biscuits, sweets, gelatine, pomeloes, pineapple, and bananas, for they are delicate feeders. Their round, well-fleshed faces are bright with well-being; all is well with the Nipponese world.

Outside the office the prisoners bow and smile politely for the newsreel photographers, knowing that a swift kick or a blow is not far behind, if they do not. The newsreel will be entitled "Happy Prisoners of War Are Grateful to the Kind Japanese for Their Humanitarian Treatment." The happy prisoners then hurry back to their camps, to rice and potato tops.

One month later the reign of terror wanes, the guard forgets, the winds change, and the rains come later every day. The soldiers loll on their guns again, sit on our steps, talk of their homes, play with our children, and smuggling revives.

But me they do not forget. In their minds I am the friend of Colonel Suga; I am not to be trusted.

I never referred again to any part of this incident to Colonel Suga. I am convinced that he knew what methods of persuasion were used on me to try to obtain a confession, for physical abuse and torture were routine procedure in the questioning of prisoners: in order to avoid being witness to this unpleasant scene Colonel Suga had absented himself from Kuching.

In meeting him later, knowledge of this scene was between us; yet neither of us would ever refer to it. We were both helpless before the violence of war: we were enemies.

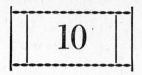

Children of Captivity

IT was the fall of 1943. A Japanese lorry drove into camp. On it were thirty-seven European women and children, people we had not seen for eighteen months, some of whom we thought were dead. We embraced, touched hands, cheered, wept.

They were glad to be imprisoned, they said, because they were with us — with their own kind. Their words brought us realization of our own solidarity, and feeling of ourselves as a homogeneous group. They brought back to us a little pride in our kind, and a warmth for each other that we had not before felt.

Here were the wives of the two Sandakan doctors, Celia Taylor and Mary Wands. Dr. Wands was in the men's camp, but Dr. Taylor was held by the military police on the charge of having assisted Australian POWs to escape. Here also was Mary Mavor, whose husband was held with Dr. Taylor on the same charge. She told me that my friend Dr. Laband, who had helped me in the Sandakan hospital, was held with the other two men on the same charge.

Dr. Alison Stookes, Val Stookes's sister, who had been doctoring all the time under the Japanese in Lahad Datu, arrived. Her brother was imprisoned now in the men's camp.

Five more children came, and twenty nursing Sisters from the Kuching hospital.

There was a drawing-together. This was the final assemblage. This was the European nucleus in this Asiatic country for victory, or defeat, or death.

We had met with tears. But we were determined not to shed them again — unless they were tears of joy.

The mothers were much criticized in Kuching. People said that we should not have been there at all, with our children. But no one had as terrible doubts about this as did we.

The women without children used to say to the mothers, "I don't see how you stand it! It must be hell being a mother in this camp!" It was hell, but it was heaven too. In that wallow of captivity known as Kuching Internment Camp, there were just thirty-four good reasons for staying alive, and those were our thirty-four children. We brought them all through.

One of those babies was born in internment, and one came into prison camp when she was only two months old. Three were under six months of age and still nursing when they and their mothers were imprisoned. Seven were the same age as George, two years old when imprisoned. The eldest child in Kuching entered camp when she was seven.

The children were mischievous, wicked, naughty, profane. They learned deceit, they smuggled, and sometimes I fear they stole, but never from each other. They fought and they kicked; they were tough. They had to be.

They learned to be hungry, that hunger was the natural condition of life. They learned that a meal was a big event, and eggs better than gold, a piece of rotting fish was a luxury, a banana was a treasure. And that all of these articles were contraband, and only to be spoken of in whispers.

They learned that everything must be hidden from the Nips. When soldiers searched the premises eggs went under the house, oil went to the latrines, sugar went into the drain.

They learned to bow politely to Japanese officers; what they did behind their backs I shall ignore.

They learned to be generous, they shared everything, even the unsharable. They were helpful, even to jobs beyond their strength. They were sympathetic, their faces of sorrow when they saw us in trouble were almost unbearable. They were cheerful, resourceful, brave, and *they* did not complain.

Those children were: Fiona and Fenella, Anne, Rosemary, Danis and Dandi, Edith and Eddie, Yin Shing, Susan, Alastair, Bryan, Jan, Isabelle, John and Dickie, Carol and Michael, Sheena and Ranald, David and Derek, Jimmy, Vicki and Thérèse, John and Margaret, Peter and Frankie, Tony, Mitey and Kusha, Julie, and George — children of captivity.

Now camp work grew heavier, mothers grew more worn and nervous, and children grew wilder, running in packs like wild animals. As nervous pressure on the mothers increased, physical strength with which to meet it decreased.

We talked to Mother Aubon of the English Sisters' barrack, of our worries. She listened sympathetically, and reversed her former decision that she could not spare a Sister to teach the younger children. She reorganized the community work program of the Sisters so that Sister Frances Mary and Sister Clitus from Sandakan convent, who were trained teachers, should join Sister Dominica with the medium-sized children, of which George was one, for two hours of schooling every morning.

I didn't care if George learned anything or not, but the idea that he would be watched over for a short time daily by the Sisters, and that for part of the time while I was away working he would be out of trouble, gave me new hope.

There were a few frayed-out school readers in camp that the older children had brought in. These we now attempted to duplicate on scraps of paper, with pencils. We also made alphabet sheets, and Sister Frances Mary made wooden squares with letters, to teach the children their letters. Pencils and papers were both contraband in Japanese eyes, consequently most of them had been confiscated, and they were now scarce and precious. However, the children finally collected a pencil each, and chewed the ends and broke the points with the same agility as do children outside prison camps.

School was held in one end of the chapel barrack, and it was no more popular with our children in camp than is school generally. George wept each morning when it was time to go, because he said he didn't want to learn. Sister Frances Mary agreed that he didn't, and nearly wept too. She said he didn't like to concentrate. But I remembered that I didn't at his age, and my brother didn't, so I looked it up in *The First Five Years of Life*, which volume was confiscated repeatedly by the Japanese — and recaptured as often by me, by my telling the Japanese that the book was necessary to the welfare of the camp children. I looked up "concentration" in the book, and ceased worrying, for apparently normal children didn't like to concentrate.

In spite of George's effort to the contrary he actually learned to read a little, while in camp, sounding the words tearfully, as he bent over his ragged, grubby, homemade reader.

When the Sisters' efforts to teach the children were brought to Colonel Suga's attention by Dorie and Sister Dominica, he was interested and pleased; it all fitted in with his idea of our ideal concentration camp. He sent a blackboard and chalk for the teachers, and allowed small slates and pencils to be purchased for the children, through the office.

In time the children were allowed out of the camp for a weekly walk, up the road to the top office and back. The teaching Sisters took them, and on no account was a mother or secular woman allowed to go. We had too much interest in the men. Occasionally Colonel Suga distributed sweets or biscuits from the veranda of his office to the children, and always one biscuit at least came home to Mother.

Shortly after school commenced for George and his gang,

Companion Irene, a Church of England teaching companion for the Society of the Propagation of the Gospel, took over the six smallest children for two hours of organized play, the play equipment being camp mud, mud, and mud.

Those women who taught our children worked hard and grew worn, and tired, for them, and their faces became drawn and thin, but never did they cease to smile, and to be patient and kind. They followed the words of Christ, and suffered little children to come unto them.

It had been raining for three days and nights, and our camp was a muddy and depressing sight this Sunday morning. The children were cross, and the mothers were cross, and the sentries were cross, and the sugar ration was late, and the rice gruel was burned.

But the rain had stopped at last, and the children had escaped eagerly from inside their prison barrack. The compound was full of half-clothed children wading in lakes of dirty water, splashing each other, and throwing mud.

Apart from the general crowd stood two little girls and one small boy, with their faces pressed against the barbed wire, just inside the gate by the sentry box, looking hopefully down the road.

The girls had worn dollies tied across their breasts, after the fashion of Malay mothers and babies. Their dresses and the pants of the little boy (who had only pants) were worn and faded, and they had no shoes, but the faces of all three were bright with excitement.

For approaching the camp they saw a large gray motor car with a red flag on it. All motor cars were a welcome excitement to them, but this special large gray one with the red flag on it was, in the children's mind, the king of all motor cars — for it carried the King of the Camp — Colonel Suga — and biscuits!

The three children, Anne, Rosemary, and Jimmy, were

panting with hope as they watched the car approach. Slowly it entered the camp compound, stopped by the road, and the rotund Colonel got out and disappeared into the barrack of the Pontianak Sisters.

The three children raced over to the parked car, where the Nipponese chauffeur now sat alone. With an ingratiating look at him, they quickly insinuated themselves inside the open car door, and seated themselves on the padded seat. The chauffeur grinned. It was common knowledge that although the adult prisoners were kept in their place, the children could get around the Colonel.

. Once inside the car and seated in satisfying pomp the girls nursed their babies, while they joined with Jimmy in playing the popular game of "Going to see Colonel Suga." This game consisted of Jimmy's pretending to be Colonel Suga, and pretending to distribute Suga biscuits, sweeties, and fruit.

The game was progressing favorably when the Colonel himself returned unexpectedly to the car. The girls were slightly, very slightly, embarrassed, but not Jimmy.

"I was just pretending to be you, Colonel Suga," Jimmy smiled, "and I was doing what I thought you'd do, and I was giving me and the girls biscuits, and taking us for a nice drive." Jimmy made this diplomatic explanation in the disarming voice of seven years old.

The Colonel smiled, and looked thoughtfully at the expectant children. Then he saw his duty, and he did it.

"You come with me for a drive, and then to my home for breakfast," he said chivalrously. The children beamed on him happily and without surprise; the Colonel had lived up to his reputation.

The car started, the sentry saluted, and in another moment they were out on the open road, breathing free air.

The children settled back in delight. They knew that this great event would swiftly be broadcast all about camp, and before their return they would be celebrities.

As the car rushed along towards Kuching it was unnecessary for the Colonel to talk, as his guests entertained themselves. Every green field and flaming canna, every house and building, every motor and rickshaw, every cow and bullock, dog and cat, every bird in the sky, was commented upon. To the prison-bred children the trip was a series of miracles, culminating in the final perfect miracle of arrival at the Colonel's house in Kuching.

Here the children disembarked confidently, and entered the low tropical bungalow.

Like a good soldier, the Colonel's first thought was for their stomachs. He had his orderly set before them a feast: biscuits, cakes, rambutan, cups of milk with sugar, and cups of cocoa with a great deal of sugar. And when the milk and cocoa were finished the cups were refilled with coffee, sweetened again with more sugar. And when the coffee was finished, the sugar could still be scraped out of the bottom of the cups. This sufficiency of sugar was to the small captives the test of a perfect meal.

When they had eaten all that they could hold, and that was a lot, and had fed fruit to the Colonel's pet monkey, and looked at the picture magazine, the *Nippon Times*, and examined the Colonel's pictures and trophies, which Jimmy particularly admired, they went outside in the garden.

Here Rosemary and Anne went mad with joy. Their delight in seeing roses, and orchids, and congea, and daisies, and rhododendron, and Ixora, and canna, and balsam again, after a year and a half in the dusty and beautyless surroundings of prison camp, was complete. Jimmy pulled off an occasional marigold head, but his interest was centered in an argus pheasant feather he saw on the Colonel's veranda.

Seeing the girls' joy at the flowers, Colonel Suga cut an armful for them to carry back to camp. Then with their arms full of neat packets containing more cakes and rambutan, a few tactful copies of the *Nippon Times*, for propaganda pur-

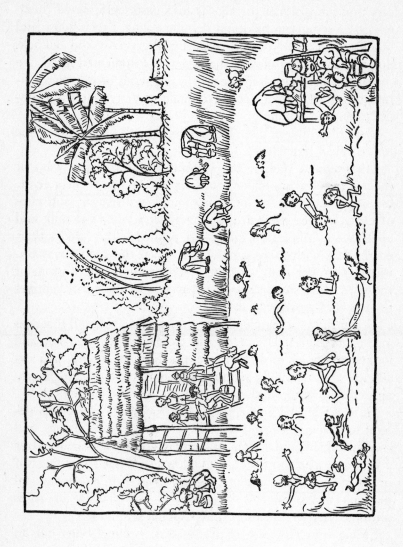

poses, the argus pheasant feather, a packet of real toilet paper, and the flowers, the children piled noisily into the gray car with the red flag, and started home again.

The journey back was all too short, as the sights of Kuching were again absorbed by the enraptured eyes of the excited children. All too soon the barbed-wire barricades of the camp appeared, the sentry saluted, and the car stopped outside the gate. The children jumped out and waved a warm goodbye to the Colonel.

The treat was over, but there was still great satisfaction ahead, for the thrilling story of "What I did at Colonel Suga's House" would be told and retold to the rest of the camp children for many days to come.

Meanwhile the Colonel himself must have smiled with satisfaction. It is not often that a military man achieves a bloodless victory.

The camp water supply was sometimes cut off. At such times it was necessary for us to go to a pond a mile away for bathing and washing, and to carry water home in empty gasoline tins for camp use. Mothers and Sisters found the journey inconvenient, but the children enjoyed the sport.

One night I started a bedtime serial for the children. I didn't know it was a serial, or for the children, when I started it; I thought it was one short story for George alone, quietly told, to put him to sleep.

Usually at twilight George and I retired inside our well-patched mosquito net to bed. We listened to the children singing, and then I told him stories for a few minutes, and then he went to sleep. His favorites were: the story of Daddy shooting the elephant, of Daddy knifing the python, of Daddy shooting the deer, of Mummy shooting the crocodile, of Mummy taming the apes, and so on. With repetition the elephants and pythons and deer and crocodiles and apes perhaps multiplied, and their measurements perhaps extended, and their strength and passion perhaps increased. I won't say they didn't! We strive to please!

And we pleased. Soon I found that eager small faces were being held quietly and breathlessly to our mosquito net, small noses were rubbing against its grime, small ears were being patiently strained to listen, small voices were asking anxiously, if I hesitated while adding feet to the python, length to the crocodile, or strength to the ape, "And then what? Tell us then what? What happened then?"

I couldn't say "Go away, this is only for George!" when this was all done so delicately on their part. No noises, no rude arrangements beforehand, no asking to come inside the net, no asking anything — except just to hear! Just small white shapes creeping up from the barrack, and standing patiently, anxiously, pantingly, waiting to learn if it was one elephant, or ten, which that intrepid, magnificent, daring, dauntless, fearless and fine Big Game Hunter, "Keith of Borneo," had just shot that night!

So "Keith of Borneo" had to live up to his audience. I never did enjoy letting fact bind my fancy, and now, with my chosen clientele, we cut loose from all truth.

There were we, surrounded by barbed wire, held captives by the Japs, with four feet by six to live in. But we traveled the jungles through, we journeyed by air and by sea, we conquered the infinite spaces, we wrestled the bloodiest beasts, we slew the blackest villains, we married the blondest brides — and for that time in the dusk and gloaming of prison, we went free.

After we had made the jungles safe for the tiniest toddler, we turned to Jack the Giant Killer.

". . . Just a small fellow like Vicki there, he was, and brave like Vicki, too. With blond hair, like Vicki's. Now Jack was very clever, and farseeing, like John, I think . . . And, say, when Jack shinnied up that beanstalk — no, I think it was a very tall coconut palm like the one that grows outside our camp — well, when old Jack shinnied up that coconut palm, and got to the top, he found — Now what do you think he found, Thérèse?"

Thérèse, who has seen her father beaten up, in prison camp: "He found a gun to shoot all the Japs with!"

"No, he found a road that led to a house. And in the house he found a very big meal laid out for him on the table. Now, what do you think he found on that table to eat, children?"

Margaret, who is nine, and remembers home: "He found chocolate cake and strawberry ice cream."

George, who knows only captivity, and to whom the height of luxury is . . . "He found an egg!"

Thus began the serial. . . .

For months we lived with Jack the Giant Killer, who slew giants, killed Japs, came in an airplane and dropped parachutes with sweets in Kuching camp, put his grandmother through college, married and had many progeny, and in time became a very good friend of the brother of the slain giant, who was a good giant, and whose name was . . .

It was simple to run a serial, for the children were thoroughly oriented before the story began. Better oriented than I, who couldn't always remember what I had told. So we always started the story thus:

"Now, children, who remembers what happened last night?" And apparently I was the only one who didn't remember.

But none of this put anybody to sleep, including me.

Jack girdled the world from Holland to visit Thérèse and Vicki, to England for Susan and John, to China for Edith and Eddie, and home to America for George. Jack girdled the world; we went with him in spirit, but meanwhile our bodies grew thinner, weaker, more tired. And in time, then, for me even to unroll a serial took too much energy at night.

So I put Jack to bed early one evening, surrounded by his friends, his giants, his Kuching meals, his Borneo jungle pets,

his war bride and his offspring, his airplane, his ox and ass and dog and cat. I put him to bed — and he never got up again. Said Vicki "But what happened? What happened then?"

I: "Nothing happened. He just went to bed. He's tired and he's staying there, that's all. That's the end."

Our barrack was regarded by nonresidents as a dirty hole, a stinkhole, a pesthole, a hellhole. It was Hades let loose on a rainy day. It was the final crash of a brass band throughout feeding hours. It smelled of kids, pots, and wee-wee. The noise started at 6 A.M. and continued until 6 A.M.

But there was one hour after supper at night when the type of noise changed. The children were all in bed then, the mothers were too, being too exhausted for anything else. Then took place that sudden transformation to which children are subject when the dusk falls: thirty-four little devils become thirty-four little angels. They smell good, they speak sweetly, they squeeze your hand, they even want to kiss you — and they sing! Tragedy came and went in our camp, but we never missed a night of singing.

"Kiss Me Good Night, Sergeant Major"; "Good Night, Daddy and Jim"; "Christopher Robin Is Saying His Prayers"; "I Think When I Hear That Sweet Story of Old"; "One Finger, One Thumb, One Arm, One Leg"; "Hark, the Herald Angels Sing." And always without fail, to end up with, in bed: "God save our gracious King . . . God save the King."

I can never forget the sound of those children's voices, singing — with nothing to sing for. If their song could have been broadcast to the outside world I think that hearts would have broken. I have stood outside our barrack at night, listening, and weeping with pride and love and sorrow for those our children.

I said to begin with that we brought them all through alive. But perhaps they brought us through alive.

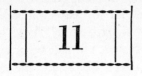

The Enemy

NEKATA and Kubu, the chief inquisitors, accompanied by five military police officers and five guards, arrived in camp at 8.30 one morning and ordered everyone to leave the barracks and remain outside. Armed guards were then stationed about us, while the officers entered the barracks to search. Fortunately they started at the end barrack from mine, searched thoroughly in the first two, less so in the third, and were as exhausted as we were by the time they had reached the fourth barrack, in which I lived. Usually searchers paid particular attention to my belongings, searching eagerly for diaries; today they confiscated my old bankbooks and were satisfied.

In the middle of it all Colonel Suga and two cars with visiting personages arrived. Apparently Colonel Suga did not know about the search, which was being conducted by Nekata, and he had brought the personages to see his Ideal Internment Camp. Lo, there were the Happy, Cheerful Internees outside under a clump of rubber trees, hemmed in by sentries with guns, the daily work of the camp suspended and the kitchen empty, while the military police probed our personal luggage. Suga gave us one look, then walked hastily away towards the chapel barrack, beckoning the personages to follow.

But one personage appeared to know me, and dallied behind to call me out of the crowd, addressing me as follows:

"You look poor, Mrs. Keith."

At first I thought he meant my clothes, then realized that he referred to my health.

"Yes," I answered, "not much food now."

"You like lice?"

"Yes."

"You like lice — or bled?"

This stumped me for a moment, then I answered "Both."

"You hungry?"

"Yes. We have few vegetables, and little food now." Meanwhile I was wondering whether I should grasp the opportunity to complain, or follow the Spartan line.

The personage, "You like fish?"

"Yes. We also like meat."

(People about me whisper loudly, "Ask for eggs," "Ask for potatoes," "And pork," "And milk.")

I: "And we like eggs — and milk."

He, in surprise: "You have meat, and eggs — and milk — every day?"

I: "No! No! No! We never have! Only greens, and a little rice. I say we *like* meat and eggs and milk."

We both gaze at each other uncomfortably, and then he retreats. This business of being a humanitarian, and a conqueror, is confusing.

The search continues until two o'clock, by which time we have headaches, and the Japs have more pens, pencils, fountain pens, marriage licenses, and snapshots of dogs, ships, and friends, as souvenirs.

We had just been reminded with especial emphasis one day to take our washing off the line, in order to make the camp look neat, to clean our barracks, to keep up our morals, to be happy, to keep well, and to be clean. With which advice, our rations for the day were cut.

This concatenation of circumstances warned me that there

must be either more Japanese generals in town, or Japanese gentlemen of the press, to enjoy the sight of our well-being, and help eat our rations.

Shortly after noon I was ordered to come to Colonel Suga's office. Here I was introduced to the editor of the *Domei News*, a man of perhaps forty years, large for a Japanese, with an impressive head, a strong chin, and eyes which were almost Occidental in shape. He was very much a modern Japanese, and his manners showed familiarity with Western custom. He spoke quietly and with dignity.

After we were introduced, Suga and Nekata left us alone together in the office, with the interpreter, which was unusual. I wondered if the editor had asked him to do so.

Speaking through the interpreter, and sometimes directly in poor English, he asked me to tell him "my thoughts," which subject is a favorite with the Japanese. I always disliked volunteering anything, as it was safer to wait for direct questions, and then answer yes or no. However, I answered him that I hoped the war would end soon, which seemed quite harmless.

He answered that all men felt the same about this. His was not the typical Japanese answer, which usually was, "Not until the British are beaten!"

He then said, "Please give further thoughts."

I answer, "My principal thought is for my son, three and a half years old, who is here in camp with me, and about whose welfare I am very worried."

He replies, "Do you not think of your country?"

"I know nothing of my country now. I have heard no news for two years. I pray for its welfare, I can do nothing more. But with my child, it is necessary that I work for his welfare daily."

He replies, "Japanese women authors forget everything except their country, they forsake children and husband, and travel every place, writing and working for their country."

I: "I would be happy to travel and work and write for my country, but as I am imprisoned here it is impossible for me to do so." Editor nods his head in agreement here, and I continue, "My country told my husband and myself to remain in Borneo at our jobs before the Japanese occupied Borneo. That was our duty to our country. This we did, and when the Nipponese arrived they interned us. We are still here, doing the only possible thing to do for our country, which is to wait, with what patience we can."

After this I become silent. Editor waits hopefully. I am determined not to volunteer anything about conditions of internment, either good or bad.

So Editor and I sit silent, staring at each other gloomily, until both glances become glazed. He wipes his brow with his hands, and says he is very fatigued from many interviews. I ask through the interpreter if, as Editor is very fatigued, he would like me to leave. Editor quickly shakes his head, and requests me to produce more "thoughts." He then volunteers that he has read *Land Below the Wind*, and that he likes it, and asks me if I am "poetist." I say, no. He asks me what form of writing I do. I say stories, articles, and a novel.

Again conversation languishes. Editor presses me again for more "thoughts." I say I hope some time in the future his country and my country will be friends. Editor then answers in very poor English as follows: "Your country is very grasping, and the British grab many countries for themselves. But now Nippon needs those countries for herself. Therefore Nippon must fight your country."

I ask Interpreter to ask Editor if I am correct in understanding that he thinks our countries will *never* be friends. At this question Editor smiles, and hastily shakes his head, and replies that he agrees with me that he hopes our countries will be friends. He then signifies that the interview is finished, and asks Interpreter to "tell Mrs. Keith that he likes her hope for the future." I leave, bowing at the prescribed degree, and leaving an Editor seemingly as exhausted by the interview as I.

The next day I was again ordered to come to Colonel Suga's office, this time to bring six children to "make pictures." I assumed that I was going to be sat down before some visiting officer and ordered to record his features, receiving at best a banana. What part the children were to play in this scene I did not know, but I always felt safer when children were invited, as it implied that the Japanese were about to demonstrate their well-known thesis of kindness to children.

I put on my "office dress." This was not my best white sharkskin, which was only used for the Japanese when I was under orders to "be neat and clean" — and they had forgotten the order today — or for meeting my husband. I put on the "office dress," a very hole-y, very shrunken, blouse and skirt which looked as an internee should look, worn and thin. It was better propaganda than wearing my best.

Then I collected George, and eight others. It was difficult to limit the children as they all wanted to come; I hoped that the Japanese wouldn't notice the extras.

At the office we were turned over to the news photographer from *Domei News*, and some Japanese newsreel men. They escorted us behind Suga's office, to the bank of the pig pond, a very pretty location under the trees. Here a small easel with a drawing board was put up for me, a stool was placed, and the children were grouped around me, their hands filled with sweets. I was given some paper and crayons and told to sit down and draw "beautiful scene," while my photograph was made, to illustrate "Artist at Play," following chosen profession, encouraged by Japanese protectors, in Kuching Internment Camp.

But my spirit was not in it — and I looked it. Speaking in English and French, the photographers kept urging me: "Look happy, please. Please be happy! Not look sad! Not look sad. *C'est triste! C'est triste!* No good for picture now! Must be happy, please! Please be happy!"

For once I had the upper hand; they just couldn't make me look happy. The children collaborated with them 100 per cent, eating, and laughing, and eating, and one of them falling in the pond. But I just sat and looked sad, with much satisfaction.

A few days later Suga gave me one of the prints. I looked sad.

The next day "The four most beautiful women" were sent for, to quote the Japanese. These were Babs Hill, Betty Hopkins, Jo Clifford, and Marjorie Colley. They furnished the beauty, and the rest of us contributed make-up, hair-dos, shoes, costumes, and advice.

They were taken in an army truck to Colonel Suga's garden, led out under the trees, their arms loaded with flowers, their expressions approved of. Then the cameras clicked, their antics were performed, and their beauty and glee recorded.

The next day a lorry came to take mothers and children on a newsreel bathing party. The order was that we must wear bathing suits, and go in the water. The number was limited to twenty only. Most people wanted to go, so they drew lots for it. I didn't compete as I'd had enough.

When the truck came the disappointed ones dashed out and tried to get on, too. Nekata and Suga, who were following the truck in Suga's motor car, ordered that all should go who could get on board. Double the originally specified number went. After they left I felt sorry for George, who was broken-hearted, and I thought that perhaps I should have gone.

The party came home in a few hours, full of thrills. They had gone bathing in the pool in the Kuching Museum Park near the Rajah's Palace. As most of the women didn't have bathing suits, a variety of combination garments had been used, which hadn't stayed on very well in the water. Jessie, who couldn't swim, had carried two-year-old Isabelle into the

pool. The bottom of the pool was slippery, and Jessie had slipped, and shot off into deep water, letting go of Isabelle, and sinking.

A Japanese guard from Formosa dove in and rescued Isabelle, while the women pulled out Jessie. Meanwhile the cameras recorded it — Jessie ought to get a Japanese iron cross for this. Isabelle was O.K. immediately, but it took fifteen minutes of resuscitation, by the Japs and the women, before Jessie became conscious.

When Jessie breathed once more, everybody sat down on the edge of the tank, and drank very sweet coffee out of a bucket.

We heard the next day that a party of Australian officers had been taken to the pool to be photographed, stood on the edge of the pool in Japanese-supplied bathing suits, photographed standing and waving, photographed drinking from cups; then taken home without going in the pool, or having anything to drink from the cups.

There was one phrase that our ears were always awake to, whispered ever so gently by a passer-by: "In the guardhouse — in the cells."

The one condition that truly enlisted the sympathy of every other woman was to have your husband in the cells. They tried to keep it from you, you usually heard it last of all, and when you finally knew, they said, "Don't worry," "He's being well-treated, we've heard," "The guard said he was fine," "Really, I'm sure they won't beat him up." And then, "We'll tell you honestly if we do hear anything bad."

But they always knew, and you knew too.

Only one woman had ever been sent there. She was put in for six hours, for smoking a cigarette outside the barrack. She refused to talk about it afterwards.

But our husbands had told us about the cells. They were

like dog kennels, to be entered on your hands and knees. Once inside you lived as no dog did, in your own filth. Only occasionally as a favor was a prisoner allowed to the latrine, and he could not bathe. His food was rice and salt. He had no mosquito net or covering, and the cell was damp and the mosquitoes were bad.

Throughout the day the prisoner was made to kneel in the middle of the cell, away from the wall, with his hands behind him, sometimes with a pole through his arms, in front of his elbows. Soon the blood would not circulate in his legs, and he fell over; he was kicked upright by the guard; when he could not stay upright he was kicked down again; and so on.

The guard's business was to mistreat the prisoner, and he attended very well to his business. Burning with cigarette butts was only one of his minor jobs. The cells were punishment; there a prisoner lost any remnants of the right to protest anything. Prisoners had come out deafened, and without their eyesight.

All this we knew. The whispered word of "the cells" in connection with our husbands turned cold any warmth in our hearts.

On March 13, 1944, at twelve noon when I came home from work in the field, Sister Frances Mary came to me and whispered that Sister Stephanie had seen Harry taken by on the road, under guard, towards the cells. A weight descended on me.

That day there was nothing definite, and the next day somebody said that a Sister had seen him, when she was going up to the office to sew for the Japs, and that he was free. The next day Dorie came to me and told me that she had been informed officially through the office that he was in the guardhouse. And the next day she told me he had been freed. And the next day retaken.

After five days of rumor, Colonel Suga sent for me to come to his office. It was 7 P.M. and he was alone; he had set the hour late, so that he might be alone.

He told me that Harry had been sentenced to twenty-one days heavy imprisonment in the guardhouse, "For being an accomplice, and for assisting in the plot, in Sandakan, of the escape of the Australian prisoners of war." He said that a letter and map had been found connecting him with the case.

He said he had kept Harry's case from military court-martial, and under his own jurisdiction, and this accounted for the light sentence, but that he still feared that his sentence would be overruled and the case taken out of his hands. Then Harry would either be executed, or imprisoned for the duration of the war outside of Borneo. Harry had requested him to keep these facts secret from me, but he, Colonel Suga, believed that I should know the exact truth, and he wished to tell it to me himself. He then said, "Do not worry!"

I, knowing that Harry had felt a responsibility to stay clear of escape plots for the sake of George and myself, said, "I do not believe the accusation is true."

Suga answered me, "Your husband has signed a confession admitting its truth."

He then said, "I had liked your husband. I considered Mr. and Mrs. Keith to be my friends. For that reason I have risked great trouble for myself, in order to save his life. The Japanese Military Command would be very angry if they knew what I have done. I do not even know that I have saved him now."

He waited a moment, and then asked, "Why do you and your husband have hostility for the Japanese? Why should he assist in a plot against them? You have told me that you do not have race prejudice."

I answered, "I do not have race prejudice. But in war it is kill or be killed. Your people started this war. The war makes us enemies, although I would rather be friends.

"I do not know what my husband did, or why. He has told me nothing. I only know that you accuse him of this.

"But I know that he is not hostile to the Japanese race, or to individual Japanese. But because the Japanese are his enemies, it is his duty as an Englishman to help the Allied cause if there is opportunity. Just as it is your duty to stop him from so doing."

Suga looked at me, and said, "I think you are hostile now, Mrs. Keith. Now you hate me, because your husband is hurt."

I said, "No, I do not hate you. I hate war, which makes us enemies. I hate the qualities which war forces on us. And I believe that you also hate war."

He was slow in answering me. While he hesitated, I felt between us the realization that we understood something of each other, that we had a desire to believe and trust each other, that we were both sick of war, sick of hatred, sick of killing, sick of the harshness of this life. That we were sick of being wary with each other — but that we knew we must be. I felt that we would have liked to meet as two human beings, but we could not, because we were enemies.

At last he answered me, "I am a soldier, therefore I cannot say what I think about war. Perhaps when the war is over — I can talk with you about it."

But I knew and so must he, that the war could not end with both of us alive. With defeat or with victory, there would be death for one, and life for the other.

I said, "Whatever my husband did, he did because he felt it to be his duty to his country, not because of racial hostility. Unfortunately your duty and his duty conflict."

He said, "You look very melancholy and you are very thin. You should take care of yourself. Please do not worry."

Throughout all my contact with Colonel Suga I had never asked a personal favor from him, although he had given me many opportunities to do so. I had made up my mind that unless the time should come when it was vital to the life of my husband or child or myself, I would never do so. This was not all pride; but partly a feeling that I wanted to hoard up every generous impulse towards me that Suga might have, for the possible time of crisis.

I said to him now: "My husband is more dear to me than anything in the world except my child. I thank you for helping him. I believe that you have acted as a friend. You tell me he may yet lose his life, or be imprisoned in a cell for the rest of the war — and then you tell me not to worry! I do worry! I beg you to do everything in your power to save him. He is a prisoner and helpless; he is no menace to your country now. You have told me many times in the past that you would help me, if you could. I have never asked you for anything. I ask you now to save my husband."

He answered: "I promise that I will do all I can do. But you understand it is dangerous to my position. I ask you not to repeat what I have said to you."

I said, "I will never do so, while we are enemies."

He then said, "I promise you to help your husband. I like your son George very much. Teach him to be sincere also. Teach him to feel as you do, and not to hate. I will give you some biscuits, and two eggs for George."

I went home then.

Three days later Colonel Suga called me. He said that he wished to warn me that he did not think he could keep my husband's case from going to a military court-martial, as the military police had reopened the investigation. In that case, he could not save Harry from execution. If I was questioned myself, he asked me to remember my promise to him not to tell of his intervention.

I told him that I would observe my promise to him. I asked if there was any chance to save Harry, in any way. He said, not if the military police reopened the case. I said, "Please keep trying. This means more than anything in the world to me."

For nights I could not sleep. Eleven o'clock, twelve, one, and two, with cigarettes to mark the hours, then an hour's sleep, and awake at four or five. I begged bromides from Dr. Yamamoto, but they did me no good.

Four days later Suga called me again. He said the military police had abandoned their pursuit of the case; that he believed my husband's life was assured. That he had done this for us.

I had no words. I sat and looked. I tried to think and speak. I was too exhausted with anxiety to say or do anything. I felt to myself, There must be a sign I can give to show what I feel. There must be a symbol, a word, a gesture, that means what this means to me: Life out of Death.

But I knew there wasn't. I knew that I was just one other creature on the surface of the world that was totally inadequate to what life asked of it. One other creature who lived, loved, and hoped, without quite knowing the why or the how. Without ever being able to express the terrible beauty and agony, the terrible joy and sorrow, of this being. I wanted to praise God and to praise Suga, and to reach out with my heart and grasp Harry. But I couldn't do any of it.

"Thank you," I said.

Then Easter Sunday came, and a message from Colonel Suga that Harry had been released and was to meet me. We met. Harry looked very ill, showed physical signs of abuse, was nervous, unstrung, and distraught, but — we met.

Whether Colonel Suga told me the truth, that he had saved Harry, I cannot prove, but I believe that he did. Other people have disagreed, have said it was a put-up job to show his power, or that he was an opportunist — that Harry was lucky and Suga took the credit. I believe that Suga wished to save him, and did so.

I still do not know my husband's full story of what occurred, for he promised secrecy. I still do not know what dangers he ran, or why. But I know that he lives, while there are wooden crosses in Kuching for the officer and soldiers who were accused in that case; that the other civilians were only released from the cells by death, and by peace.

Harry was still in the guardhouse in March 1944, when the first and only Red Cross parcels to be received in Kuching throughout the war arrived.

A small amount of clothing, a few underthings, a few yards of dress material, ten pairs of women's shoes, four pairs of children's shoes, some hairpins, face cream, and tooth powder, came for our women's camp of two hundred and eighty.

Food packages arrived also, approximately one package for every six prisoners in Kuching.

The clothing and comforts were addressed to "American Internees," the food packages to "Prisoners of War, and Invalids." It was stressed by the Japanese that the shipment came from the *American* Red Cross, which surprised me, as I thought the Red Cross international.

As the packages were addressed to "American Internees," they were turned over to the four Americans, Betty and Marjorie from Manila, Mary Dixon, a missionary, and myself, for distribution.

The four of us were called to the Japanese offices, and each one was given a pair of men's army shoes, and a food package for herself, as the perquisites of Americans. As we returned down the road to camp with our arms full, the soldiers and the priests along the route, who knew by rumor what had been happening to us, whistled "Yankee Doodle" as we went proudly by.

Mary said that it was good to be an American today! Marjorie said it was good any day! Betty said, "Gosh, I'll sure be glad to get some shoes on again," and "Gosh, do you see that chocolate and powdered milk in the food box?"

George dashed out to meet me, and was frantic with excitement at the sight of the new shiny tins in the food package. He and I opened the box together, and all the children crowded around and everybody looked at and felt the tins, and admired and Ooooh-ed, and I wondered anxiously what to do about it.

In that box, in shiny new tins with bright American labels, were the following foodstuffs: one pound tin of Klim, one tin soluble coffee reinforced with dextrose and maltose, one package Kraft cheese, two tin openers, three tins corned beef, two tins Spam, one tin salmon, one tin sardines, four tins butter-spread, 1 box prunes, 1 tin meat paste, one tin grape jelly, two packages chocolate ration, a package of lump sugar, and six packages of Chesterfield cigarettes. All the tins were reinforced with extra food elements and packed for Army use. I had never thought to see such things until after the war.

After looking at the contents I removed the cigarettes and then turned the food over to Lilah, who was the children's barrack master, for use of all the children. I suggested that she might keep the food and distribute it on George's birthday. I had arbitrarily changed the date of his birthday celebration to April 10, in the hope that Harry would be out of the cells by then.

At seeing the food change hands so rapidly, just when he thought it was going to be his, George wept. Not from avarice, but because he wanted to open it immediately and eat it now.

Forty-six similar food boxes also arrived in camp for community distribution.

Now the Americans had the appalling problem of trying to divide ten pairs of shoes amongst two hundred and eighty people, and to distribute one portion of food for every six people. Everybody needed clothes and shoes, but some were in greater need than others. The only thing to do was to ask everyone to submit her requirements, and try to distribute the articles according to greatest need. When a number experienced the same degree of necessity, they had to draw lots for the article.

There were ten pairs of adult shoes, and the majority of people were barefoot. Each person tried on the shoes, and then competed for the size that fitted her. There was more sorrow than rejoicing at the results.

I was better outfitted than most, and did not want anything for myself, but I did covet a pair of shoes for George, who had none. There were thirty-four children, six of them had shoes. Four pairs of Red Cross shoes had come. The children fitted these on, and were proud to have them for even a moment. Then each registered the size he was competing for. We had eight children on each of two pairs of shoes, and six on each of the other two pairs, and they drew lots. George didn't win.

The forty-six food boxes were turned over to the community kitchens, their contents to be distributed to everybody equally bit by bit at mealtimes. A small amount was to be put away for emergency.

Each meal now there was something exciting. One wonderful day the coffee drinkers were served coffee at 10 A.M. Another day we had chocolate pudding, made from rice, cocoa, and sugar. The tinned meats, fish, sausage, and such were combined with rice to make cakes, in order to make them go further.

The powdered milk was divided equally per capita, each person receiving about 3⅔ ounces of the powder. I thought it should all be given to the children, but we did not agree on this. It was thrilling to see powdered or any kind of milk again. Tinned butter was divided, ½ ounce per person, about the amount an individual at home eats per meal. When one has had nothing but rice and vegetable soup for two years, and tea to drink, even a taste of any luxury is exciting.

The pleasure the children had with even their small portions of food was immeasurable. George would follow me home from the kitchen when I brought the dinner tray, leaping like a retriever pup to see what was on the tray, and shouting, "Sausage roll! Chilren!" or, "Fish, Chilren!" And one thrilling day he shouted, "Prunes! Chilrens!" and each person was served with seven stewed prunes for dinner!

A few days later "the Americans" were called to the office again and presented with 100 cigarettes, unpackaged and unlabeled, and four packages of pipe tobacco, and one pipe. We

learned later that the goods had been held up by censorship and finally removed from its packages and delivered to us unlabeled, because of something which was printed on the label. I suppose it was some wartime advertising slogan which proved offensive to Japanese sensibilities.

Most of my cigarettes, and the pipe and tobacco, I saved to send to Harry for his birthday, or whenever he got out of the cells. It was amusing to see how anxious the Sisters were to receive the tobacco, and pipe, and cigarettes, as they wished to turn these over to the Brothers and Fathers in the priests' camp.

On April 5 George was four years old. It was his second birthday in prison camp. Harry was in the guardhouse. George had no present from him.

At midday, Lilah and I got out the box of Red Cross food. We opened everything and divided each item into thirty-four sections. It required mathematical precision, but we did it. Every child then brought a bowl or plate to us, and watched with shining eyes.

We filled each plate with little mounds of salmon, sardine, butter, Spam, ham, jelly, meat, prunes, chocolate, cheese, and we had made a milk pudding with milk and rice, which we added. Then we called for cups, and distributed coffee with sugar. And all mothers were rewarded for being mothers, with cigarettes.

Each child took his plate, said "Thank you" politely, said "Happy Birthday" to George, and scurried home. Each face was pale with excitement. This was not fun or pleasure. This was tense, terrible, earnest participation in Paradise.

I had wondered beforehand if I was wrong in not saving the foodstuff for George, to feed to him over a period of time. But when I saw those faces I knew I was right.

George's melting gratification in having something to give, his pride in being a benefactor, made him swell all day long before my eyes, until by nighttime he was twice-normal. How I loved him then!

12

Endurance

In May 1944 Shihping Cho was informed by the Japanese office, through our camp master, that her husband, Henry Cho, was one of seven men taken into custody on an unstated charge, and held for questioning in the guardhouse. Betty Weber was told that her husband, Harry Weber, was another of the men. Dr. Alison Stookes's brother, Val Stookes, was another, and Babs Hill's husband, Stanley, a third. The women were brave, but remembering what I had felt when Harry was in the cells, I knew what they were hiding.

Shihping tried to laugh and talk naturally with Edith and Eddie. She was very good at it, and everything went well, until suddenly her voice would become shrill, and she would scream at them to be quiet — and then look over at me and say apologetically, "I feel a little nervous!" I wanted to help her, but there was nothing to do.

Babs Hill was young, and seemed unfitted to have hanging over her the responsibility of Susan, who was ill, and of her husband's unknown fate. I remembered those two so well from Sandakan days, when they were madly in love, always together playing tennis, holding hands down the road, holding hands in the movies, always smiling and teasing.

Betty showed her worries by snapping everybody's head off, until no one dared to go near her. She worked harder than ever at community cooking, did three people's jobs, and gave her own food away recklessly.

Alison Stookes was depressed, but tried hard to fight it off. She was assisting with the camp medical work now and that helped her. Her brother was her idol.

Other men being questioned at the same time were Le Gros Clarke, the former Government Under Secretary of Sarawak, a man by the name of Crawford, and a British soldier, name unknown to us. Young Abbott of the Sandakan Civil Service was in separate custody.

After they had been two weeks in the guardhouse, we heard that the men had been moved to the Kuching jail, where they were questioned by the military police. After four weeks there, Cho, Hill, and Clarke were released and brought back to the Kuching prison camp. The rejoicing in our camp by the wives of Cho and Hill was dampened by the fact that Weber and Stookes had not been released.

The Sunday after her husband's release Shihping received a verbal message from him: "I have answered all questions with a clean conscience. My character remains unsullied. I have emerged with all honor." It was so typical of the Consul that Cho and I laughed gently together.

Shortly after this Cho and Hill and Clarke were returned to the cells, for further questioning. Then after some weeks Weber and Stookes were brought back from the Kuching jail, and they with Hill and Cho were told that they were to be sent to an unknown destination. They were permitted an interview with their wives in the office, under guard.

Betty told me that when she met her husband that day she found his hair had turned white during the weeks of imprisonment. He asked for permission from the Japanese to make his will and have it witnessed before being taken away. He was ill then with beriberi.

Shihping said that her husband was quite cheerful. He said the Japanese could prove nothing against him, and that he believed the tide of war had turned in our favor. We felt more hope for his survival, because he was an Asiatic, and might be better able to deal with Asiatics.

I couldn't bear even to look at Babs Hill, or to ask her about Stanley.

Dr. Stookes was not optimistic, his sister said. I was afraid that he knew what was coming. He has had a great deal of illegal contact in the past with the British soldiers, whose camp adjoins the men's camp. He has tried to help them with medical advice and care, and with smuggled food and drugs, and the Japanese may have knowledge of this. Stookes has been a reckless smuggler all during camp life, frequently running the blockade on Berhala Island. Ever since his days as an aviator in the First World War he has lived life at a reckless pace. He is brave himself, and expects others to be; he gives of himself without counting the cost, and accepts in the same degree from others. He will not learn caution now, I am sure, nor retreat from his gamble with fate.

Celia Taylor has just said good-bye to her husband after seeing him again after months of torture and questioning. The Japanese still accuse him of having helped Australian prisoners of war to escape from the POW camp in Sandakan; the same charge brought against Harry. Dr. Taylor is ill with beriberi. She doesn't know where he is going or what his sentence is. Gerald Mavor is with him. The last time I saw Dr. Taylor was in the hospital in Sandakan when I had malaria and he gave me a tin of milk to hide in my luggage for George.

Mama Baldwin, a Scottish woman of seventy years, and the mother of nine children, is no longer in doubt. She has just been informed by the Japanese that Baldwin, who was chief engineer of the *Baynain*, died of dysentery while a prisoner in Tarakan, Dutch Borneo.

But Mama has the heart of a lion. Never does she fail to sing, on Christmas Eve, St. Andrew's Eve, New Year's Eve, or any evening when she thinks we need it. To listen to Mama

Baldwin sing "Auld Lang Syne," in a prison camp at the age of seventy, with knowledge of her sons in German prison camps and fighting, with her husband dead in a prison camp, with hardships and illness and suffering to bear herself, is to hear fate defied by a brave woman. We who say we can't bear it, have something to learn.

About now the Japanese imported Miss Asaka, a female interpreter, to deal with us ladies — feeling that they needed stronger meat than little Wilfred. Asaka was the kind of Oriental female that you never read about, with all the gentle sensitivity of a keg of nails, a heart of stone, the tenderness of asphalt, the voice of a streetcar going down a long tunnel, a chest like a barrel, and legs like concrete columns — but she *could* speak English.

She was said to be a widow, her husband dead in China, his ashes by her bed. The Nips, who had an extraordinary sense of propriety at times, commanded one of us to live outside the camp with Asaka, to chaperone her. Most of us preferred captivity, but several for their own reasons tried. One smuggled and got caught, one argued and got slapped, one played with soldiers and was sent to the guardhouse, one wept all day alone, one slept all night not alone, one was too clever and spied. In the end the Nips gave up. Asaka lived alone.

Most of the time she wore military uniform; later, when bombing started, she wore a siren suit with a long zipper opening, known to everyone as her Yankee pants, one Yank and they're off.

With the arrival of Asaka camp searches became more thorough and systematic, less inspirational. But with all her cast-iron exterior she was more scared of the Nipponese officers than we were. I didn't like her, but I was sorry for her; life couldn't have been worth much to her between the Nips and us.

Towards the end of the war when fighting was heavy over

Borneo and we all expected to be blown to bits between friends and foes, she said to me: "You needn't hope for the Allies to come to Kuching and rescue you! If they do come, the Japanese will cut you to pieces first. We Japanese go crazy when we fight!"

About this time, also, Sister Leontine, one of the Dutch Sisters, celebrated her golden anniversary, of fifty years wedded to Christ.

A symbolic wedding was held, with Sister Leontine dressed as a bride in an old evening gown borrowed from one of the secular women, with a veil and train, with little Dutch Thérèse dressed as flower girl, with songs and prayers, and afterward all the camp was invited to come and congratulate Sister Leontine.

The Sisters had been saving their rations for days, they had smuggled madly beforehand, a feast was achieved for the order, and a special tidbit of food was given to every child in camp. Sister Leontine looked happy, but dazed. All this for her? It was the biggest celebration that had ever occurred in camp. Sister Leontine could scarcely take it all in; the Mother had to help her to keep her wits about her on the receiving line, when everybody shook her hand.

The next day Sister Leontine was not well. Then for days she could not see people. Then she made queer noises and did odd things in chapel. Soon we understood. Sister Leontine's Golden Anniversary had marked her last clear thought.

For a while she lived in the barrack, then she went to one of the hospital beds in camp. Then she went to live in the chapel, curtained off from the rest of the room. On moonlight nights her calls and cries were very mad.

She could not sleep, we could not sleep. Two Sisters lived with her, night and day. The nights became wild with her screams. The guards never went near her.

We told the Japanese that we could not stand this.

The Dutch Fathers were sent into camp, and built a small

palm-leaf house in the middle of the vegetable patch at the foot of the camp ground. Here two Sisters went to live with Leontine. All day, Sister Leontine sat in front of the house with her head bowed on her knees; all night she sang and cried.

The Japanese gave us a young female pig. "Raise pigs," they said, "and stop complaining about food."

"Raise pigs on what?" we said.

"On garbage."

"*We* eat the garbage."

"Don't argue. It is an order."

How one raised pigs from one lone female was not made clear. However, we named her Salina; the kids doted on her, and, being a Borneo pig, she raised herself. But she didn't get fat, and she didn't get pregnant.

One day we had an electrical storm. Lightning struck all around us, and Salina, obediently raising herself on garbage under a near-by tree, was killed. Instantly the body was raced to the kitchen, the throat was cut by a Dutch Sister, an expert in slaughtering, and the carcass was divided amongst our three groups: the Dutch Sisters, the English Sisters, and the women and children. One pig equals pork stew for two hundred and eighty hungry people.

I dreaded breaking the news to George that Salina was dead; but he had to know before dinner. "Poor Salina," I said, "she's gone to Pig Paradise!"

"Hurrah! Pork for supper! Chilrens! Pork for supper!" said George.

The Sisters in their way were equally practical: "The Lord has provided a feast for All Saints' Day," they said.

We reserved ten spaces in one barrack for sick people. These spaces were always full. If you were sick, you took your bed with you. The Sisters took turns nursing.

I woke up one morning in this camp hospital ward instead of my flat. I asked how I got there; all I could remember was shaking with chills the afternoon before in my own quarters, and thinking sadly that I had no more quinine.

Sister said I was brought into hospital the night before with a high temperature and delirious. I had said the war was over and I was going home, and I headed out through the barbed wire several times. As they were afraid a sentry would shoot me, the doctor moved me into the hospital, with a Sister to watch over me.

I remained there two weeks. Penelope moved into my space in the mothers' barrack, and took care of George, who became a reformed character. Everybody said he behaved much better with her than with me. He didn't miss me, but I missed him.

There was one little Belgian woman in the ward, and the rest were Sisters. The Sisters wore nighttime bonnets to save their head coverings. At seven every morning the priest came to give Holy Communion. The Sisters lay like dead Crusaders, hands crossed on breasts, mouths open, awaiting the Host. The priest administered it, and a look of satisfaction crossed their faces. A few minutes they lay in meditation, the ward so quiet, a Presence there. Then up they popped, adjusted caps and nighties, called for tea.

Mother Lucila, an English nun, was having hemorrhages from stomach and intestinal ulcers, and said to be dying. There were no drugs or food, no manner of giving a blood transfusion. A little ice was sent in by the Japs for ice packs.

One night she started to die at midnight. The only light in the ward was a small coconut-oil lamp, of the Sisters, which was carried from bed to bed.

At 2.30 A.M. Mother Lucila's Sisters were awakened and called for last prayers. A ghost procession of white-robed women, led by three russet-clad Slot Sisters, the holiest of any, passed my bed praying, chanting, and singing "Mary, pray for us. Save her soul. Save her soul," and surrounded Mother Lucila's bed.

I had been trying to doze inside my mosquito net, but this finished me; I sat up and joined in. Mother Rose came to me, and talked for a minute, and said, "Dear little Sister! She is so happy! We are all so happy. She is happy to go. See, she has a smile on her lips!"

For hours there was the sound of vomiting, gasping, groaning, singing, and chanting, while Sisters went by with blood in bowls. Until 5.30, the Sisters prayed: then Mother Lucila opened her eyes very wide and looked up at the faces above her and said, "The Dear Lord is not coming for me yet. Go home, dear Sisters, and sleep." The Sisters went home, and Mother Lucila fell asleep. From then on Mother Lucila got better.

Every few days Dr. Yamamoto came, stood in the doorway with Little Napoleon pose, one hand in shirt front, the other behind him, holding — guess what? — green bananas! Bellowed out, "Gibson!" Then with an expression on his face which was a blend of naughty boy having a joke at elders' expense, benevolent despot distributing alms to the groveling poor, and Charlie Chaplin imitating a Nipponese soldier, he distributed the bananas, one per patient. We lay supine, hands cupped on breast as in communion, awaiting the handout. Into each pair of hands Dr. Yamamoto himself, in person, not a motion picture, jabbed a banana.

The first day Yamamoto found me here he said, "Keif-kah? How do you feel, Keif?"

"Horrible!"

"Ha-ah-ah-ah!"

Dr. Gibson came to me hastily. "Oh, she's better, thank you, Doctor, much better." It was a matter of pride for us to be "better."

Yamamoto: "Eh? Better-kah? Keif better?"

I, determined: "No, I'm not. I feel very ill. And I won't be any better until I have more quinine. The doctor hasn't enough quinine to give me the full dose; she can only give me ten grains. Will you send me some quinine?"

"No quinine-kah? Hah! Hummph! Hah! Quinine very difficult! Nobody has enough. Hah! . . . Yes, I send you quinine." Then to the doctor: "I send you quinine for Keif. Understand? For *Keif*. You give *all* to *Keif*."

This meant he would send full dosage of quinine for me, all to be given to me instead of being divided amongst all malaria patients, a few grains per capita, as community medicine.

The quinine came. I was up in five days. I had offended against community law, but I was again able to do community work, and to take care of George.

One month later Yamamoto again found me in the hospital bed, hands folded, waiting the green banana.

"What? Keif again? What disease?"

"Malaria. Will you please give me more quinine?"

"I think not malaria this time, Keif. No, no, no. I think influenza. Much influenza in Kuching now. I think very good you gargle." Demonstration here. Then hastily, to prevent my asking for a gargle, "Hot water very good to gargle!" From which I judged he was short of quinine.

"This isn't influenza, Doctor. I know it is malaria. If you will send me some quinine, I will be all right."

"Quinine! Quinine! Quinine! You always ask quinine, Keif! I always give! Ha! Ha! All right, all right, all right. I send!"

He proceeded on the banana tour — exit with clicking heels. Each patient relaxed from the death rigor to look anxiously at her banana and see if it would ever ripen.

Again Yamamoto did what he said: quinine arrived for Keif.

During that stay in hospital I got down to eighty pounds.

Shortly after I left the ward there was a recurrent outbreak of dysentery, the ward was full, women lay languishing upon their beds, unable to eat anything. Dr. Gibson pleaded for

milk and eggs; they did not come. But Yamamoto came —
with green bananas!

I thought a great deal in hospital, and mostly, about one
thing: how to get a hen.

Somebody had had a great idea. Our diet was carbohydrate.
The children must have protein. If you got a hen, and fed
the hen rice, and the hen laid an egg, you had protein. That
was the origin of the hen racket.

I did the mental work in hospital; as soon as I got out I
traded a black velvet dinner gown to a woman who wanted
it, I don't know why, for a white cotton sheet. The Chinese
outside of camp had the hens; they wanted white cotton
goods, none of which had arrived in Borneo since we had
been cut off by war.

I made the deal through a Japanese guard. The sheet was
worth a hundred dollars cash, and was to be traded for two
laying (emphasize *laying*) hens, worth fifty dollars each.
The guard was to procure the hens from a Chinese farmer,
the guard probably receiving a third hen for himself, or keeping half the sheet.

After I gave the guard the sheet, a period of suspense followed. He was shifted to another camp and couldn't get in
touch with me, the price of hens went up, and sheets went
down, a smuggling scare ensued.

The guard and I trusted each other, because each of us had
something on the other: we were equally anxious not to get
caught. But if the guard was caught with identifiable goods,
I might be traced; or if he was questioned too closely under
torture, I would be.

One evening at dusk he returned, and called for me. I went
to the wire. In his arms nested a hen; number-one laying hen,
Hetty. We welcomed her. I had never before really noticed
a hen, except in gravy on a platter. I saw that this one was
undersized, moulty, had catarrh, and rattled. But the test
was, did she lay?

George adored her, grabbed her, held her, frightened her, let her loose; Hetty squawked and ran out through the barbed wire. We followed in agony, and stood at the wire making noises like fresh worms, hen food, bran mash, little chicks, or anything we thought a hen would like. Hetty didn't give a damn. Just out of reach, she squawked and scratched and clucked and rattled. Never had I hated the barbed wire more. This went on for hours; George and I and our neighbors alternately enticing and cursing. Then the guard changed, and an old pal of George's came around. We begged him to shoo Hetty in. He shooed. Hetty came. We fell on her, and tied her firmly by the leg under my part of the barrack, kindness to animals or no.

The next morning I was in the kitchen getting tea. A shout came from George, from Shihping Cho, from all the mothers' barrack: "Come quick, come quick!" I ran. There stood Hetty in the garden, looking surprised. Beside her was an egg. We looked at her in awe. That egg was worth two dollars.

It was three weeks from dinner dress to egg. Hetty laid forty-one eggs before she went broody, and thereby established the camp record. They were like ping-pong balls, with shells like cellophane — but they were eggs, and George had protein, one egg's-worth per day.

Then there was a long wait before the arrival of the second hen. The guard was held in the guardhouse for questioning; I swore off smuggling, and gave up hope. But one month later the guard came back, and this time he brought Letty. Letty was a healthier, happier, wholesomer hen than Hetty, but she knew less about eggs. Everybody said, "What a beautiful hen!" and Letty fluffed, and scratched, and goggled her eyes, and did her droppings daintily, but didn't do her duty. She ate too much and laid too little. I studied her, fed her everything I could spare, did everything but push an egg in in one end and pull it out the other. She laid just often enough to keep me hopeful.

I fed Letty and Hetty with part of my rice ration, and

with scrapings of bran which I pinched from the cattle shed when I was working outside. I took them out worming in the garden attached to my wrist by strings, as each hen was only permitted to worm its owner's garden. In time every inch of our grounds was dewormed, and the only worms left in camp were in people's intestines.

The hen racket grew. At one time the Japanese office had allowed the Sisters to accept a gift of several hens sent in to them from their Asiatic Sisters in the Kuching convent. Also several hens had been sent in as gifts from the Indonese. This nucleus of eight legitimate hens was now lost in an illegitimate population of more than one hundred smuggled fowl.

Two rival organizations formed: the Hen Owners' Union, and the Gardeners' Guild. The hen owners sponsored proteins, and the gardeners sponsored vitamins. The gardeners said that the hens scratched up their gardens, and the hen owners said that the gardens took up worming space. I had both hens and a garden. George was quick to throw stones at other people's hens in order to save our worms for Hetty and Letty.

My garden produced potato leaves for vitamins, and chilis to make the leaves edible, as we had no salt. I couldn't grow potatoes because my garden allotment was too swampy, and George and I were too hungry to wait six months for them to mature.

The hen owners were always in trouble. Threats were made against the hens' lives, but two things saved them. First, the hens ran faster than the ladies. Second, no one would have dared to kill a fifty-dollar hen that laid a two-dollar egg (later eggs went to twenty dollars); it would have provoked homicide.

The hen owners met regularly to decide what we would say if the office ever asked us to explain the number of hens in camp, and accused us of smuggling. At first we were going to say that our hen was one of the eight legitimate ones belonging to the Sisters, but when the camp total exceeded one hundred this ceased to be practical.

I decided to deny Hetty and Letty completely. Nobody could prove they belonged to me, except by the fact that they came when I called them. If an officer asked if that hen belonged to me, I would say, What hen? Could I help it if a hen flew over the barbed wire and laid an egg under my flat?

The hen racket lasted with me until the next rice cut. I already had to give George some of my rice ration, and couldn't spare the rest for Hetty and Letty.

George and I couldn't afford to kill and eat the hens; we didn't want a feast. We wanted the minimum amount of food for living, for the maximum length of time. So I traded Letty to the Dutch Sisters for use on a feast day, in exchange for a sweet potato a day for six weeks for George. They were better gardeners than we, had used human excrement from the first to fertilize with, at a time when we still shuddered at it; now they were harvesting sweet potatoes. This potato — it was to be delivered to George at eleven every morning, in the Dutch kitchen — meant security for George for six weeks; that was long enough ahead to look. During the six weeks there proved to be three feast days, and on these days George was given *two* potatoes! How he sang to himself those days, as he ate!

Letty I gave to Bonita. She managed to feed Letty until peace came, and in addition shared the eggs with George. After armistice Letty went into a stew, and George and I helped to eat her. George loved Letty, but he loved her best in the stew.

How we did long for beauty: beauty of sight, sound, odor, beauty of thought! We dreamed of hearing symphonies again — opera, jazz — or whatever meant beauty of sound to the dreamer. We dreamed of beautiful flowers, places, sights, beautiful clothes; in our dreams we smelled perfumes, and fragrances, ginger bread, the sea, and the flowers. The scent of roses and violets haunted me, night after night I put myself to sleep by remembering it. And day by day I smelled latrines.

We had latrines made of rotting wood, now, with half a dozen separate compartments with eye-high divisions between, divisions which soon became waist-high as we stole the planks for our furniture. Once established in a latrine, one looked down into a lava flow of dung through bore-holes which were round, oval, or square, according to the designer's conception of women's behinds.

We always thought that some child would fall through a hole one day: and one day one did.

Mitey — a Javanese — was the tiniest, daintiest little girl-child in camp. She was mocha-colored — skin, eyes, and curly hair.

One night at dinnertime when the mothers were standing in line outside the kitchen waiting for soup, word came that a child had fallen into the lats. We raced for the latrine to see whose child, and arrived just as Mitey was being fished up by a Dutch Sister through the outside opening from which we emptied the latrines. Despite her protective coloration, Mitey looked desperately dungy.

As Mitey's mother was working in the kitchen, Mitey was

instantly engulfed by other mothers and raced to the bath-shed, the principal maternal emotion just then being one of relief that it wasn't your own child. We wanted to give her an antiseptic bath, but the only antiseptic in camp was Friar's Balsam, so we boiled her instead, and gave her a dose of salts.

The next day Mitey was fine, and the latrine was ordered emptied.

We asked the Japs for a children's latrine then, submitting a design with a clover-leaf bore-hole, proof against falling through. They admired the design, but didn't give us the bore-hole.

Our attitude towards the waste products of living had changed. At first in prison camp we had shuddered over the latrines, held our noses, asked to have the excrement removed. Now we hoarded it, and rationed it, per capita, per garden. Dysentery and doctor's orders did not stop us. Fertilization makes vegetation; and hunger outruns hygiene.

I often thought, by contrast, of the orchid-colored, smooth-tiled Ladies' Rooms at home, with Kleenex, Cutex, Kotex, pale soap, faint scent, and "This Room Perfumed by Kush-Nu."

Food fastidiousness had disappeared. Prisoners pushed flowers, grass, weeds, dogs, cats, rats, snakes, grasshoppers, and snails down their gullets, where desperation plus the force of gravity carried it to their stomachs, the stomachs hurried it on to intestines, which hurried it on to the next place. The following day, we, as gardeners, passed it back to the potato beds. Somewhere along the yards of irritated mucous membrane we received the impression that we had had a meal.

If it was possible to hate one season more than another in camp, I hated Christmas. Then was the time one wanted to give — gifts, joy, happiness. Then was the time material and spiritual paupery hurt. Christmas 1944 was the worst.

The Christian religion taught us that one thousand, nine hundred and forty-four years before the Saviour of the World was born. His promise was Peace on Earth, Good Will to Men. He showed us the way by love. The irony of celebrating His birth and teaching, while we were following their antithesis, overcame me.

So then we had a rice cut, George had a toothache again, I heard Harry was ill, and Christmas was coming.

I wanted to cut it all out; I felt that I could not pretend. I suggested that as both energy and materials were nonexistent now, we should keep Christmas as the Sisters did, as a religious festival only, and agree not to give any presents to our children. If no child had anything they could not compare, they would not be sad.

But the majority of mothers felt that the children would be disappointed if they did not receive gifts, as we had made things for them the two previous Christmas seasons in camp. And if some children had gifts, then they all must have.

So the Christmas rush started. We cut off sleeves, shortened dresses, cut off collars, sacrificed anything to get bits of material out of which to make presents. Many of us had slept in evening dresses for a year or so, our nightgowns being worn out; now the good parts of these were sacrificed. We unraveled stockings and socks to get thread to sew with. I had one pair of kid gloves which I cut up to make dolls' shoes. In the excitement of creating we sacrificed anything. Out of bits and pieces of every sort of material we made small dolls and fancy animals, and never have I seen their like for originality. Nothing was what it seemed to be.

Their bodies were made of flesh-colored underpants or nighties or beige stockings, and stuffed with *kapok*, tea, or shredded rags. Hair was made of hemp, unraveled from the ends of rope, or else of wool. Faces were embroidered on, or rubbed on with pastel, or painted. I had a few pastels which the Japanese *Domei News* reporter had given me when he had posed me for a propaganda picture of "artist at play" the year before; these I used combined with my own lipstick and rouge, to paint faces. I put the pastels on with a wet matchstick to make them more lasting, and finished each face with a coat of my face powder.

The Christmas before I had done fifty dolls' faces for people this way, and nearly exhausted my make-up and my patience. Now I said that I would trade each doll's face for a scrap of extra food, or smokes. The barter did not discourage trade as much as I had hoped.

We cut blocks of soft rubberwood and carved small toys; we used liquid rubber tapped from the rubber tree in camp to glue things together with. And anything with any claim of edibility was bartered for, and hoarded for the day.

If I hadn't been exhausted anyway, if I hadn't grudged the energy and time, if my heart had been in it, it might have been fun.

The day came. The children went wild. The barrack was bedlam, the holiday bustle was there, the excitement and comparing and quarreling. Each special Sister came along with a food tidbit for her special child, and contributions arrived all morning. Gifts came from their fathers, permitted by the Japs: scooters, swords, guns, carts, and blocks, made of soft rubberwood, put together with nails made from the twisted-off barbs of barbed wire.

The Japanese office sent word that we were to meet our husbands for half an hour, in the field outside the barbed wire. We put on our make-up and went.

Lieutenant Nekata was there, looking benevolent or malevolent, according to your interpretation of him. Miss Asaka was there, announcing and pronouncing the rules and regulations and taboos of the occasion with her own natural vocal arrangements, which surpassed any ordinary loud-speaker. The armed guards were there, sweating and prodding their way amongst us. Colonel Suga was there, sweeping by in his motor car, he bowing, we bowing. Sweet biscuits arrived to be distributed to the children.

We sat with our husbands quietly under the trees. They held their children lovingly to them, and yearned over them. But the children would not have much of that. They were outside the barbed wire today, in the fields with the trees and the stream, running wild, climbing trees, picking flowers, burs, buds — any living wild thing — running free. Fathers were secondary to freedom.

Harry looked ill, always more ill, and more thin. At the end of half an hour the parting came. As always, I felt that I had forgotten the most important things, that all I should have said was, "I love you."

The men were mustered and marched off down the road.

Some looked back striving to hold the moment longer. Always there was the feeling that danger, destruction, death, would strike before we met again. Always each meeting seemed the last. I looked after them as far as I could see. Was it better, or was it worse, to meet like this, I wondered.

In the afternoon we had the Christmas tree. It had been sent from the men's camp with all the decorations on it, made by the civilian men and the British soldiers, and arranged for by George Colley, the American from Manila.

The tree was pleasant, a small Dacrydium with bending boughs. Flowers and tiny scraps of colored cloth or string or paper were used to make it bright. There was a present on it for every child from the sender, and a few children had additional gifts. The smaller gifts were hung on the tree, and the heavy ones placed under. It was like every Christmas tree, the shrine of great promise.

A Christmas angel in spangles with limbs of seduction and face of enticing dissipation teetered drunkenly on top, created by a British Tommy, in likeness of a prisoner's dream.

Long before the presents were distributed the boys had spotted the best ones. These were two wooden motor trucks, a train, and a large and splendid ship carved of rubberwood. These were outstanding and stupendous, they were manly and pretentious. All over the tree were hung various colored stuffed animals and dolls which represented Mama's garments and undergarments of the past — most ingenious, considering — considering! The materials for these had been sent to the men to work with; and there were giraffes, tigers, elephants, zebras, spotted ponies, dogs, cats, bunnies, and golliwoggs — whimsical, fanciful, phony. We thought they were wonderful, considering . . . considering . . . But who wants to consider?

The boys looked at this stuff lethargically, and even the girls were blasé. There comes a time when Mama's clothes should either be buried or burned.

But at the foot of the tree the boys all crowded, and handled, and grabbed, and dribbled on, and panted over the trucks, the boat, and the train.

George said happily, "That's mine, isn't it, Mum? That big big big boat?"

"I don't think so, darling. That is so very big it must be for the biggest boy. But there is *something* lovely for you on the tree, I know."

"I want the boat, Mum."

"But all the boys want the boat, and they can't all have it. You must wait and see."

"But I want it, Mum."

"Wait and see."

The distribution started. George waited breathless and confident, to receive his boat. I was praying; if only one child could have that boat, it might as well be George!

One by one the gifts were distributed. Still George didn't have his, and the boat was still there. And then George was handed a white pony with red spots and an orange mane and a beautiful Christmas card, "To George."

"Say Thank You, George."

"Thank you. But when do I get the boat?"

"That is for somebody else, dear."

"I don't want this pony. I want that boat."

"I think we'd better go home now, George." Something was about to start!

"I won't go without my boat!"

Just then the boat was presented to Vicki! It was actually taken and held by Vicki, and it was removed by Vicki.

George watched it go. His world broke into bits. This was worse than the war, or being hungry, or toothache; this was the end of everything.

So he acted accordingly.

Oh, George, my darling, I know just how you feel. I would have got it for you if I could. I didn't know in time.

But it was too late then for me to make one, or smuggle one, or steal one.

It wasn't nice of you to throw that pony on the ground and

stamp on it. It wasn't nice to scream and shout, "I hate that bad-smell pony!" It wasn't nice, but I know how you feel.

Dusk comes, quiet comes, children sleep. Christmas is over again. I say my prayers: "O God, before next Christmas comes, give me a boat to give my son."

There was something that kept us going in Kuching, beyond just rice and greens. Each one of us was beginning to know that it is not enough to exist, that one must have a reason for existing. "Man liveth not by bread alone, but by every word that proceedeth out of the mouth of God," was never so true as in prison camp. And the less bread there was, the more we needed the Word.

The word that proceeded out of the mouth of God for me was the warning not to be consumed by hate. Hate is a wasteful emotion; for my own sake, I didn't wish to hate the Japanese, or the people about me.

Every night when I lay down beside George I was filled

with love for him. Every night we said the Lord's Prayer together. I was not praying for an answer, or to praise the Lord, but to ease myself. I was looking for rest and peace, and a way to make life bearable, when it was not bearable.

With George beside me I could know that love holds together in time of danger, love soothes and strengthens, love builds up, where hate destroys. I could pray then to love and to God, the two inseparable.

I went to bed at dusk most nights, and lay awake several hours before sleeping. I got up several times during the night to smoke cigarettes, because of hunger. I went out to the latrines several times each night as a result of improper diet. My ribs and shoulder still pained me and kept me awake. I had time at night to think.

I thought of all the young men of all races, who were dying all over the world in battle, who had at some time lain like George at their mothers' side. When those boys died, what did they die for? How often must they have asked themselves this question. I could not believe that their answer was "For hate." Hate is worth neither living nor dying for.

We in prison were now the mistreated ones. Yet it would be only a matter of time, and the turn of the tide, before we would be the abusers, and our captors the abused, because we had in ourselves the same instincts for brutality. War evoked and exalted these instincts. It was war that we must hate, and not each other.

It was the practice of the Japanese to make us unwilling witnesses to their abuse of our fellow prisoners. These exhibitions were public, and the victim was detained in public view long after punishment. A dog may hide away when in pain, but not so a prisoner.

During these episodes I have never seen a victim fail in fortitude, or lose the dignity of courage. At such times the thought came to me of Christ, who suffered persecution bravely on the Cross. It was not Christ who was shamed, but the persecutors. Watching these men and boys who were so brave I saw that the only shame for them would be if they should ever change place with their persecutors.

I had often to observe the actions of one handsome young Nipponese soldier. He was always in charge of the guard that herded us women out to haul firewood, outside the perimeter of the camp. He was tall for a Japanese, with unusually nice legs, of which he was very proud. He treated them tenderly, clothed them with the Japanese rarity of well-fitting trousers, and ended them in well-polished army boots.

On the road down which we carried firewood we usually passed British soldiers at work. They were almost naked, without shoes or trousers, half-starved, and scarcely able to carry the loads under which they struggled. Our handsome guard could never pass by one of these soldiers without kicking him on his naked body with his own well-booted foot.

We always pretended not to see, walking with eyes ahead and with expressionless faces. But under our breaths we muttered "The swine, the louse, the filthy Jap." I know that we despised this boy as he could never have despised us.

This Japanese lad had another victor's gesture. When displeased, annoyed, fed up with life, he would call a British soldier out of his group, and command him to stick out his tongue. He would then snap the man's jaw to on his tongue, with a swift uppercut.

Unwillingly I witnessed this boy's progress throughout two years of war. I made up my mind then that I would sooner see my own son die of starvation, in camp, than live to grow up and be like that. I learned then that I hated the spirit of brutality in man more bitterly than I hated anything that the Japanese could do to me.

Last Gasp

NINETEEN FORTY-FIVE came. One year before, we had celebrated the new year with the false rumor of the collapse of
Germany: for one month we had believed it. This year we
celebrated nothing. One year before it had seemed incredible
to us to still see no Allied planes in the air above us. This year
we expected nothing.

What we saw, when we looked up to the heavens, was
worse than nothing: it was two inexterminable little Nip
planes that lived in the shrubbery near camp. Buzzing daily
above us these little planes with their glaring "poached eggs"
on the wings were the symbol of Nipponese supremacy.
While the Nips still fluttered in and out over the Eastern
battle front in playthings like this the Allied menace could not
be very near.

With the new year came a cut in the rice ration. The
physical strength of the women was decreasing rapidly. We
were ordered to work outside the camp for six hours each
day, digging in the fields. I was one of the few able-bodied
ones left. I had been working as a substitute when women
became ill; now, however, for me to accept even partial ex-
emption from full-time physical labor, because of writing
for Suga, became impossible.

I went to Colonel Suga and told him that I must cease writing, and go back to work in the field.

He said, "But I have excused you!"

I said, "You have ordered us to turn out so many women every day as a working party. You exempt me personally from going, but somebody has to fill my place. There is no one more able to go than I. All are now unwell, I must help."

He made no further comment. Perhaps as patron of the arts he had been satisfied. I went back on the work list. But the Japanese office forgot to discontinue the three-dollar salary and this was paid to camp funds until peace came.

With each anniversary I looked back and counted the waste. Each year I had gained nothing. I had lost joy, youth, accomplishment, love. I had retained one thing only, life.

Life is worth much; I did much to keep it. I learned to do anything, or die doing it. I ate, or didn't eat, though I preferred to eat. I lived with germs, and did not die of them. I was unsanitary, and escaped the diseases of dirt.

I endured pain, when discomforts and annoyances seemed unendurable. I looked at death without fear, though I did not want it; but my ungenerous living frightened me.

I doubted the existence of anything beyond myself, but more than ever I needed something. As life grew grimmer my only sign of something beyond was the constant search and desire for it.

The circumstances of prison-camp living brought out the worst in us. The struggle for survival of the fittest in primitive circumstances is not a show-up of one sex against the other, but a show-up of anybody who competes.

We had two virtues: good cheer, and courage. The morale in camp was always good. We knew the only way to make camp life bearable was to laugh, not cry. Tears and gloom were resented more than vice.

A stranger coming into our camp would not have guessed from the atmosphere that all of us were hungry, many were suffering from physical complaints for which we had neither remedy nor palliative, and all were sick at heart. For on the surface we were cheerful. The Japanese officers, when inspecting our camp, often turned this quality of cheer to their own credit; they said that one could see by our cheerful attitude that we were well-treated.

Some of this cheer was pride: we were determined to show the Japanese that Western women did not complain. We had many opportunities to hear about the virtues of Japanese women in contrast to Western women.

We had pride amongst ourselves. One was ashamed to complain, when all had cause to do so. The heroism of a few was noticeable. It is impossible to exaggerate the mental torture experienced by those women whose husbands had been taken from camp and either were held without communication in Japanese prison cells, or had disappeared from their knowledge completely. And yet, they were brave. Almost everyone in camp displayed physical courage; we came to accept discomfort and pain as normal conditions. The old, the ill, and the frail attempted and accomplished impossible physical tasks, survived impossible illnesses, and evaded unavoidable death.

In the men's camp there was only one coffin in use, this with a false bottom. With each burial the coffin was lowered into the grave, then the bottom was released and the body fell through into the dirt. The coffin was then brought home and dusted off for the next corpse. This custom was established when a glut of corpses created a firewood shortage. But in the women's camp, each body went to rest, and remained there, so we believed, in its own coffin.

A Sister was dying.

For months past the weary process had been going on, for leukemia is a slow and despoiling, but inexorable, disease. During a period of many days only Sister Antonia's strong heart had kept her alive. To palliate her illness and its resulting agonies Dr. Gibson had just one remedial therapeutic aid, soda bicarbonate. There had been little food in the camp diet that the Sister could eat. Rice gruel alone sustained her now.

Her final breaths were coming. Her fellow Sisters visited her, whispering and genuflexing and praying, and then passing out of the ward with long, mysterious faces, and dry, mysterious eyes, and plowing feet and whispering skirts.

At the other end of the hospital ward three little girls lay in hospital beds, Edith, Margaret, and Anne.

Edith was Shihping Cho's five-year-old daughter. Her illness was due to eight decayed double teeth, and her gums were abscessed and covered with gum boils. The decayed teeth could not be removed because anesthetics were not obtainable, and the shock to the child's nervous system of removal without anesthesia would have been too severe. Edith had been suffering from this septic condition for months, and was also anemic and undernourished.

In the bed next to her lay Margaret, who was ten. She had a "tired" heart, and wept with the pains in her legs and arms. Rheumatism, the doctor said, caused by malnutrition and general debility.

Anne was the third child, with straight, fawn-colored hair, and wistful brown eyes. Her body scarcely caused a wrinkle under the sheet which covered her. Anne was always having to take it easy, and the other day when she became unconscious in Sister Dominica's schoolroom the doctor took her into the hospital for rest and care. Hers was a case of heart weakness, also caused by malnutrition and general debility.

These three were hospital cases. What they needed was not medicine or doctoring, but food: eggs, milk, meat, vegetables, and fruits. And these neither hospital nor doctor could supply. In Kuching itself they were difficult to obtain and expensive; for internees they were impossible.

The beds of the little girls were covered with their home-made dolls and small playthings, but the children themselves spoke in whispers. They cast anxious glances down the ward towards the dying Sister's bed. Frequently in the midst of their play their attention focused thoughtfully on the mysterious parade of whispering, praying Sisters as it rustled by them.

"Everything is all right," the doctor had assured them many times. "Quite all right! Do not pay any attention!"

But they were not reassured.

Now a Sister is dead.

We pause in our work in the kitchen to watch the body pass by. The hearse is a stretcher on four wheels, the coffin is a rough wooden box, the cover is held down by two bent and rusted nails. The pall is covered with scarlet cannas and balsam, flowers which have been planted by the Sisters and have bloomed many times since our arrival in this camp.

The stretcher is pulled and pushed by half a dozen Roman Catholic priests. Behind them follow some twenty-five Sisters, and a small body of secular friends. By special permission this funeral party will be allowed to go on foot to the Kuching cemetery, about two miles distant from our camp.

It is high noon, and the sun is blazing. The Sisters in their white robes move slowly in the heat. Many of them wear woven grass coolie hats, or Dyak hats, balanced on top of their white veiled heads. A few carry black cotton umbrellas.

The procession passes out of our gate and moves on past the sentry. Down the road, in front of the men's clinic, it pauses. Soon it is joined there by another coffin, this one draped with a Union Jack and carried by soldiers. In it is the body of a British soldier who has died this morning. The tropical climate allows for no delay in funeral obsequies.

Along the road to Kuching travel the two dead bodies.

Slowly they pass by the pleasant fields, the bending trees, the shining sky, the grazing cows, the dogs and cats and birds and squirrels and free live things — all simple things that speak

of life and happiness — all things that the two captives have
longed once more to see. Now this today they cannot see.
Their eyes are closed, their senses are forever stilled.

A Sister is dead; a soldier is dead. Two prisoners are freed;
two captives have returned to their Homeland.

As these eldest and more feeble nuns die off, the erudite
Mothers who are left declare that these deaths are a sign of
another move coming soon. For the Lord in His kindness is
sparing the sick, the weak, the aged from the exhaustion of
another camp migration — even from the exhaustion of that
journey for which we all pray, the exodus from prison into
freedom.

Of the soldiers' deaths we can no longer keep count.

Here in captivity the natural processes of life are reversed.
In the outside world things are born, and things die. Here in
this camp things die; but they are not born.

Every change was for the worse. Rules increased, food decreased, work increased, and strength decreased. Disappoint-
ments multiplied, and optimism was never verified. Hope itself seemed only a refuge for those who would not face facts.

Our food ration, then, as supplied by the Japanese per
person per day, was as follows: one cupful of thin rice gruel,
five tablespoons of cooked rice, sometimes a few greens, a
little sugar, sometimes a little salt, and tea. This was what
the Japanese expected us to live on. Or did they expect us to
live on it?

Additions to this diet were sweet-potato tops, which we
grew ourselves. We used the tops because we were too hungry to wait for the potatoes to mature. Every square foot of
the camp was in use for gardens, but the soil was exhausted,
and we were exhausted. The last eight months of imprisonment it was almost impossible for us to do heavy work, but
we did it. We arose before sunrise to finish the work inside
camp, and then went outside the camp to work for the Japa-

nese. By nine o'clock in the morning we were worn out.

By now soldiers were trading for and buying skinned cats and rats, people were eating snails and worms, all of us were

eating weeds and grass, and plenty of us would have liked to eat each other.

I had meals of banana skins stolen from Japanese refuse barrels and boiled into soup.

March twenty-fifth came like any other day. At 10 A.M. two little Poached Egg planes scooted hastily out of their underbrush and puttered across the sky. Their shadows crossed the field where I dug; I knew how the sun must shine on their red egg centers; I heard them, I didn't look up.

Half an hour later we gardeners sat down to rest, heads on hands, cold tea beside us, eyes down. We heard a drone. The sound grew. The sound swelled. We squinted an eye. There were specks above. More Japs? we said. . . . They don't make that sound! We squinted again. The heavens rolled, the clouds shook, the sky filled — there was the roar of bomb on bomb! Not Japs! Not Japs! *Not Japs!*

OUR PLANES!

We believed it. They could be none other but ours. And at that moment patriotism returned; love of country, love of our own magnificence, pride of being the biggest and best.

The planes moved above us in the clear sky, majestic and deliberate. The sun blazed from their wings, the sky filled with their sound, and the earth lay helpless beneath. Up and down Kuching River they bombed, and in the vicinity of camp, and then turned unhurriedly and flew away. There was no single shot from Nipponese defenses.

And yet we were not mad with joy, not yet did optimism revive. In my diary I wrote:

First Allied planes seen today. Three years ago I would have been delirious with joy. Today I have neither energy nor heart for excitement. Too little food.

With the Allied Forces over Borneo the Japanese paper money, known as "banana currency" because of the banana trees pictured on it, was decreasing rapidly in value. The guards were becoming anxious to acquire our gold jewelry and diamonds, cotton material of any sort, and men's clothing, and by this time there was just one thing that mattered to us — food.

The guards would force the Chinese outside to sell food to them for cash; and they would then deliver the food to us in exchange for our valuables, or trade the goods to the farmer for the food and keep a cut from food and goods as commission.

What little jewelry I had with me in camp I had taken for sentimental reasons. I had my engagement and wedding rings sewed inside the overflap of a blouse pocket, and these I never parted with. My other pieces were old family keepsakes of gold, several set with diamonds. I had my sorority pin, which had been especially set in my college days with a diamond from my mother's ring.

My first jewelry trade was a heavy gold chain, a keepsake from my English grandmother, which I traded for four bottles of coconut oil, normal value about ten cents a bottle. Oil was important, as we had none in our diet.

I traded an old gold brooch, with a topaz in it, for two *katis* (2 2/3 pounds) of *blachang*. *Blachang* is a rotted, native-made fish paste. After liberation, when the American Navy came into camp, I opened my *blachang* tin and let a sailor take a sniff. If a sailor could faint, he'd have fainted. He said, "Oh, lady, not even a sailor could take that!" But *blachang* was rich in protein, and it was salty, and we'd had no salt, and we loved it.

I traded a gold watchcase of my mother's, which had been made into a locket to hold my mother's and father's pictures, for forty eggs, one bottle of oil, and a bottle of Japanese toothache remedy for George.

I traded my sorority pin for forty eggs and one bottle of oil. In normal times eggs had been three cents each. This trade meant two eggs and a spoonful of oil every day for twenty days — safety for three more weeks for George.

The racket in diamonds was going well until one woman got nervous and broke the market by trading a ring with three diamonds in it for the food value of what the rest of us were asking for one diamond. This market break took place while I was making the deal with a Nip guard for my sorority pin. He had promised me forty eggs, four bottles of oil, and five hundred dollars banana currency, and had left the five hundred dollars with me as security, while he took the pin to town to a Chinese jeweler to have the diamond examined. My soldier brought back my pin and said he didn't want it, and that he wanted his five hundred dollars back. I said I couldn't give it to him as I had already spent one hundred dollars for a bottle of oil. He said, "Never mind, keep the money!" I said I didn't want the money, I wanted food! And I asked him to make me an offer for the pin.

Making this offer required three days of conversation through the barbed wire, and many visits to my barrack. Meanwhile I insisted that the guard keep the pin, knowing he would be more tempted to close with me for it after showing it to his friends. In due time, but without much enthusiasm, he brought the forty eggs and one bottle of oil; he did this, he said, because he was sorry for me. I gave him back his four hundred dollars.

The extra food which came into the women's camp in this way, during the period of least rations, was probably one reason why the women remained in better health than the men. All the camps smuggled, but the women's camp was furthest from headquarters, and our guards were in less danger of discovery. But the principal reason that we were successful with contraband was that the Japanese officers ignored our activity as long as we did not face them with it. If we were clumsy and they caught us, then to save their faces they were severe. But in the men's camp smugglers were fiercely sought after, and brutally punished.

In time the officers acquired most of these possessions which we traded over the fence for contraband.

Sometimes I enjoyed it thoroughly: my mind had nothing else to work on but outwitting the Japs, and getting meals. Other times, when I almost got caught, when consequences

stared at me, I was scared to death, and thought longingly of
the time when I could live under the law again, and not fight
it for food.

We had been ordered to clear and weed the sago acres,
a swampy plantation near the camp, about fifteen minutes'
walk away. The sago root was ready for harvest, much of it
was rotting in the ground, and we were hungry and without
food. Yet we were not told to harvest the sago, but to clear
it, and leave it in the ground. There were now eighty secular
women in camp. Of this number, only thirty-eight were
well enough to do physical work.

We were ordered to send out a working party of thirty
women daily. This left eight able-bodied women in camp to
do the community cooking, cleaning, and so on. Working
hours in the field were nine to twelve, and three to six. We
took turns going out on the working party, and on my day of
rest I stayed at home and did camp work.

As the Sisters had also to send out a working party, they
discontinued the children's lessons. But as the mothers were
the youngest and fittest group in camp, and best able to do
outside work, it was necessary for us to go. We asked the
Japanese what to do with our children. They said, "Take
them with you."

We did. The rain came daily, the sun steamed us daily. The
plantation was swampy; there were mosquitoes, bugs, centipedes, snakes — and a stream to fall in. The children loved it,
but the mothers didn't.

So we left them in camp, to run wild. At night when we
came home to them, filthy dirty ourselves and dead-tired, we
always found them in trouble: swimming in the bath tank,
wading in the well, fishing in the drinking water, stealing potatoes from the Sisters' garden, pinching somebody's firewood,
throwing stones, cutting each other up with knives, or maybe
just getting mud all over our own four by six feet of living

space. Did our kids have any rights in this world, we asked. No, they didn't.

Then the Allied planes started bombing Kuching. To leave our children in camp uncared-for, then, was torture. The Sisters came to the rescue again: they rearranged their work program so that two teaching Sisters could resume teaching, and when air raids came they saw the children safely in the trenches, which had been dug for them some weeks before by the Dutch Roman Catholic Fathers.

After two weeks of working in the sago swamp the number of ulcers in camp trebled, the sick roll doubled, and fever became very prevalent. It seemed impossible to fill our quota of workers, but like all other impossible things in camp life, we did it.

Sago root grows like a tuber under the soil, and is called in Malay *ubi kayu*, literally "wood potato," which is a very good description of it. The root is pure starch and water, and when old it becomes so fibrous that it splinters when you break it, and is inedible. But when young it is delicious roasted or boiled, or seems so to starving people. It tastes a little like white potato, but never becomes floury when cooked, just becomes more and more glutinous. The skin is poisonous, and it should be peeled off very deep, and, with or without skin, eating much sago root produces acute indigestion.

The roots grow from six inches to two feet below the surface of the soil, and above them flourishes a thin-stemmed, green, dusterlike tree which grows to be six to eight feet tall.

If we had been sent out to harvest the sago root we could have put heart in it, but to be told to clear and weed the land, while the sago went to rot, was annoying.

However, not all of the sago went to rot; we ate frantically all the time we were working. We dug it up with our hands, digging madly with bare finger tips, extracting the root, pushing mud back in the hole, huddling secretively down, and eating hungrily. We ate it raw. It was said to be poisonous, it was manured with excrement, we were forbidden to dig it; but we were hungry, and we ate it.

We became bolder, and started hiding it on our persons and smuggling it home. The roots were edible when from two to twelve inches long. I wore a man's shirt and khaki shorts, and filled my pockets, stuffed my shirt front, and held some up under my armpits. I enlarged the pockets of my shorts to accommodate the larger roots. Some tried carrying it in bags and coats, but these were always inspected, whereas our bodies were seldom searched. Safely back in camp, we roasted and boiled the roots for the children, for ourselves, for friends. Having something to give was the one joy of that job.

The guards knew that we were eating in the field; they grumbled at us, but did nothing. They, like ourselves, were tired of war, fed-up, lethargic, they hated the sago job too, they said. They said to us, "Well, if you can eat raw sago root you *must* be hungry!"

One day the guard warned us not to take any home. He said that the officers were angry with us because we were not working hard, and they guessed that we were stealing the sago. He thought there would be a search. I contented myself with eating in the fields, that day. However, many people stuffed their bosoms anyway; hunger is a great incentive, and we were used to false alarms.

At noon we were mustered on the road to go home. The ladies bulged, and the Sisters billowed. Instead of being marched off home, we were ordered to remain at attention on the road. Then approaching us we saw Miss Asaka, the female interpreter, and a Japanese officer.

Instantly we knew. Sago hurled through the air like projectiles. Without hesitation the ladies unbosomed themselves from every fold, throwing the swag as far from them as they could. The air was literally thick with it; it was anything in order to get rid of the evidence. At one moment the ladies bulged with sago, the next moment the roadside was buried under it. We ladies had no modesty, no shame.

But not so the Sisters: their swag was too well secreted. Modesty made them hesitate to expose undergarments, limbs,

and person; the indignity of exposing their contraband in its intimate locations made them hesitate, and hesitating they were lost.

Arrive Asaka and officer. Scene: landscape covered with sago root; ladies mostly not; Sisters guilty, shamed, and trembling. Asaka starts the search, pinching, patting, prodding, looking, opening, exposing. No sense of shame, or modesty for sex, restrained her; she knew how to search.

Some of the ladies still had sago; these ladies' names she took. As she searched there was a monologue from Asaka: "Shame! For shame! To steal! You white ladies! Shame! Shame!"

Then came the Sisters. What a sad exposé! Out of pants, bloomers, blouses, aprons, shirts, singlets, stockings, sleeves, came sago. Caught with the goods, there wasn't much to say. Asaka searched, and clucked, and "shamed."

The Sisters were not used to being rebuked for naughtiness, as were we ladies, and they took the scolding seriously. The Nips had always thought better of the Sisters than they did of the rest of us.

The Sisters wept. We ladies only said, Too bad, no more sago now!

That afternoon word came from the office for the guilty ones to appear. I had not been caught with sago, but I was ordered up. If the Japanese once learned your name they went on using it for every occasion.

We went. Lieutenant Nekata gave the lecture: he said that to steal was a great shame on us white people, who talked so much about being honorable. He said we should know better and have higher principles. He then asked, "Why did you do it?"

Each one answered the same: "We are hungry."

He said, "If you are hungry you should ask, not steal."

We said, "We do ask, and you do not give."

He said, "Ah, ah, ah, we are all hungry in Kuching because Allies stop ships from bringing rice to Borneo. This is the Allies' fault. We Japanese are hungry too."

We looked at him and at the guards, and then we looked at ourselves, and mentally compared our bulk and flesh.

"May we then in future take sago home from the fields when we work?" we asked him.

"Not now," he said, "because you have been naughty! If you steal again I will punish you severely, but I will not punish you this time. Go home now, and be good."

So we went home, but were not good.

In May 1945, we were given one postcard each, and told we might send it home. We were to write twenty-five words, not including the address. This happened three times a year, but this time there was something new. In addition to the twenty-five words, a certain percentage of the camp *must* include a propaganda sentence, this to be chosen from a number of sentences submitted to us.

A few of these sentences follow:

Borneo is a land of milk and honey and plenty, with fruit, glorious moonlight nights, happy days, and contentment, here among the wonderful Nipponese.

We appreciate the kindness and bounty of the Nipponese treatment.

We have learned to admire many traits of the Orient since being interned by the Nipponese, who are gentle, and kind, and generous to us.

We are allowed to smoke, sing, hum, whistle, play games, and we would be very happy if only you were here, darling. [I wanted to add, "But we do not eat."]

These kind and happy people have done so much for us. Dear ones, it is a privilege for us to be with them. But we wish that our aggressor nation would sue for peace now. . . .

I studied the sentences in order to find the least objectionable. I thought that if I used a propaganda sentence the card would be more likely to get home. Then I decided that they were all so obvious that my people would know they were propaganda.

I sent the following card:

Seven communications sent. Seven received. Health moderate. George well, energetic, roughneck, reminds me my brother.

Fed-up with war. Hopes deferred.
Borneo is a beautiful place for living, a dreamland where the scenery is beautiful, little birds sing, very delicious fruits grow, we are very happy here.

AGNES, HARRY, GEORGE

My aunt told me later that she had never felt as down-hearted about my fate as when she received that card. She said that obviously I had lost my mind.

That card, thanks to the propaganda sentence, got home. Many previous cards were later found in stacks in the corner of the Japanese Kuching office.

After the spring rice cut, the sick roll doubled, and there were deeds of despair and violence amongst the prisoners. One person could hang on while another let go. Perhaps the person with the greatest emotional capacity for realizing life fully suffers the greatest when his life sinks to a monotone of misery.

In the civilian men's camp there was a brilliant and high-strung young man who had held an important position in the Sarawak government. He was a gifted student of languages, and in addition to Western tongues he spoke Japanese and Chinese well.

He had Asiatic attachments in the town of Kuching, which brought him into notice of the Japanese *Kempi-Tai* (the military police) a number of times. Again and again he had been questioned, with all that questioning implies, in the attempt to extort information from him about them. He must have wondered how long he could remain silent in the face of torture, whether or not he had anything to tell. He had said that if he was taken again for questioning he would kill himself.

At one morning roll call this young man was ill, and did not turn out. His absence attracted the attention of Lieutenant Kubu, who was taking the muster; Kubu remembered that this was the man whom he had questioned and beaten so often before.

Unable to get his dope supply that day, Kubu was in a bad mood, fit to take insult at anything. He called the man to the office, questioned and beat him, then took him outside to the square and placed him in front of the Japanese sentry, there to stand with his arms above his head until sundown. He was then taken to the guardhouse to await requestioning by the *Kempi-Tai*.

The young man asked permission of the guard to go to the latrine. He did not reappear. The guard went to the latrine and found him lying in a pool of blood, dying. He had broken the water bottle which was used for toilet purposes, and with the broken glass had cut the arteries of his wrists and throat.

Kubu was very angry. He ordered a search of all camps immediately. A search was always a soporific for upset Japanese emotions.

The younger men buried the suicide. The ground in the prison burying plot was hard, the young men were weak and not well, an empty stomach rattles and pains and aches worse than a full one. It was slow work digging — and nothing to go home to except, Who next?

I had just finished writing the story of this man in my diary the next morning, when the word "Search" was passed along the barrack, and a guard appeared at my door.

We knew the look of search parties: several officers grumbling, one of them usually Kubu, surrounded by five or six armed guards shouting more loudly than usual. Almost always we saw them coming down the road in the distance, and were warned before they arrived. Today they had sneaked up on us, unnoticed in the early morning rush.

I had no chance to put my diary back in the tin, crawl under the barrack, and re-bury it in its waterproof wrapping. I could just get the papers stuffed inside my shirt when the guard looked in. It was safer to have them on me than to leave them in the barrack. . . . Then I followed the guard out to roll call.

We mustered in groups before the barracks. The far end from us was the Dutch Sisters' barrack, usually treated with consideration by the Japanese. But today guards were shouting and blustering, and to our surprise the officer, who was not Kubu, was feeling the women's bodies. Evidently the suicide had upset them, and they had to relieve themselves in some way.

The whispering chorus carried proceedings down to us: "He's furious! He's feeling them all over, he's feeling under their skirts. He's looking . . . ! Ohhhh — He's found something! Ooooooh! Now the Mother is explaining — Oh, he slapped her! He's furious today! Now he's on our women. He's talking to somebody. He's called Dr. L out of line. Oh, she had a cigarette behind her! She would! He's going to slap her! . . . Oooooh! She doesn't give a damn! Gosh! She can take it, can't she! He's getting madder and madder. . . . Now here he comes. . . ."

This was not a good time for me to have a diary in my shirt front. I waved a hand at the guard like a schoolchild at home, and said apologetically, *"Benjo?"* (Latrine.) While he was grumbling at me I broke ranks and ran back to the lats. There I reached high above my head and stuffed the papers between the palm leaves which formed the roof, and then returned to roll call again.

The sergeant major was there before me . . . but he'd gotten tired of feeling the females. He'd taken it out on the first groups, he'd felt 'em and smacked 'em and put 'em to bed! Now he looked at us dumbly, boredly, frustratedly; what a hell of a war, when a Jap patriot had nothing braver to do than feel under women's petticoats. For what? He didn't really know for what. . . .

So he told us to go and sit in the shade, while he went inside the barrack and searched our things.

In April 1945, when food was shortest, and drugs were nil, Colonel Suga called Dorie Adams, myself, and George to his office to a coffee party.

We had the usual biscuits, fruit, very sweet coffee, and tea. George lit into everything in such a ravenous manner that there was no need to mention that he was hungry. I could always rely on George to prove my point. The orderly could not keep up with his appetite: he had three cups of coffee, and gobbled everything from his own plate, and from the plates in the center of the table, and then began to look at mine, where I was saving my banana which I intended to take home for him.

Suga looked at me and said, "Why do you not eat your banana?"

I said, "I am going to take it home for George."

"You eat it now. I shall give you more for George." . . . Which was what I had hoped.

14

Fallen Enemy

Daily all through that spring the Allies bombed and machine-gunned Kuching, and the river, and the airdrome, and the roads and fields around us; fragments of bombs and debris descended in camp; we alternately hurried for shelter, and stood outside and gloated over Allied supremacy. And all this time, those two little puttering Poached Egg planes arose from the bushes in Kuching half an hour before the Allied planes came, and buzzed home again half an hour after our planes left. We always listened hopefully, thinking this time the Poached Eggs' landing field would be destroyed and they couldn't land. But always they found a pocket handkerchief somewhere to flutter down upon. They, in their own small way, were as invincible as our huge planes.

At first we all went to the trenches, as we were ordered to do by the Japanese. The children liked going, and were better organized than anyone else. When the signal came, George would race for home, get his grass hat, look for something to eat on principle, take the water bottle, get his waterproof cape (cut down from a soldier's), put his little stool on his back, and trot down the road to the children's trench, regardless of whether or not I was with him.

The Japanese ordered us to disguise the fact that we were females; if the Allies knew we were women and children they would most certainly bomb us! To this end of concealing our sex, we were forbidden to hang out our washing, and were supposed to keep out of sight, in the barrack if not in the trenches. Soon few people went to the trenches. Instead we sat inside in the shade of the barracks, happily free from the guards, who were hiding under the trees.

After the first six weeks of daily air raids, the exhilaration was gone. Obviously the appearance of planes had nothing to do with quick release. It was all right for the airmen up in the air, where it was a matter of a brave life or a speedy death, and meanwhile a full stomach to keep cheery on. But for us, asking ourselves every morning, Can we get through this day? . . . and every night, Can we get up tomorrow? . . . for us, those planes in their swiftness and freedom were by contrast most annoying.

The weather that summer was frightfully hot, the water pipes had been disconnected by the Japs, and we had to carry water for some distance from wells in buckets. Food was starvation level.

Night after tropical moonlight night I lay awake listening. Would the besieging Americans come up the river to rescue us? Or would the Nipponese soldiers in Kuching, who hated the POW camps, come up the road to murder us? Or would the Nipponese rabble across the pond, shouting and singing drunkenly every night, come across the pond to massacre us? Or would the slow breaking of dawn, the anticipated time for air landings, bring us the sound and sight of our planes? If so, would we be massacred before the rescuers arrived?

On those hot, black-shadowed, steeping nights, while we women and children lay in one camp and the men lay alone in another, we asked ourselves wonderingly why, in this sterile life, our bodies struggled so hard to live.

And yet, in those nights of lonely and widowed waiting, it wasn't passion and desire fulfilled that we wanted. It was the touch of the hand, the word of comfort, the laughter shared, the saving from utter loneliness by the existence, near you, of the person you loved. It was that our bodies ached for, and our hearts broke at not having.

Month followed month without release. All night we lay and listened for something in the sky; all day we plodded and dug in the earth beneath it. Again we ceased looking up. We ceased expecting release. We ceased expecting. We just existed.

The first week of August came. I knew that victory would come. I knew that Christmas would come. I knew that death would come. But which would come first? And did it make any difference?

Aside from any importance which might attach to the date August 15 in the world outside our barbed wire, we had for three years celebrated that day under Japanese command. It was the anniversary of the grand opening of the Batu Lin-tang Encampment, the Kuching prison camps. In 1942 Colonel Suga had been made commander in chief of all the POWs and internees here, and by his order we yearly cele-brated the event of our captivity. He saw no irony in this. Sometimes we got an extra banana, sometimes an egg or some sweets, on that day. But food was short in 1945, so they gave us instead a half-hour meeting with our husbands, on the third anniversary of Prison Camp Day.

Harry and George and I met under the trees outside the barbed wire. George dashed off to the field to play by the stream, while Harry and I sat and talked. No longer, now, about winning the war, or victory plans, or Allied planes, but about simple things that counted.

Just before it was time to part Harry said, "Here's some-thing I'll tell you, for what it's worth. You won't believe it, but you can laugh at it. A drunken Tommy from the soldiers' camp sneaked through the wire into our kitchen last night, and the men caught him trying to steal food. They were going to beat him up, and he said that if they'd let him off he'd tell them something that would make them feel so good they wouldn't want to beat him. He said word had come to them over the hidden wireless in their camp that night that an armistice was going to be signed today, between the Allies and the Japanese."

I said, "Well, I'll believe the war is over when I see American sailors in Kuching Square!"

The British soldiers' camp stretched along the side of our road. I was walking up that road on the way to Colonel Suga's office one day, when something caught my attention. All over the soldiers' camp I saw small campfires glowing, with little pots of various sorts smoking over them. And I thought I smelled . . . chicken! I stopped and stared and sniffed. The Jap sentry near by me said nothing. All this was unusual — fires, food, and silent sentries.

A miserably thin-looking soldier in a loincloth, so close to the barbed wire that I could see him wink at me, sang out recklessly, "Happy days are here again!" A boy near him shouted, "It won't be long now, lady!" Two others bellowed out the familiar camp phrase, "They'll be coming up the river when they come!" Somebody else chanted the soldiers' favorite:

Let the Chinese and Dyaks and the Dutchmen fight about it,
They can have their Borneo. We can do without it. . . .

and all over the camp I could hear snatches of "Yankee Doodle Dandy." I saw then that every British soldier within sight was smiling at me, and waggling thumbs up, and the Jap sentry near by, instead of shouting and shaking his gun, just glared with gummy eyes and did nothing.

I remembered what Harry had told me. I walked on, thinking. None of the scraggly Indonesian chickens that usually fluttered about on the road between camps were visible today.

Slowly I began to see the connection between the road without chickens, and the soldiers' campfires with. It had been
chicken that I smelled all right!

The soldiers would not have been killing the chickens
from which they occasionally got stray eggs if they did not
have good reason to believe that peace had come, nor would

the Nipponese sentries have been allowing them to build
campfires. That smell of chicken cooking will always in my
mind be the first harbinger of peace.

The next day the Nipponese sent us a double ration of rice
and sago flour. We had already received our August rations,
complained at their scarcity, and been answered, "There is
no more rice in Kuching." When the double ration arrived
we knew something had happened.

Meanwhile the Japanese officers denied the rapidly spread-
ing rumors of peace, and the Japanese guards believed their
officers, so convinced had they always been of their own in-
vincibility.

Then for us in Kuching began the most nerve-destroying period of the war. After peace had come to the outside world, we came nearest to being destroyed.

On August 20, at 2 P.M., pamphlets were dropped to us in the women's camp by Allied planes. We picked them up and read them before the guards could snatch them from us.

> HQ 9TH AUSTRALIAN DIVISION
> BRITISH BORNEO
> *18th Aug.* '45
>
> TO: ALL ALLIED PRISONERS OF WAR IN BRITISH BORNEO
> FROM: THE GENERAL COMMANDING 9TH AUSTRALIAN DIVISION AIF
>
> At last the Allies have defeated completely the Japanese, and the Japanese Emperor, on behalf of the Japanese Nation, has accepted unconditional surrender. The necessary arrangements for the implementation of the surrender are now being made between the High Commands of the Allied and Japanese Forces.
>
> Be of good cheer.
>
> I know that you will realize that on account of your location, it will be difficult to get aid to you immediately, but you can rest assured that we will do everything within our power to release and care for you as soon as possible.
>
> G. F. WOOTTEN
> (*G. F. Wootten*) *Major General*
> *Commanding 9th Australian Division*

Two hours later I was called up to Colonel Suga's office. Before going I sewed my hidden pamphlet inside my shirt. I thought the interview must have something to do with this news. Suga, however, greeted me as usual with small talk and tea. Finally I could bear it no longer and I asked him if there was any change in the war situation in the East.

He answered that the Allies were fighting in Borneo and they would soon try to take Kuching. Here they would converge with the Japanese forces at the site of the POW camps, where the final battle for supremacy would be held over our captive bodies. At this point in the conversation, with my peace pamphlet against my skin, I wondered which of us was crazy — Suga or I.

Suga then showed me a typewritten order to all the prisoner of war camps, commanding them to move their camps, "For the sake of your own safety," to an undesignated location. This order, Suga said, was to be given shortly. I saw that it was dated September.

I said, "If you move us again you will kill us."

Suga replied grimly, "That is my responsibility," and his eyes glittered and the tone of his voice warned me not to continue. In place of the university graduate I saw the Japanese fanatic.

I asked him if there was any change in the situation in Europe, as we could usually discuss Europe without excitement. He answered that Germany had suffered complete defeat and had accepted peace terms, leaving Japan to fight alone. The Allies had recently used a new atom bomb over Japan, the most destructive and inhumane bomb ever used. The first bomb had destroyed an entire city. He believed that his own family, resident in that city, had been killed by it.

This talk was on August 20. I felt as I talked with Suga that day that there was little protection in a peace pamphlet while the enemy still held the guns.

After the dropping of the pamphlets we became reckless of Nipponese rules. It wasn't that we felt safe, but, shoot us or not, we didn't care. As our captors were more hysterical than we at that stage, it is a wonder they didn't shoot, if only by accident. Officers and guards threatened one moment, placated the next. No one knew who was in a position to kick whom. I knew how the Japanese must be feeling, with everything good behind them, and everything bad in front. It was the identical position we had occupied three and a half years before.

During these days of uncertainty we tried to keep the facts

from the children, for fear of what they might say to the guards. But they knew that "the Japs were licked," as the older boys, John, Jimmy, and Vicki, freely expressed it, and George so confided to me. Already their attitude was veering towards that of conquerors, and they were swinging their little shoulders proudly; already George and Eddie were shouting to each other about "the dirty Japs"!

On the twenty-fourth of August the military interpreter came into the women's camp, and ordered all the women to go to the chapel at 4 p.m., saying that Colonel Suga would address us. Colonel Suga had never before spoken to us on our own ground: we had always been ordered to stand in the square and await his convenience.

At four in the afternoon the sun hung hot and lethargic in the Kuching sky. It glared in our pupils at eye level, and bored in the windows of the chapel where we sat. The heat was stifling, the room was silent and breathless, we were tense to the point of agony, and Colonel Suga was an hour late in coming.

George was with me, unusually quiet for him, feeling the tension. I prayed over and over. This was the last chance. I couldn't survive, if the prayer wasn't answered this time — God, make it peace.

I looked about me at the women in the chapel. We had stood a great deal. When the Japs cut our rations, we had laughed. When they sent us to work in the fields we had laughed. When they cut off the water, and we carried it from wells, we had laughed. When we were hungry, ill, tired, we had laughed. But now, if this promise of peace was one final joke — we could not laugh!

I looked about me and saw women who had performed impossible physical tasks, and who looked it. Faces were strained, lined, agonizingly controlled. Hands were stained and blunted and calloused; feet were bare, broken-toenailed, grimy, with sores and septic toes; clothes were worn, patched, faded, and scanty. There were only half a dozen out of the whole two hundred and forty-six who looked at all attractive and alive. Of the rest, some might regain attractiveness, but never youth again. Captivity had taken too much.

At five o'clock Colonel Suga arrived, accompanied by two military aides. As he entered the chapel, I shook with nervous tension, and my heart pounded as if with adrenalin, my hands were cold and damp. We rose to our feet and bowed. It was the last time we were ever to do so to Colonel Suga.

For the first time in our imprisonment, he spoke to us that day in his own words, without a written address. In the past his speeches had been written for him by prisoners, sometimes by myself, and at his dictation they had run to oratory and self-praise. But this day he spoke slowly, with painfully sought-out words, and carefully controlled emotion, and there was no false note. I know that the words he spoke were truly terrible to him to speak. They were the death of his pride and probably his body, and they were the coming to life again in us of these things.

Many times in the past I had watched Colonel Suga's prison audience, and felt the hidden smiles, the latent sneers, the suppressed snickers sweep through them, inaudible and invisible, but more insulting than a loud guffaw. I have seen Suga stop cold in his words when that wave of derision struck him, and turn yellow and stiff, while he reached out mentally for some way in which to retaliate against the contempt of his twenty-five hundred captives. But he, the victor, had no way to retaliate; he could shoot them, or torture them, or bribe them — the sneer would be in their hearts, though they died, and he would know it.

This day, as one of the vanquished, for the first time in camp life he commanded public respect, even from those who hated him most. We knew that we were watching him die, and that he was doing it bravely.

What he told us was this: Peace was here. The events leading up to it, and the principal causes of Japanese surrender,
were as follows: (1) The complete collapse of Germany in
May of this year, and her acceptance of the Potsdam peace
terms. (2) The use of the atomic bomb by the Allies in
Japan, a bomb more destructive than any other, and one
whose use was against international law and humanity.
(3) The declaration of war against Japan by Russia, on August 9. The Japanese Emperor could not bear to see the
misery of his people, borne by the women and children at
home who had suffered by the destructive forces of the atomic
bomb. In order to save the Japanese nation from complete
destruction, he had asked on August 15 for an armistice to
the fighting, and had agreed to the Potsdam Conference
terms.

This would be good news to us prisoners, Suga said, but
we must not get excited, or lose our control, as danger was
not over. We must obey orders and keep calm.

The Japanese Army was still undefeated. They still held
successful positions in all the occupied countries, especially
China, for the Armed Forces had not lost the war. These
forces had refused to surrender. But, as Japanese, they had to
obey their Emperor, therefore they had renounced their
Japanese nationality, and repudiated their allegiance to the
Emperor. They were determined to fight on to death, as victorious, brave, and undefeated soldiers.

This morning the Emperor had sent out three princes to
three important military positions, to attempt to persuade the
generals to follow his orders. He, Suga, hoped and prayed
that they would be successful, and the end come soon. If
the peace terms were made reasonable for Japan, perhaps the
princes would be able to persuade the Army to cease fighting.

Kuching, he said, was now the military headquarters in
Borneo. The military forces had taken up their positions in

the highlands, from whence they would resist the Allies when they came in to Kuching, and there might be fighting. He, Colonel Suga, was prepared to obey the Emperor. Our safety was his concern. But he had received no orders of any sort from anyone, and no official information. Kuching was at present unable to communicate by wireless with the outside. He would do what he could for our safety, but the Japanese officers and young men were hotheaded and fanatical, and they had the weapons. Therefore, although peace was in sight, we must not get excited, we must keep calm, do nothing to annoy, and obey orders. We must be patient, and keep up our morals.

He then read aloud the pamphlet dropped by the Allies on the twentieth, which I had concealed on my person and which probably he had on his, when we had met that afternoon. When he read the sentence, "At last the Allies have defeated completely the Japanese, and the Japanese Emperor, on behalf of the Japanese Nation, has accepted unconditional surrender," I remembered the times in the past when Suga had told us that Japan would win the war, if she had to fight for ten years longer. I felt that in that sentence the ultimate degree of humiliation for him was reached.

This was Suga's last message to us in captivity.

Suga left in his car, the same car from which he had so many times in the past distributed small packets of biscuits and sweets to the clamoring children, when he was the victor and had the spoils. George looked after him and said, "Did he feel bad, Mum, because he lost the war?"

After leaving us, Suga went to the men's camps and made similar announcements. It was obvious that he desired to avoid mass meetings, or demonstrations.

A Douglas C-47 flew very low over camp. A door opened in the center and two blond airmen leaned far out, waving and shouting and laughing at us. We had crowded to the entrance of the camp when we heard the plane flying low, and now we waved wildly back, jumping and cheering, not knowing what was happening, but sure that it was good.

The C-47 circled camp and returned, swooping even lower as she neared us. The center door opened again, the men were leaning out waving, and suddenly, to our delight, out of the door came a long torpedo-shaped object. It shot downward; then, just before reaching the ground, a parachute unfurled above it, and the torpedo settled softly to the ground, between the entrance gates of our camp. The thirty-four kids fell upon it. On the six-foot torpedo was printed the word BREAD.

People have asked me since if we raced for this first bundle of food, and tore it open, and fought over it. Such an action would have horrified us. We might have felt like it, but we could not have done it. Mean tricks we had learned in captivity, but an equal division of rations had become sacred.

In any case, half-starved though we were, that first parachute meant so much more to us than food that we were not even tempted. Even more than our bodies, our hearts had starved — for contact with our own people, for a touch of the friendly hand. The word on that parachute spelled BREAD, but it meant, YOU ARE NOT FORGOTTEN. The greatest satisfaction we could get from its contents was ours already.

Twenty-five parachutes descended that day. At first the Japanese held us back; but by the time the planes had left, we had raced forward and started salvaging the parachutes themselves, which we saw would be priceless for shirts and pants. Some of those first parachutes — made speedily into pants — were walking around on children and mothers within twenty-four hours.

In addition to bread we received that day boxes containing tinned tongue, ham, rabbit, milk, butter, chocolate, biscuits, sugar, custard powder, soap, toilet paper, Red Cross medical supplies, and a little clothing.

During all of this people continued to go mad. George leaped into the air like a puppy, women jumped and waved and screamed, tears flowed, noses were blown, hearts pounded, laughter and cheers poured out. All but myself; I went very silent, in a cold sweat, with an asinine smile, and no words for my feelings. I could only nod my head, Yes, Yes, in agreement with everyone that this was the greatest moment of *our* war.

On September third, Colonel Suga gave a "farewell party." Invitations to attend were delivered to Allied representatives of the prison camps.

Some refused to go. For the first time in prison life we were in a position to say No. As communication was now allowed between camps, Harry sent word to me not to accept. But journalistic instinct urged me on; I had a feeling that party would be unique. I had seen the mud and blood, and now I was going to see flowers strewn at the victor's feet. So I sent word to Harry by Dorie that I was going, wouldn't he go too? He would.

We arrived at the top office at 6 P.M. Here we found Colonel Suga resplendent in Japanese uniform with the same Allied World War I military decorations on his chest that Harry has. His former prisoners, now his guests, wore the new uniforms with which the Japanese had supplied them after the armistice, and the civilian prisoners wore their coming-out clothes, hoarded throughout imprisonment for the time of release.

There were about sixty persons at the table, including all the Japanese officers of the camp. Victims and torturers mingled nervously. Lieutenant Kubu, the chief inquisitor of the camps, sat across from me. He was a drug addict, and particularly cruel when his supply ran out: he would get it on Fridays, and on Friday night one could ask him for anything and get it, but Monday to Friday he was bad.

This night he asked me who my favorite English author

was. Every time we met, which was on all camp searches, Kubu always asked me this question, both of us being, he told me, "literary." I replied with a different author each time, but he always gave me the same answer: "Kipling is the favorite author of the English people." Kipling, with his White Man's glorification, was not the favorite author of the Japanese people. Tonight I told him that Dickens was my favorite author, and he rallied me with "What? Not Kipling?"

Dr. Yamamoto sat next to me, and was as usual very polite. We talked little, and he ate scarcely anything. The atmosphere was too tense for any jokes.

Miss Asaka sat between two civilians from Harry's compound; the attempt to force fraternity by intermingling friend and foe was obvious. Her train-announcer's voice penetrated the strained laughter of the others, but nothing could penetrate the dead silences which frequently occurred.

We were seated at a long U-shaped table in the top office, which had been built for Colonel Suga a year before by the POWs. When it was near completion, the workers had collected the bedbugs which abounded in the POW camp, and established them in the cracks of wood in the new offices. I was reminded of this story tonight by a young Australian officer near me, who muttered a sinister question in my direction: "Do you itch yet?"

Lieutenant Nekata sat at the center of the U-shaped table near Suga. He spent his time jumping up and down pouring drinks for prisoners of higher rank. Suga himself was surrounded by Australian officers, as a tribute to the Australian liberators who were now on their way to us.

The meal consisted of soup, beef, pork, fried rice with meat, vegetables, bananas, jelly, hot water in cups, and cigarettes, followed by local "whiskey" made from pineapple juice. As the whiskey was passed around, Colonel Suga commented, "This whiskey will be very strong for you, because you are unaccustomed. It is for a toast." So we waited to drink it for the toast.

When we finished eating Suga arose to speak. His hands were shaking, and he cleared his throat constantly, and mispronounced his words. I had never heard his English so bad. His words were:

"Peace has come. The Japanese have surrendered. That is good news for you, but not good for us." (Here a nervous laugh, not echoed by anyone else.) "I am very sorry so many prisoners have died. This seems to some of you to be due to some neglect." (Here followed a completely unintelligible flow of words for several minutes.) "I am very sorry for the relatives of the dead people. I also am a relative of dead people. I thank the representatives of your camp for work and assistance in running these camps. I hope there are no hard feelings or thoughts of revenge with you. I hope sometime we can be friends. Let us drink now to better feelings in the future. Cheerio."

We drank. With the unpremeditated, involuntary motions of people hypnotized, the glasses were raised and lowered, and the whiskey slipped down our throats. I felt then that no comment could ever be made on this party which could equal the party.

These men had been our torturers and executioners, they had starved us, and left us to die from disease. But this was war, the object of which was to kill; this was legitimate murder and destruction. If there had been poison in the soup and arsenic in the drinks tonight, I could have sympathized. But to sit here as guests, with our stomachs full and smirks on our faces, and wish each other well, was perversion of every instinct.

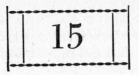

15

Old Lady

DESPITE starvation and abuse, the soldiers had one thing that we did not have to keep up their morale — they had authentic news of the outside world.

Throughout their imprisonment a homemade radio was concealed — and functioned — in the British soldiers' camp. On this wireless the first news of peace was heard, on the night of August 14.

In the Australian POWs' camp in Sandakan the Japanese had discovered a similar secret radio set in 1943, the radio from which we had received smuggled news reports when we were on Berhala Island. This discovery had made the Japanese suspicious of the existence of one in the Kuching camp, and they searched constantly to try to uncover it. Memory in this camp of the execution of a number of Australian POWs as a result of the discovery of their radio made our soldiers more wary in hiding their own.

The radio was never referred to in camp by name, but spoken of as Granny, Mrs. Harrison, the Ice Cream, the Old Lady, and several less polite terms. Knowing that the lives of its inventors and protectors were forfeit to its discovery, as well as the welfare of the whole camp, a security service of men was formed to guard the Old Lady. These kept guard on the Japanese guards, with more efficiency than the guards kept guard on them. Night and day a signal system of songs, whistles, and bird noises kept the Old Lady vigilant to the approach of danger in the shape of guards, officers, and *Kempi-Tai*.

At first the soldiers' camp had electric lights, and while this lasted the radio was run by electricity. Later when the electricity was discontinued, the radio ceased to function for a four-months period, during which time the men were busy at work making a hand-power generator. It took them only one month to make the generator itself, but it had taken them three to make the tools with which to make the generator.

This hand-power generator was run by a flywheel, which was disguised as a barrel top. The wheel was turned by one man, and had to revolve at the rate of three thousand revolutions per minute in order to generate sufficient power for the radio. The man who turned the flywheel was given extra food and care in camp, and developed huge muscles in one arm and side from turning it. After sixty seconds of turning, the sweat poured from him like water, and he could turn for only a few minutes at a time.

With the exception of the four months' silence during the construction of the generator, the radio never ceased to function throughout the entire life of the Kuching prison camps. Only a dozen or so soldiers in camp were trusted with the knowledge of how, or where, the Old Lady was hidden, or were given at first hand the news that she brought — because of the necessity for secrecy, and the great risks attached to her possible discovery.

But rumors which they knew were based on fact reached all of the men, and these cheered and interested them. Fully as important as the news itself was the fact that the camp knew that in spite of everything the Nipponese could do, despite threatening, searching, watching, and listening, the Old Lady still thwarted discovery, remained alive and well, and was functioning regularly. This heartening defiance of the enemy gave them courage to live and the will to endure, when nothing else might have done so. When peace finally came, the Old Lady's welfare was considered to have been such a vital factor in keeping up camp morale that some of the young men who were responsible for her birth and preservation were later awarded military decorations for their accomplishment.

The manner of the Old Lady's concealment varied through the years. At first the wireless set was buried in the ground, and dug up every night for use; but this was hard on the Old Lady's guts, and also on those of her caretakers. In time a recess was made in the walls of the kitchen, and here she was incarcerated behind a false wall, which had nightly to be opened up and then replaced after use. In the end a table with a false-bottomed top was constructed, and she was hidden there, behind a drawer. Here she lived contentedly until the end of the war. On this very table the Japanese officers would frequently sit, drumming nervously with feet and hands, while directing the search of the guards in the kitchen, for the Old Lady's hiding place. Frequently during the Old Lady's clandestine life she was so near to detection that her protectors must have lost some of their longevity, even if escaping immediate execution. But the Old Lady never choked a valve. True to feminine instinct, she was at her best when surrounded by anxious males.

During the first year, the news that came over the radio was typed out and sent to a Chinese in Kuching, for the information of the Asiatics outside. Soon the Nipponese became suspicious, the Chinese was executed, and all concerned took warning. From then on, the news was kept inside the camps. Here, for a while, a weekly report of the news was smuggled to the camp master of the civilian men's camp, to the British officers' camp and several other camps, as well as to the soldiers' camp master.

But as the events of war grew more unfavorable to Japan, the Japanese increased their efforts to locate the hidden news organ; searches increased, and the mere existence of an optimistic atmosphere or a cheerful expression was enough to focus suspicion. Lives hung on secrecy, and few can keep a secret even at that price. It was decided to keep the Old Lady's babblings exclusively military, and only the sergeant major of the camp itself and the British officers' camp master were informed of the news. It was particularly desired to keep the news from the civilian men's camp where the husbands lived, for the reason that this was the only camp which was presumed to have contact with the women's camp. Possible meetings of husband and wife, and ensuing indiscreet confidence from him to her, followed by the indiscreet confidences of the wife to everybody, were greatly feared by the Old Lady's soldier protectors.

What they did not realize was that it was not our husbands who were indiscreet. Every British soldier who came in contact with us, passing on the road, on a working party, or emptying latrines, succumbed to the temptation to try to cheer us up. When we whispered an anxious "Any news?" to them in our surreptitious passings, they whistled, sang, whispered, and shouted the events of the week at us, if there was anything good to tell. They loved to give us a thrill, and "make the girls happy." What saved us and them from destruction was the fact that we didn't take them seriously; by the time I reached the armistice stage, the thing that made me laugh most bitterly was a soldier saying, "It won't be long now!"

The story of the Old Lady was told to me by a number of young men seated around the false-bottomed table which was her last hiding place, with the Old Lady sitting on top in state. When I asked them, "Who is responsible for this great lady's birth, breeding, and condition of vigorous health?" each young man pointed at another, and said "He did it"; then finally, "Well, we all did it together."

But when I said, "I mean who was the expert? Who was the doctor who delivered her, and throughout her lifetime diagnosed and treated her complaints?" they all pointed together to one modest young man, and said, "He was."

This young man was Sergeant Leonard Beckett, a radio mechanic by profession. His responsibility was so great in the building, care, and use of the Old Lady that during his life in camp he was relieved from all community work to take care of her.

So humble were her beginnings, and so simple and inanimate the articles which finally in her being gained life and functions, that the Old Lady seems to have been truly created, rather than built. The origins of her component parts were as follows:

The *receiver* was made from the stolen steering damper knob of a Norton motorcycle.

The *coil* was made from a Gibbs bakelite shaving-soap container.

The *variable condenser* was made from biscuit tins, stripped and remodeled.

The *resistors and valves* were made over from old hearing-aid amplifiers belonging to a deaf civilian. Without these, there could have been no Old Lady.

The *resistor condenser panel* was made from bakelite linen from an old map container.

The *high-frequency choke* was made from a Colgate's shaving-soap container.

The *humdinger or small rheostat* was made from stolen old brass, bakelite, and wire.

Insulation was supplied by pieces of airplane glass stolen by soldiers working at the airfield.

The *ignition coils* were stolen from an old gun battery.

The *rectifier* was stolen by a soldier when on a working party in Kuching.

A *fixed condenser* was stolen from a motorcycle in Kuching by a soldier on a working party.

And the *generator* was made of scrap iron, soft Swedish

iron, and copper, these materials being stolen from the Nipponese stores, or salvaged from old machines, by men on working parties.

The Old Lady in the altogether was hidden in a soldier's mess tin, an unrewarding place for the only lady in the soldiers' camp to sleep.

While awaiting liberation I was requested by Colonel King, the English medical officer who had been in charge of the British soldiers' camp during captivity, to visit their camp. If I was going to write, he said, I must know the truth. So Harry, two other civilians, and I accompanied Colonel King into camp the next day.

When I entered the soldiers' compound I was instantly struck by its utter barrenness compared to our own. It was an eroded brown wasteland crossed by washed-out gullies with row after row of withered palm-leaf huts with ragged, limping men coming from them.

I asked why the soldiers had no gardens, and was told that it was because their working parties had been so large and their outside work so heavy that they had no strength or energy to garden for themselves. A consistent program of starvation, overwork, torture, and beating had made anything beyond mere existence impossible.

In camp there were seven huts used as sick bays, in addition to the hospital barrack across the road. An eighth hut had just been allocated because of the rapidly increasing numbers of ill men. Number Nineteen was known as the Death Hut, devoted to dysentery patients and to the dying.

The huts were built like our own barracks of palm leaves, and had the same solid wooden shutters, which, when they were closed to keep out the rain, kept out all light and air. Even when I saw the soldiers they were still lying on the bare floor. Only a few had mats or blankets to lie on, and mosquito nets, and these had been sent in by the Japanese after the armistice.

Before Colonel King took me through the sick huts he asked me if I had a strong stomach for shocking sights. I said that I hoped I had. When I saw the conditions I was not concerned about my stomach, which had stood up to everything for years, but I was disturbed at the distress which I feared I might cause the patients. They were almost naked, covered with ulcers, and in such a state that I felt they would resent my intrusion, if they had strength for resentment. If they had any active wish now, it must be to crawl away from all eyes and die.

But I found I was wrong. Great as their physical misery was, their boredom was even greater, and this I could relieve. For they, like the stronger men in camp, were avid for sight, sound, or smell of a woman. Soon we all talked together, and examined ailments together; soon we could scarcely move through the huts for patients describing their symptoms and showing their wounds. Finding that they liked seeing me helped me to move naturally amongst sights which Colonel King had properly described as shocking.

The bodies of all the men were shrunken from starvation, with the bones showing like skeletons, the skin dried and shriveled, while the skulls with their deep-set eyes seemed unnaturally large.

All patients had ulcers caused by malnutrition and lack of circulation, many covering an entire leg, chest, arm, or thigh. Many had a gangrenous condition of feet, hands, testicles. Some had a condition of the fingers and toes which can only be described as dissolving away; the tips of the digits were open and bloody and they seemed to be bleeding off.

I was told that of 2000 British soldiers who had been brought to Kuching from Singapore as prisoners, 750 now survived. Of this number 650 were ill, and not 30 men in the whole camp remained strong enough to form a working party.

Four years before, these soldiers had been fittest of the fit. This was what a war fought in captivity had done for them. I

SANDAKAN. 1946. Former Site

was glad I had seen them. I would never forget them. I wished that anyone who spoke philosophically of "the next war" could see them.

When I put George to bed that night I looked at his little boy's body, ribbed through with the fine, strong bones that are the right of youth. And I remembered the fine, strong bones that had once been in the bodies of the young men down the road.

After George was in bed I sat down to drink coffee, and Nishi, the tall young guard from Formosa, came in. I asked him to have a cup of coffee with me.

He was the guard who had saved Isabelle from drowning on the bathing party at Kuching, and he had always been good to the children, and especially so to Edith and Eddie, and George. He had brought them sweets when he came to camp, and brought Edith a pair of shoes from Kuching. He had always been kind to the men's working parties in camp, and never struck or bullied anyone.

While drinking his coffee he told me that the Australian forces were expected to occupy Kuching tomorrow. I asked him, "What will happen to you?"

He looked at me without a word, opened his hand palm upward with a gesture of helplessness, and shook his head.

vernment Buildings and Shopping Center

It was hard to realize that these men who had been all-powerful over us were to be helpless now in our hands.

Then I wrote him a letter on a piece of Red Cross paper, addressed to whoever might come. I said that he had been kind to his prisoners, that he had saved a child from drowning, and helped us when he could. I asked that he be given merciful treatment, because he had earned it.

He took the letter and thanked me, finished his coffee, and got up. He went to George's mosquito net, where George had popped out his head, and kissed him good-bye. He took my hand to shake it, started to speak, and stopped. I looked in his face to see why. The tears were rolling down his cheeks and he couldn't speak. He held my hand a minute and, with tears falling, bent over it. Then he straightened quickly, bowed, and was gone.

I went to bed. As I lay beside my own son that night I asked myself: Why must all young men throughout this world make the choice, to either kill, or be killed?

And I knew there could be no good answer.

16

September 11, 1945

No C-47's came at eleven o'clock that day to drop food for no C-47's dashed by at arm's length.

Instead the planes overhead were high, remote, and austere. They were in the air over Kuching vicinity for several hours. This dignified conduct on their part suggested to us that activity was at last taking place on the river.

At four o'clock that afternoon we were told by Dorie Adams that the Australian occupying forces had come up the river and landed at Kuching. They were on the way to us now, and would take surrender of the camps as soon as they arrived. There would be no preliminary warning. If we wished to see them take over we must be ready to leave for the square at a minute's notice.

I warned George then to stay close at hand, but I still would not let myself believe that the day had come. Not until I had laid eyes on those Australians. Most of us felt the same way. Long disappointment had taught us.

At five o'clock the call came. GO TO THE SQUARE. AUS-TRALIANS TAKE OVER IN THREE MINUTES.

For one minute then I stood quite still. I knew in my bones that this time it was true. With all of my being I gave thanks to God. It was over.

Then the camp became madder than ever. Most of the women tore off their patched old clothes and hurried into the one decent dress which they had been saving for years, for this day.

I looked all about me for George. No George. All over camp I ran. Still no George. All right, George, you little so-and-so, I thought, I'm not waiting for you this time. You can just stay behind.

I give one final shout of "George," and somebody shouts back that George has already gone up the road with some of the children. How quickly they have learned that they are free — they are free — to run up that road, I think. I am late, I run towards the camp entrance and start up the road.

"Mum!" George's small voice calls faintly from far behind me in camp.

I stop, George is covering the ground after me as fast as possible. "Hurry, hurry, or we'll miss the soldiers."

"Mum, my belt's busted and my pants are falling off." Whereupon his pants fall off. George arrives with tongue out and pants in hand. On go the pants, on goes the belt.

"Now hurry!"

Up the road we race. The road to captivity before; now the road to freedom. Here to the left of us is the hospital ward, here is the morgue where the bodies of men have been piled like fish in tins, here is the clinic, where men begged for, but didn't receive, medicine from Yamamoto, here one bowed low in passing, Jap doctor in sight or not. Here is the sentry box. Here one bows to the Nipponese guard — or used to do. There is no guard here today. Here was the scene of endless tortures for the men.

Here on the right hand is the British soldiers' camp, the camp of skeletons, which move laboriously, slowly, weakly; that they move at all is the wonder.

Here is the Dutch camp, beyond it is the civilian men's camp, across from it is the priests' camp. All camps are empty. Everyone who can walk, creep, totter, crawl, is on the road moving towards the square. And this is the same road down which we women have so many times in the past dragged, carried, and stumbled under the weight of heavy rubber trees, to be used for firewood.

Now we are in the square. This was the place for public meetings when we as prisoners were harangued by the Japanese. Here Colonel Suga has frequently addressed us.

His words have been: "This is going to be a long war, ten years more at least. The Nipponese are going to be victorious. Your Army and Navy are being defeated. The Nipponese never give up. I know you are homesick. I sympathize with you, I am very kind. You are prisoners. You must obey me."

This square was the place for public punishments. Here George and I have stood in the sun at attention for punishment. Over here is the little green mound with the main sentry box. The sentry used to stand in the box under the tree in the shade. The victim stood in the road in the sun. Perhaps he held a heavy weight at arm's length above his head, perhaps he squatted, perhaps he knelt with his arms at right angles in front of him. When he fell over he was kicked until he got up, and when he could no longer get up he was just kicked.

As we pass the gate of the civilian men's camp Harry joins us. All three together, we push forward into the square, which seems already full with the two thousand prisoners. There is a small platform at the far side, with a Union Jack now flying above it.

I look about me for the Australians, for we have heard that five hundred of them are here. But there are only a few to be seen, tall, straight-featured, strong young men. There are more American sailors to be seen than Australians. I have said in the past, "When I see American sailors in Kuching Square, I will know we are free."

We learn later that most of the Australian soldiers are busy moving about the city of Kuching, trying to appear like five thousand rather than five hundred men. The Nipponese still have under arms in Kuching, and unsurrendered, five thousand soldiers.

Now Colonel Walsh, the highest ranking officer amongst the Australian prisoners of war, steps onto the platform and calls the crowd to attention. He then presents a huge, blue-eyed, red-cheeked Australian, who is Brigadier General Eastick, R.A.A., of the 9th Australian Division, in command of the landing force. He also presents Captain Jennings of the United States Navy, who has accompanied Eastick up the river. Captain Jennings is the perfect picture of what a captain in the Navy should be.

Brigadier General Eastick then speaks in a cheery, booming voice. "I feel deeply honored to be the one to bring relief to you today. I will read a message to you from Major General Wootten, who commands the 9th Australian Army Division which sets you free.

" 'We are sorry to have been so long in coming to you. Because of your position up the Kuching River and because of difficult fighting conditions in Borneo we have been slow in getting here. We have not had the shipping available to come in to you before, or to take you away. You have been patient for a long time. But today I greet you as a free people again.

" 'We expect to take you out of Kuching as quickly as possible. The sick will be taken care of first. Some of these will be taken tomorrow to Labuan, the headquarters of the 9th Division in Borneo. The rest of you will be taken out day by day as shipping space becomes available. In Labuan you will be given medical and hospital care, rest and every aid toward regaining your health, while you are waiting for transportation to your homes.

" 'We have brought with us three Padres, Roman Catholic, Church of England, and Congregational, as we expect that you will wish to hold thanksgiving services tomorrow.' "

While Brigadier Eastick is speaking we in the crowd come a little nearer to realizing that we are FREE. We are beyond words, our hearts hammer and bang, our pulses throb, our throats ache, we weep and we cheer. We strike each other's backs and clasp hands. The children are held high in the air. But they are quiet now, for our tears astound and frighten them. Harry attempts to lift George to his shoulder, but he is still too weak; a friend lifts George up instead.

Then over this sea of hysteria Captain Jennings speaks. Here are his words:

"Today is my first experience of this sort. It is worth many a battle, and many a long, hard night on the sea. THIS is what we have been fighting for."

It is the one perfect speech that I have ever heard, it is the only speech I ever wish to hear, but it finished composure. Captain Jennings himself, they tell me, ended his words in tears. Anyway, no one was ashamed of crying that day.

Everyone now having had a good cry, the next best thing was for the war correspondents and photographers to get busy and carry the drama to the outside world.

Eastick and Jennings were photographed shaking everybody's hands, we were photographed with and without tears, the rescue forces were photographed, and the children were photographed eating chocolates, lollipops, chewing gum, which every single soldier and sailor gave them with a grin.

When the 9th Australian Army Division and men of the United States Navy came to us in Kuching, we had nothing. We were hungry and they fed us, we were ill and they cared for us, we were ragged and they clothed us. We were anxious and they reassured us, we were hysterical and they dealt tenderly with us. They came into our camp and cooked for us, chopped firewood and carried loads for us, nursed our sick and took care of our children. Every jeep, DUKW, motor truck, boat, became a plaything, every soldier a friend and father.

These men came into Kuching with blood on their hands,

from heavy fighting in Borneo and the Celebes. They were soldiers known for their toughness, taking no prisoners, observing no laws; yet never did we hear from them a word of impatience or anger, a rough speech or a curse, or see an unkind or unpleasant action. To us who were weak and were helpless they were gentle as angels from Heaven. We became proud then of men, as we had for years been ashamed. We wept for their kindness, as we had not wept for abuse.

Those young men were for that time a part of all goodness and virtue, a part of all love. They brought us liberty and freedom, and something even greater — belief again in the decency of men.

The most dramatic picture of that day was never photographed.

Harry and I stood at one side of the crowd waiting for George to disentangle himself from a newsreel. The crowd still faced towards the platform. Skirting uncertainly along the edge of this crowd came a small, very small, very short, khaki-clad figure, his sword smacking his brief legs, his heels clicking, his little fatigue-shirt tails flipping. It was Colonel Suga, alone, ignored. He trotted all around the outskirts of the crowd. No one smiled or spoke or saluted. People didn't fail to see him: he just didn't exist any. more for them.

A month before we must have stood at attention, saluted, bowed at a fifteen-degree angle, while all the Nipponese soldiers in sight would have shouted, grunted, banged their guns, and acted in correct Nipponese style.

Suga wove his way to the forefront of the crowd near Eastick and Jennings. Here he hesitated, stood and waited patiently, finally pressed apologetically forward, waited again, and in due time received a nod from them, and then a careless word of dismissal. Then he turned and trotted back again in our direction.

I hoped he wouldn't pass near us. I wanted to turn my back and not see him. For three and a half years I had been sorry for us, and now I didn't want to have to be sorry for him. I didn't want to speak to him, the favor of Colonel Suga was not to be sought after. And I knew Harry would hate speaking to him. But I was sick of hatred in any form, turned either upon me or on somebody else.

Suga came towards us and, as he drew near, he looked straight at us. Harry and I both said, "Good evening, Colonel Suga."

He stopped, took off his hat and said, "Good evening. Have you met the American naval captain, Mrs. Keith?"

"Yes, thank you, Colonel Suga."

"I hope that you and Mr. Keith are both well?"

"I am well, thank you. My husband is not."

"Ah-ah. Very sorry. Good evening."

He disappeared into the crowd, and ceased again to exist. I said to Harry, "I didn't think you'd want to speak to him."

"I didn't. But I felt sorry for him. He was so alone."

We saw him just once after that. The next day the Union Jack was formally raised over Suga's head office at the top of the hill. I watched him stand at salute while our colors went up. He stood alone, a little small man, the only Japanese amongst us. After the salute his sword was taken in surrender.

The next day he was flown to Labuan, Borneo, headquarters of the 9th Australian Division, to be questioned in regard to the mistreatment of prisoners in Borneo.

It was getting late now and photographers, correspondents, generals and captains, rescuers and rescued, were exhausted. George and I said good-bye to Harry at the entrance to his camp. George was tired, and I lifted him to my back and we started down the road pickaback. Everybody was dragging along to his camp now, completely exhausted. We hadn't the emotional strength even to be rescued.

The camp was quieter than usual, even the children's barrack was quiet. We had supper and the children fell into bed. I wanted to make some notes about the day, but it was dark, I could no longer see — and there was no further need for secrecy.

I went across to the English Sisters' barracks. There I found Mother Aubon and said, "Could you possibly let me have a little piece of candle to write by?" Candles were priceless, but the Sisters always had them for mass.

"It was a great day," sighed Mother Aubon, producing a bit of candle from under many petticoats. "A very great day. Now you must go back and write something wonderful about it."

I went home and lit the candle, and sat down and tried to write. I wanted inspired words, but I couldn't find them. I wanted some way of explaining to others what had happened to us that day. I wanted to tell them what it meant to be captive, and then to be free.

What it meant to be free! I saw again in my mind the figure of Colonel Suga, who didn't now even exist.

I put down the pencil and blew out the candle without having written a word. I was tired in every part of me, mind, body, and soul. I lay down by George. His legs swarmed all over my side of the bed. I pushed and prodded my way in beside him. He turned over in his sleep and started grinding his teeth. Worms again, I thought.

I put my hand on his cheeks, which were cool, and felt his feet, which were warm; I touched his hair, which was soft. There is nothing I can say as wonderful as George, I thought, and went to sleep.

There was just one good thing about the road that led to the women's camp: you could see the blue-green hills of Kuching in the distance, hills that meant freedom to me. Today I look at those hills and walk up that road to the prison square, a free woman.

This square has been the core of our prison. Here has taken place the worst and the best of our time. In all my life to come I must remember it as I have seen it, day by day, month by month, year by year, with broken, starving, beaten men in it, half-naked, thin, and grim. With the Japanese sentry staring blankly ahead, with Colonel Suga's car racing past, with Japanese guards laughing in the road, with the sun beating down. With George and myself hurrying past, eyes averted from suffering, to Colonel Suga's tea parties.

Into this square today we come to give thanks to God for freedom. Both those who believe and those who do not believe; we have all learned to say our prayers.

All the prisoners who are able to walk are present, perhaps fifteen hundred, and there are many Australian soldiers and American naval men. Three Padres who came with the Liberating Forces officiate. The service is to be nonsectarian; they distribute printed thanksgiving texts to us.

The service begins. I have a text. I try at first to follow with my lips and voice, as I do with my heart. Soon I cannot go on; I stand silent and shaken while the service proceeds.

For years now I have been laughing, in order to hide my tears. Today laughter stops, and I cry.

I put my smoke-stained handkerchief over my eyes. George holds my hand, he knows that something too great, too beautiful, too happy, too wonderful for words is happening to us. He knows there is more than the chocolate and milk, the bread and butter, the tins and the chewing gum, that has come into Kuching with these soldiers. He knows there is friendliness, love. He holds my hand, he squeezes it, he understands.

Not since the first week on Berhala Island has he seen me break. Then there were terror and strangeness and fright. Today all about us is kindness, kind faces, protection, and love. Today in Kuching I weep tears of thanksgiving to God for His blessing. Today my son is born again into freedom and love.

George and I leave the square and go hand in hand across to the men's camp, where Harry is lying on his bed.

Here I meet an American naval captain whose home is in Hollywood, close to where my home has been, near now to that of my aunt. He gives me news of my world.

I learn now, by official communication, that my mother died in 1943, without hearing that we were still alive. That at the time of her death it was not believed that George and I could survive the violence of war and the long period of captivity. Harry hears that his father died in 1943. There is word that my brother is married.

Captain Hawkins insists now that I must send a letter home to my aunt in Hollywood. This letter he will enclose in an air-mail letter to his wife.

He even puts the paper and pencil in my hands, saying:

"Write it now. Go on, write it and send it home now. Please do — Go on. My wife will see that your aunt gets it immediately."

They are so kind, I think to myself, these young men are so kind and strong and sure of what to do. I hope my George will be like that.

So I write out lethargically my first message from freedom.

We are all alive. George thin, but well. The day we have lived for has come at last. There are no words to tell you what this means to us. I have no words to say what I feel. Peace and freedom at last. Thank God.

Twelve days afterward, this letter is received by my aunt in Hollywood. I learn later that it is the first news of any sort to tell our relatives we are alive and free. My aunt tells me that when Mrs. Hawkins brought her the letter, she wept from joy.

It was George she thought of first, she said. "He is the future, he carries on the spark." That went to my heart — it was my feeling throughout captivity: our children were the future, their lives at least had been worth fighting for.

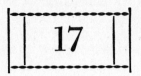

17

Road Home

THE sick people were evacuated first from Kuching, and the families with children next. As Harry and I were walking malaria cases, and we had George, we qualified twice over for a quick release.

Early one morning Harry arrived at camp and we prepared for immediate departure. We couldn't take much luggage, so first we removed my notes from their hiding places and condensed them. We ripped open George's stuffed toys and sleeping mats, and broke open his false-bottomed stool. I crawled under the barrack and unearthed rusty tins, and went to the lats and fished two bottles out of the drains. For the first time I assembled what for three and a half years I had been dispersing.

These notes went back to the second night of imprisonment on Berhala Island, when I had written by candlelight, "We cannot live through many months of this!" These first entries were full of emotions, mostly unpleasant. As time went on, they became less passionate and more disconsolate, then they became mere records. "Rice v-short, 5 tblsp. per day. No sugar now. Salt ration discontinued. Traded Harry's white jersey for twelve eggs." And at the end, to commemorate our day of liberation, there is one sentence: "I have lived long enough, having seen this day."

We unpacked these notes, and wrapped them in an Australian newspaper. They made a bundle about twelve inches by twelve inches square, and six inches tall.

"Well, there it all is," said Harry gloomily. "But I don't think you can take it in the plane." Harry was always gloomy about my luggage, whether it was twenty-three pieces on my first journey to Borneo, or a bundle of notes in prison camp. It is a principle with him to act as if I have too much luggage and too little sense. This old gloom about the luggage quite rejuvenated me. It reminded me of every trip we had ever taken together, even our honeymoon.

One thing that I had sworn to through imprisonment was that I would get my notes out, or die in the attempt. When Harry left for his camp, he picked up my bundle of notes, and said to my surprise, "I'll just put these in my own bag, to take on the plane as my luggage. You have enough to manage with George." Perhaps he was afraid I'd leave George, and take the diaries.

As soon as Harry left, an order arrived saying we were to leave immediately. "Leave everything," it said, "especially bedding." (With bugs in mind.) "You are going to a Rest Camp in Labuan, where everything is provided." I couldn't believe, after prison experience, that there was any place in this world where living conditions would not be improved by having George's pot, an enamel mug, my wooden clogs, a blanket, a bottle of drinking water, and a pinch of salt, with me. But I left them.

We left camp by bus, and drove through Kuching, where the local natives and inhabitants cheered us on the way, and the children almost fell off the truck waving. We arrived at the landing field and saw in its bomb-torn condition an explanation of delayed air communications, for landings were still perilous.

We were loaded into a C-47 Transport, which had been stripped to its essentials. It was overloaded and slow, and it took us three hours to get to Labuan. We were all very cheerful and ate Australian milk chocolate and smoked Australian cigarettes. I said that I longed for something fresh and green, and the pilot produced a half head of lettuce, and we divided it out leaf by leaf. Then somebody said he would like to have

an apple again, and three apples appeared, and were divided amongst us. The children all had turns with the pilot. I received the general impression that the kids flew the plane most of the way.

Mid-afternoon we landed at Labuan.

Here at Labuan the fates of our ex-guards pursued us. They in their turn were now confined behind barbed wire, were mustered in labor squads and turned out to work, were put in the guardhouse and cells, for discipline.

Poker Face, the sergeant major, met with a fatal accident; Fish Face was beaten to death. The Wife Beater, Pimples, Little Pig, Swatow Bill, met with accidents. TB was placed in the cells, where he benefited by his Japanese lessons to us as to how the victor deals with the vanquished. The Fishwife, who had always been athletic, was persuaded to run an interminable race around the perimeter of the camp. Other guards — Dopey Dick, Big Annie, the Yokel, Comic Cut,

Stammering Stephen, Piano Legs, Mad Harry, the Weasel, and *Benjo* (latrine) Bill — were also given opportunities to experience the punishments which fitted the crimes.

The fate of Tasty, the Japanese ration master, was an unknown one, but we hoped he was doing well. He had done more to save us than many an Allied bomb; he was our Number One smuggler.

What happened to the young Formosan guard who had told me good-bye with tears I was unable to learn.

In general, the stories of the fate of our guards were told and received with relish. A favorite internee theme in the old days had been the description of how we were going to treat our captors when we were free. I had heard women say, "Wait until our turn comes! Then we'll make them suffer as they have made us. I should like to get hold of their Japanese women and children and make them live as we live!"

The officers of the Kuching camp were taken for questioning. Lieutenant Nekata attempted suicide, cut his throat, was nursed back to life to await his trial. Dr. Yamamoto attempted suicide, was frustrated, repeated the attempt, and the final outcome I did not know. The other officers followed suit but determined efforts were made to defeat their suicides in order to bring them to war crime trials.

Now in Labuan the last chapter was written of Colonel Suga. The last chapter of a little Japanese man, onetime graduate from the University of Washington, patron of the arts, recipient of World War I Allied decorations; a military man with shaven head; a sick man with diabetes who eats no sugar; a soldier who likes children; a little man with a big sword; a religious dilettante, born Shintoist and turning Catholic; a hero and a figure of ridicule; a Japanese patriot, Commander of All Prisoners of War and Internees in Borneo . . . and a human being. Now in Labuan is written the end of Colonel Suga. He cut his throat and bled to death in an Allied cell, on the day that Harry, George, and I left Kuching for freedom.

The end of his life, but not the answer to the query of his being — was he good, or was he bad? Were we better off, or worse, under a Western-educated Japanese who knew Western ideas? Did he have more prejudice against us, knowing *our* racial prejudices? Could he have helped us? Did he try?

I shall say first the good things that I know of him. He was courteous to all in the women's camp, and kind personally to many. He bowed when he might have beaten us, he smiled when he might have kicked. Courtesy does not fill empty stomachs, but it soothes worn nerves, and most Japanese officers I met neither soothed nerves nor filled stomachs.

Colonel Suga's picture of himself was as the cultured and beneficent administrator of the ideal internment camp of Kuching. He was always kind to the children, often brought them biscuits and sweets, supplied means for their teaching, gave them what liberty he could. They all liked him.

He had good and kindly impulses, and a real desire for interracial understanding. He was kind to me personally. I believe that he saved my husband from death.

Against this, I place the fact that all the prisoners in Borneo were inexorably moving towards starvation. Prisoners of war and civilians were beaten, abused, and tortured. Daily living conditions of prison camps were almost unbearable.

At Sandakan and Ranau and Brunei, North Borneo, batches of prisoners in fifties and sixties were marched out to dig their own graves, then shot or bayoneted and pushed into the graves, many before they were dead. All over Borneo hundreds and thousands of sick, weak, weary prisoners were marched on roads and paths until they fell from exhaustion, when their heads were beaten in with rifle butts and shovels, and split open with swords, and they were left to rot unburied. On one march 2970 POWs started, and three survived.

The Kuching prison camps were scheduled to march on

September 15, 1945, had peace not intervened. It was this abandoned order which Colonel Suga had read to me on the day peace pamphlets were dropped.

I have since heard reports of other Japanese prison camps outside of Borneo: in most of them conditions were better than ours, in few were they worse.

For these black chapters in captivity Colonel Suga, commander in Borneo, must be held responsible.

What his orders were I do not know. No doubt he must obey them, or risk himself. Whether he attempted to save us I do not know, but I do know that it takes more even than physical courage to stand up for human values against patriotic zeal, in wartime. Until the gun is held at your own head, until the whisper comes of "Traitor," you cannot know what you will do.

Colonel Suga was accused by the Japanese of being prejudiced in our favor, and accused by us of unnecessary brutality. We knew that he vanished on the eve of particularly cruel orders, given or carried out, as he had vanished when he knew Nekata was after me. In the cause of humanity, he might have helped us, but in wartime the cause of humanity is lost.

In this weighing of a Japanese military man I consider two things. First, that all these horrors which I have described are war, which itself is a matter of life and death. War is the acceptance of suffering and atrocity, and the sacrifice of decency and good thinking. War itself is the crime against humanity. When we accept war we accept war crime; we then have no grounds to complain.

Second: We in Kuching suffered under Colonel Suga and the Japanese. The entire family of Colonel Suga was wiped out by the atomic bomb at Hiroshima. Colonel Suga himself cut his throat in the Allied cells, in Labuan.

Honors in suffering and atrocities seem even.

When details of Colonel Suga's death were made known in Labuan to the liberated prisoners of Kuching, the comments were: "Only half an hour to bleed to death? Not half long enough for him to suffer!" "Too good for him!" "I wish that I could have had the old bastard to finish off!" "They ought to have kept him alive to prolong his agony!" "Slow torture is what he needed!"

Lieutenant Tàkita Nekata,
War Criminal Number 3.
Executed by hanging, after
cutting his own throat.

Some of my papers from "captivity," which he must have had with him, were returned to me at Labuan by the Australian Command.

Here we learned also the fate of several European parties who had attempted to escape into interior Borneo, as I had one time planned to do, before the Japanese invaded Borneo.

Shortly before the Japanese military forces landed at Miri, North Borneo, a party of European men, women, and children, missionaries and families of government men, decided to retreat from there to Long Nawang. Long Nawang was an abandoned Dutch military outpost in southern Dutch Borneo, about six weeks' river travel inland from Miri.

After the Japanese invaded Borneo no news was heard of this party for a year. Then rumor of the presence of escapees at Long Nawang was brought to the Japanese, who went up the river, shelled and captured the Dutch fort. The Japanese then shot the men who survived the battle, and took prisoner the women and children. After holding them for two months as prisoners, the Japanese killed the children before their mothers, then tortured the women to death.

The husband of one victim, and father of two others killed in that party, had remained at his government post to meet the invading Japanese. He was taken prisoner when they landed at Miri, and confined with my husband in Kuching throughout the war. He survived.

Most escape stories demonstrate the fact that the Japanese were angered by the idea of people running away from them.

Here at Labuan I learned the end, or perhaps the beginning, of the story of Celia and Jim Taylor. Celia, who in spite of ill-health was one of the bravest, least selfish, and most hard-working of our community workers, had always told me that she believed steadfastly that she would find her husband alive at the end of the war. And hers was one of the few stories to have a happy ending.

Without having heard any news of Dr. Taylor since peace came, I came at Labuan upon these two walking together, alive and hopeful. Together they told me his story.

After leaving Kuching he had been taken to Singapore and there imprisoned in Changi Jail. He was ill and weak from abuse and starvation, and in this condition he had just managed to survive, until the Allied Forces came into Singapore and freed him, after peace came. Gerald Mavor, from Sandakan, who had been imprisoned with him on the same charge, had died of mistreatment. Gerald's wife was now in Labuan also.

Dr. Taylor told us that upon his release he had tried to ascertain the fate of his wife, but could get no news of her, as the search for lost persons was an almost hopeless one. As he had no news of her, and was ill himself, he decided to return to his home in Australia, and await news there. As a first move towards home, he flew from Singapore to Labuan, there to await a plane for Australia. Here, at our rest camp in Labuan, he came upon his wife, who was also waiting for passage to Australia, and they had met by accident just before I found them.

I saw before me two middle-aged people with worn, strained faces and hardened hands, dressed unbecomingly in Red Cross clothes which didn't fit, two people who had lost health and youth as well as everything material in this war. Dr. Taylor was very lame from the effects of malnutrition, and Celia was thin and tired.

But I looked in their faces and I saw there something that held me·more than beauty would have. I saw what one seldom sees in the sleek, well-fed-and-cared-for faces, the well-adjusted expressions, of middle-aged people at home: I saw the emotion of love. Seeing them thus reassured me. Hate is strong and destructive, but love alone is nourishing; love alone can survive.

Here in Kuching Shihping Cho and Betty Weber and Babs Hill were searching for news of their husbands, who had been taken from Kuching prison camp a year before. Here also Alison Stookes was on the same mission about her brother.[1]

We spent five days in Labuan. Our camp was located at one end of Labuan Island, and Port Victoria, the American Naval Headquarters, was at the other. The approach to our camp was via the beach at low tide, and there was no approach at high tide.

The children were frantically happy. They rode up and down the beach with the soldiers, in jeeps and motor trucks all day long, they went to sea to bathe in DUKWs, and they saw as little of their mamas as possible. In short, they joined the 9th Australian Army Division.

But the adults — the coconut palms swayed over us, the South China Sea played at our feet, the tropical sun, moon,

[1] On the North American continent now, I have received a letter from Shihping Cho which tells me that her husband was beheaded in Borneo five weeks before the armistice. She is living now in Nanking, China, and finds difficulty in getting the proper food, drugs, and living conditions for Edith and Eddie, who are both unwell as a result of their years of imprisonment.

Betty Weber has written to tell me that her husband was also beheaded in Borneo just before the armistice.

Dr. Val Stookes was beheaded.

Le Gros Clarke was beheaded.

Babs Hill's husband is dead, either beheaded, or dead of dysentery, we are not sure which. Young Abbott died of dysentery.

and stars did their best for us, but the lure of the tropics was dead. We just wanted to go home.

While waiting transport home I agreed to make a broadcast to Australia telling of the liberation by their forces. Just at the end of my broadcast, two United States sailors in dungarees appeared at the tent door, and handed me a letter. The letter said that if Harry, George, and I would be in Port Victoria, Labuan, at 11.30 this day, we would be placed on board a U. S. Navy PBY-25, and headed for the U.S.A. The plane would be held as late as noon.

Harry, George, and I had been, as always, an International Problem. Harry was a British subject, and I was an American citizen; his legitimate channel for help was British, mine American. His legitimate destination was England via Australia, mine was the United States. But despite divergence of means, our one aim was to arrive as quickly as possible at the North American continent, where we had what we wanted most in this world: a home, a family, and a chance to be alone together.

It will sound unbelievable, to those who have not had our experience, that we were not rejoicing throughout every moment, after release from captivity. But physically, mentally, emotionally, there was nothing left in us with which to rejoice.

For three and a half years we had lived with war and hate, and the conditions produced by them, and we had been nearly destroyed. We had come to believe that if we could get back quickly to our love and affection for each other, to our life together, then we might become again a part of life, instead of death. If we didn't, then that for which we had survived was in vain.

It was 11.30 when I read the good news that we were to leave for the United States in half an hour.

"We'll borrow a DUKW to take you up the beach in, and then we'll pick up the jeep where we left it," said the sailor confidently. "Where are your things?"

I rush to our tent for Harry and George and the luggage. There I find Harry has already been informed that we are going to leave by plane, and has hurried to the camp head-quarters to get official clearance papers, as we are under military discipline in camp. On his way he meets Penelope and Geoffrey Gray, and tells them of our imminent departure.

Penelope and Geoffrey, who are the kind of people who always meet the emergency, hurry along to our tent to proffer help. When I arrive, Penelope is already waking George, who is sound asleep on his cot.

Early that morning, while joy-riding in a DUKW, George had fallen out of it and hurt his arm, and Harry had taken him to the doctor while I was writing my broadcast. The doctor thought it might be a greenstick fracture, and as the arm could not be X-rayed until afternoon, he had suggested the application of a temporary plaster cast. The cast was placed on his arm with the united effort of doctor, nurse, and Daddy. George was brought home to me. I examined him, and found that the cast was on the well arm.

Confronted with a plane trip to Manila, and George with one good arm in a cast, and a possible broken one unprotected, I ask Penelope to take him to the doctor and see what can be done, while I pack.

Just in time, Penelope returns with George. The injured arm is bandaged, and the doctor sends word that it must be X-rayed as soon as possible. The sailors arrive with a jeep; George, the luggage, and I are stowed, the sailors jump in, and we go to the office to pick up Harry.

With Harry on board we proceed to the water's edge where we change to a DUKW, and on it we wallow through the surf towards Victoria.

We pass the recuperation camps for liberated soldiers, and

see them smoking, eating chocolate bars, lying leisurely at the water's edge, laughing and joking. Already there is a remarkable difference in their appearance. After years of undernourishment, a few weeks or even days of concentrated foodstuffs put on flesh more quickly than is normal.

We pass working parties of Australian soldiers; all are smiling and cheery. There is a distinct type of Australian physiognomy. They are tall, lean, long-boned; their faces are strong-featured, with rectangular jaws, thin, straight noses. Their eyes are wide-spaced, as if they had spent their time looking into pleasant places, rather than squinting through keyholes.

All these men smile and wave at George, who is perched on top of the DUKW. George has met thousands of soldiers in the five days since he has been freed from prison, and is close friends with all of them. It isn't George each soldier sees, when he looks at this small boy; it is his own little son or brother.

After twenty minutes in the DUKW, we arrive at the place where the motor road from town ends in the water. Here we find the sailor's abandoned jeep, and shift hastily into it. Meanwhile the time is ten minutes after twelve. The plane was due to leave ten minutes ago.

We stop and telephone Navy H.Q. The man at the other end of the telephone tells us that the Catalina has just been released. No, wait, she is still at anchor! They will hold her for us until 12.30.

"We *must* get there," I beg Number One sailor.

"We'll make it," he promises. The Navy is as determined by now as we are, to get us on board that plane.

We race down the road. The jeep has no springs, the road no paving, our behinds no padding, our luggage no locks. The two young sailors sit in front with their long legs doubled up, their angular chins resting on their knees, chewing gum incessantly. George, inserted securely between them, also chews gum incessantly. Harry and I bounce around in the back seat, pursuing and retrieving pieces of luggage which try to leave us. Through Victoria we race, past a few indignant M.P.s. "We're not stopping for those guys!" says Number One.

We arrive at Navy H.Q. Here the young naval lieutenant who is responsible for arranging our trip is waiting anxiously. He jumps on the running board, and directs us to the landing float. Here we say good-bye to our sailors, and board a Navy launch.

From this day forward I am unalterably prejudiced in favor of the U. S. Navy. Our air passage out of Borneo was *ex officio* and without benefit of rule, but I think it was most surely in keeping with the best tradition of our Navy to answer an S.O.S. We were three human beings greatly in need of help, and the Navy answered our call.

In the midst of mutual benedictions, between the Navy and ourselves, we arrive beneath the wings of the most beautiful amphibian that I have ever seen.

With little effort on our part we find ourselves standing on top of the Catalina, bound for Manila. We call back good-bye to our naval friends. Then we are gently lowered into a large dark hole, which proves to be connected with the business part of this amphibian, and in due time, after progressing like worms through wormholes, we arrive in a luxurious cabin, with deep upholstered overstuffed seats. For the first time in three and a half years our behinds rest in luxury again.

There are bunks overhead, into which the handsome young men attempt to dispose George, who is now half-asleep from exhaustion. "Poor little fellow, he's worn out!" But not until he is quite unconscious is Poor Little Fellow disposable overhead. Meanwhile he chews more and more gum.

Now the plane leaves the water, and rises in the air, and we look down for the last time on Borneo. The water below us remains blue, jewel-like, vivid to my last glimpse, and the

coast with its green tropical islands is like a miniature aqua-
rium scene. Seen from the air it is again the Borneo that I first
loved, eleven years ago — the land of romance and adventure.

In that Borneo I have lost my home, my worldly belongings, my youth, my strength, and my unborn child.

Can I ever bear to go back again, I ask myself.

The final answer may only be told with time. But a chill
of cold physical nausea went through me then.

One of the tall handsome Navy lads leans sympathetically
over me. "If you feel ill, why don't you let me put you in
the berth up there? I guess you're glad to get out of this place,
all right!"

"Yes — I am!"

But another handsome angel appears with his hands full of
something very savory-smelling, wrapped up in paper napkins. "Say lady, what you need is food! How would you like
some good old American hot dogs with mustard on 'em? And
some American coffee, and American cigarettes?"

Even Harry arouses to this.

"How do you think we'd like 'em?"

Hurrah for the U. S. Navy!

18

Three Together

IN Manila we boarded an Army Transport headed for the United States. It should have been the happiest moment of our lives. But we were poor subjects for freedom; slavery had unfitted us.

Starvation and illness were with us still. Although I was gaining weight rapidly, my flesh was numb from lack of circulation. My skin broke and bled at any knock, and no sores would heal. My fingers were infected at the base of the nails and had been discharging for months, to such an extent that I now had difficulty in picking things up. My sight was affected by malnutrition. I could not read through a page of print, nor focus my eyes to watch the cinemas which were shown every night. Harry suffered from the same troubles, and was also running a temperature from malaria. In addition to losing all our material possessions in Borneo, we had lost health, and the good years of life. Could we ever come back? We didn't think that we could.

There were fifteen hundred passengers on board, liberated American POWs, GIs, officers and wives, several Chinese families, the Filipina wives of United States military personnel who were taking the last chance of free transportation to the United States, where citizenship by marriage would now admit them, an American Negro GI with his handsome wife and children, a number of Franciscan nuns, and about a hundred civilians like myself who had just been liberated from Japanese prison camps.

The women, children, and officers slept in overcrowded cabins, or in bunks on deck. Fourteen hundred men slept between decks and on the promenade deck. Women, children, and officers fed in the dining saloon; the fourteen hundred stood in line on the troop deck for food, where they waited several hours for each meal.

There were some thirty-five children on board, most of whom had spent their childhood in prison camps; they were unused to plumbing, chairs and tables, European food served on plates in a dining room, knives, forks, and spoons to eat with. To fight for existence was their training, liberty and sufficiency were new to them. The mothers were like myself, sick and tired, nervous and apprehensive, without clothing and comforts, tired to death of the struggle.

I acted as commissariat for the Keith family. Harry was in sick bay part of the time, and when he got out he was too weak to stand in line on deck and collect his food. George, who was unused to either food or eating utensils, lost his appetite, and found meals with me in the dining saloon a strain, which was nothing compared to what I found them with him.

Usually I ate alone, as quickly and lightly as possible, collected the remnants, and carried them above decks to my family. If I missed a meal, we all went hungry. In my feeding system I was aided by the stewards, who picked me up when I slid downstairs with the tray, dusted off the cream puffs, and started me upstairs again. I soon ordered dry meals, which could be brushed off and swept up easily.

The one thing that worked on the transport was the hot-air system, which functioned continuously. All orders were broadcast over the loud-speaker Public Address, known as the Public Abuse system. Announcements ranged in subject matter from vomit to virginity. The style varied, some being worded like pep talks to public-school boys, others being the tight-lipped warnings of prison warders to life-sentence prisoners. But they all had one thing in common: they were addressed from a superior being to greatly inferior ones. The Japs had told us that we were a fourth-class nation; we were addressed now as members of the animal kingdom. After listening to what the GIs had to swallow I thought better of the enemy.

The first Public Address message in the lounge before sailing was inspired by the fact that Harry and other husbands had complained at being told that they would not be allowed into first-class quarters at any time during the voyage, to see their wives or children. The following message was then addressed to women and children and a few officers:

"If you don't like your quarters on the ship, get off. I don't know what you are accustomed to, but you're in the army now. You are all under military discipline, and if you don't behave I'll put you in the brig on bread and water for seven days.

"The husbands of most of you women are quartered below on the troop decks. If you have children your husbands will be allowed to enter first-class quarters for a short time daily to help care for the children. If they don't take care of the children, and just play around with you girls, they will not be allowed up.

"You are not out of danger yet. Carry your life belts at all times. These waters are full of mines. Are there any questions?"

Old Lady: "About those mines! Is it really dangerous?"

"Don't you worry! We haven't had any accidents yet, and we are very clever at navigating this ship."

Ten minutes later, while weighing anchor, the ship backed into a stationary barge, and had to remain at anchor twenty-four hours for examination and repairs. While waiting at anchor we saw in the distance the blazing hulk of the ship ahead of us, which had just run into a mine.

Next day P.A. resumed over the loud-speaker: "I am not satisfied with the conduct of parents and children. Children must not come in the lounges. Fathers will not be allowed up from the troop deck unless they spend more time on deck with the children, and less in the lounge on romance."

Next day: "It has been rough lately and some of you have been seasick. If you must be sick do it in the proper place. If you vomit on the deck or the lounge you will have to clean it up yourself.

"Young ladies who sleep in the deck dormitory must be in their beds, their own beds, by midnight."

Next day: "The children are too noisy. If their conduct does not improve I shall turn the children and mothers out of their cabins, and assign them to bunks on deck."

Next day: "The children have been fighting. If this continues I shall put all the children in the brig, and feed them through the grating, and turn them all over to the police upon landing, and fine all their mothers."

I almost hoped that this would happen; I thought it would be the best news story of the war, if the children who had been imprisoned and starved throughout three and a half years in enemy camps returned to their native land confined in the brig of a United States transport, fed on bread and water.

Physical conditions on the ship were luxury compared to our past life; anyway, we would have come in a rowboat to get home. But in the past we had been the captives of an enemy race. When the Japanese browbeat, bullied, and humiliated us I had been able to comfort myself by saying, "But Americans don't do that!"

Meanwhile, sitting in the lounge talking, listening to the radio broadcasts, we learned the pay-off. The world had not changed. The Anglo-Saxons still despised the Jews, the Jews the Filipinos, the Filipinos the Negroes, the Negroes the Chinese, and the Chinese everybody. The Americans hated the English, the English hated the Australians, and everybody hated the Russians, who hated each other. Love of country flourished, while love of humanity withered; worship of God was present, and following of Christ was absent. This was the victory we had won. This was the world men had bought with their blood. This was peace.

We listened to descriptions by the soldiers of their rough treatment of the enemy, which they felt that we as ex-prisoners should enjoy. Sometimes I asked them, "Why did you do that? Did you enjoy doing it?"

The answer was, "They did it, so we did it too." Or else, "Oh well, they had it coming."

I noticed a tall, unusually husky young POW on board who had both his hands bandaged. His story was quickly told. He had incurred these injuries the day after he had been liberated from his prison camp in Japan, by beating the Japanese commandant and the second-in-command of the prison camp. He had beaten them with his fists until both Japanese were dead. He had broken his hands in the process.

Confused though our thoughts were as to the ideology of war, I did not believe that we had fought it in order to retaliate in kind for the actions which we condemned. But war brutalizes all whom it touches; if it did not do so it could not be endured.

As we approached the shores of the United States I began to worry about my identification papers, which had been confiscated in prison camp. I began to wonder if I could get into the United States again without proof of citizenship. I saw about me all colors and states of citizens-by-marriage, with proper passports, while I, who was born there, had nothing. I visioned Harry and George being torn from me and admitted to the United States as visiting British subjects, while I, because I clung to admission as an American citizen and had no papers as such, was turned away. I saw port officials shaking their fingers at me and saying, How can you *prove* you were born there? Port officials never take existence as any proof of having been born at all.

Then the weather turned very cold. We had no warm

clothing, as the Red Cross in Manila could only supply tropical things. Harry and many men did not even have blankets for sleeping. Everyone crowded into the lounge, and there were dozens of sitters per chair. The children were overwrought and excited and noisy. They were not welcome in the lounge, the decks were too cold for them, the cabins were too crowded.

The children would play, wrestle, sing, and fight on the stairs and in the corridors, like a mass of struggling worms. I understood P.A.'s sentiments, but didn't know what to do about it; they had no place to go. I used to take George and stand in the woman's toilet for an hour at a time while I tried to keep him quiet.

Then George, thank God, met Edward. Edward was a GI, twenty-one years old, with the face and sweetness of a child, and the bulk and fortitude of a man, and three years of prison camp behind him. He kept George on the deck with him all day rolled up in his army blanket, he played with him, bossed and bullied him, made him behave. George soon worshiped Edward, and so did I.

Then George came down with bronchitis, and the doctor said, Put him to bed. I was putting George to bed, George was resisting loudly, the other women in the cabin were looking unhappy, I was wondering how we could live through it, and how soon we would be locked up in the brig, when there came a knock on the door. George stopped with his mouth open. Enter Edward, with permission to visit his sick pal, George.

Edward puts George to bed, gives him his medicine, tells him a story, sings him to sleep, looks down on George and says, "He's such a purty little fellow! Gee, you couldn't get cross with him!" Exit Edward. God bless Edward. Edward does this daily until George recovers.

As soon as George was able to creep out again he took up quarters on deck with Edward. The men told me he was well-behaved, a fine little fellow, a swell American kid, lady, no fooling. They said, "Sure we like kids! Get us some more kids, lady, let them all stay out here with us. Those guys over there want some kids too, lady!"

I said, "But aren't you too crowded?"

They said, "Say, we're used to being crowded, lady, that don't mean nothing to a GI."

So then the Franciscan Sisters, the Dominican Brothers, the lady refugees, the single gentry, the officers and their wives, and an occasional bold husband, sat in the lounge and listened to P.A., ration hints, strikes, transportation difficulties, reconversion programs, rum and Coca-Cola, refugee stories; and swapped prison recipes for making edible garbage; matched up atrocities, and wondered nervously what it was like at the other end.

While on deck in the mist, the GIs moved up and rolled over and made room for the children, played with them, teased them, scolded them, peeled their oranges and unfroze their milk for them, told them not to swear, gamble, or lie, told them to do what their mamas said. Told them that America was a swell place to come home to, and Oh Boy, aren't we glad to get there!

And the children looked and listened and learned; learned that if America was like what the GIs remembered, then it sure was a swell place to come. And thus, in the arms of the men who had fought for them, our children came home to their native land.

I have said that the darkest hours of my life were the forty-eight before the Japanese occupied Sandakan. Almost as despairing were the last forty-eight hours before we touched America again.

Harry and I had lost our nerve, we had no heart to fight longer. The world awaited, and we feared to meet it.

We had one hope left, one faith placed in one person, who

could change the aspect of things for us if anyone could. From childhood, Al, my brother, had been best friend to both of us. All the way home we hoped and prayed that he would meet us; we said all night before the vessel docked, "If only Al is there!"

The transport had been scheduled for San Francisco: at the last moment her course was changed to Seattle. Privately warned of this, unable to get rail transportation, Al, and Tiah his wife, started to drive to Seattle. They had a motor accident, chartered a plane, and got there. When the ship nosed coldly against the wharf they were on the dock waiting. From that moment when we saw them, Harry and I took heart.

They fed us and clothed us, they bribed a hotel room for us, they gave or loaned us what they had; Tiah gave me her coat, and Al gave Harry his. They said we looked fine, that we were wonderful, that they were proud of us. They gave us faith in ourselves, and hope in the future. Three days later when we left Seattle we were beginning to be human beings again, instead of Displaced Personnel.

The first thing people asked me when I came back was, Did I believe I had been right in staying in Borneo?

All through my married life I had felt myself to be part of my husband. We were one in bodily desires, in dreams and laughter, and in pleasures of the mind. When war came to him I could not remain outside, safe, comfortable, prosperous, alone. If I had spent those years in freedom, I know now we could never remeet.

I will never be free of those prison years. I would kill myself sooner than live them again. But except by death I would not avoid them.

In estimating the cost to us of captivity, I think the things that really mattered were: the utter waste of those years, the child that we lost, and the children that we did not have; the entire absence of beauty, either physical in our surroundings, or emotional in our living; the arrival at disillusionment in ourselves and others, and the consciousness of human suffering which has become part of us forever. Those things, even more than physical pain.

Now in the security of peace we come together again. With the touch of our hands we put from us that awful aloneness, with the warmth of our bodies we lose the chill of the deaths we have seen, with the beat of our hearts, life is born out of lonesomeness. Thus together we liberate each other; together we escape from captivity.

While in captivity, I thought I had become hard, cold, tough, unable to be hurt myself, and ready to hurt others without a qualm. But now I am free I see that I am, as George would say, just an old softie again.

I hope that the hard manual tasks which I learned to perform under the Japanese will from now on be wasted achievements in my life. I hope that in my future life the necessity to smuggle, fight, and beg for food, as I did in Japanese prison camps, will not occur. Those years in Japanese prison camps prepared me for nothing which I hope to meet again.

But those years of captivity convinced me of two things: that there is no war without captivity, both of the victor and of the vanquished. And that there is no life with captivity.

I know now the value of freedom. In all of my life before I had existed as a free woman, and didn't know it.

This is what freedom means to me. The right to live with, to touch and to love, my husband and my children. The right to look about me without fear of seeing people beaten. The capacity to work for ourselves and our children.

The possession of a door, and a key with which to lock it. Moments of silence. A place in which to weep, with no one to see me doing so.

The freedom of my eyes to scan the face of the earth, the

mountains, trees, fields, and sea, without barbed wire across my vision. The freedom of my body to walk with the wind, and no sentry to stop me. Opportunity to earn the food to keep me strong. The ability to look each month at a new moon without asking, How many more times must this beauty shine on my captivity?

I will never give up these rights again. There may be more to life than these things. But there is no life without them.

From out of war, from out of death, we three came home to the North American continent. Here in spring we watched the yellow and the purple crocuses appear, the purple poly-anthus and violets, the pussy willows, plum blossoms, and forsythia. The trees that were dead swelled with life, and the plants that had withered turned green. The rain smelled of new life, and new earth; death and decay seemed far removed. Once more we were warmed with the sweetness and virtue of life in its seasons.

Once more we lived through night and day together, as we had dreamed. We found again affection which existed in every act. The last embrace at night, the first cup of coffee in the morning, the fresh taste of toothpaste in your mouth, the cigarette before breakfast, the clean smell of the morning air, the newspaper to open and someone to laugh with you at Dopey, the warm kitchen with the smell of toast, and the knowledge that you are not alone. All this we had remem-bered, lived for, almost died for — now we had. We lived again, and took heart.

After I had been home for some time, living in peace on this continent, with rest, good food, and vitamin pills, the continued pains in my chest, side, and arm, and inability to use one hand normally, sent me to a doctor. His examination of me, and X-rays, revealed the scars of two broken ribs, evi-dence of an injury to my shoulder socket, and an injured ten-don in my left arm, the results of Nekata's questioning in

Kuching. In due time, after treatment, these improved, and now for the first time in three years I can lie on my side and breathe without pain.

The doctor was the first person to whom I had ever told the story of how I received from Lieutenant Nekata six eggs for wounded honor and broken bones. I had had three reasons for keeping silence in the past. At first in camp I dared not speak, from fear for myself and husband; and then I wanted to forget; and then after peace came I did not want the victors to take revenge upon the vanquished for brutality, which is the guilt of war, more than of the individual. I knew what it was to be helpless in the hands of the enemy. Those reasons are now invalid, and the villains of the story are dead.

In talking with the doctor, I broke through the aura of horror and ignominy with which I had come to surround the affair. I saw the occurrence then for what it was, just one more incident in war.

I told the story to Harry then, but I wasn't sure how he would take it. One anticipates some emotion from a man when telling him that his wife has been attacked, kicked, and beaten. Subconsciously I think I expected a little melodrama.

There was none. He knew, even while I was telling him, what I was going to say. I saw in his face, as he listened, distress for me, and regret, but no surprise. I saw an acceptance of brutality and a resignation to suffering which those who do not know captivity will find it hard to understand. He took it all for granted; he could feel no private resentment that this had happened to his wife.

I saw that we had come far from our old concepts of honor and disgrace. In war, we women must fight with all of ourselves, whether we are fighting against Japanese soldiers or atomic bombs.

Now with regained health, I see my native land. Here I see everything: health, decency, comfort, and virtue, beauty, and love. We of all this world today have peace, security, and plenty.

We are free under law from starvation, from persecution, from fear of our fellow men. We are free to eat and sleep, to work and pray, to love and dream. We are free to choose the right.

I am proud to call myself American; but I do not call America mine. Its goods and plenty, its products, its people, its great ideals, and its freedom belong now to the world.

Today we live in a world, not a state. Discoveries of science eliminate space and time. We have become a body of human beings, not of nationals. The responsibility of the entire body is ours. No matter how good our own conditions now, we cannot ignore starving Europe, a demoralized and fighting Asia.

With return to health my husband was recalled to Borneo after only six months at home.

He has written to tell me how Borneo has been laid bare by friend and foe. The land has been burned clean by the Japanese, and bombed flat by the Allies. Wherever you dig there are bones, and the dead stick up out of the soil. The natives and Chinese have been murdered or bombed, and the Eurasians have been wiped out — they didn't please anyone.

The collaborators have been shot by one side for betraying, or by the other side for failing to betray.

Of the Kuching prison camps the Japanese officers all are dead, either by their own hand or by execution as war criminals.

In our own personal household Ah Yin has died of ill-health and undernourishment; Arusap, who retreated during the war to his native interior village, still flourishes as Head Man. Usin is dead. Ah Kau survives as cook. Anjibi and Herman, the *wah wahs*, are dead of starvation.

One by one now the surviving Borneo Asiatics creep in from the jungle, the river, the hills. They are starving, and 95 per cent of them are ill with malaria or dysentery. There are insufficient food and clothing and drugs in the country to take care of them. Relief channels contribute little. These people risked their lives to give us the food that saved us; we owe them a debt that we would not ignore.

British North Borneo has now ceased to be the only surviving Chartered Company, and has come under the Colonial Administration, of which my husband becomes a part. He is in charge of food production.

And so he returns to Borneo. Again, as in prison, we say that we cannot bear it, to part. And again, we do bear it.

At each stage of the journey we call back to each other, holding that last look, touch, sound, as he races further away.

I go with him to say good-bye in Seattle at midnight. Twice I leave him, twice go back to the station, back to the platform, the train. Then I get in a taxi, and weep. The driver turns to me and says, "I'm sorry, lady."

I go north to Victoria, Harry goes south to the boat. He telephones me from San Francisco, again good-bye, good-bye. He telephones me from Australia. His voice is strong and clear; it diminishes the universe, makes overwhelming our love. We speak at twelve midnight, my time, through stars and night here, through the sunlight between, through layers of air and weather, into Australian dusk. He calls back to me, and I answer: "I love you." We must hold to that, till we meet.

I shall return to Borneo in May if my health permits, taking George with me. George has recovered completely. His body fills out, he grows inches, his cheeks are red apples, his feet are huge, his hands tough paws. The baby is gone. This is George, young North American, scooter-rider, roller-skater, marbles expert, stone-thrower, tough guy — with blackberry jam on his face. This is George, who is this continent, vital, energetic, robust, intelligible.

This is George, until bedtime. Then, as in prison camp, sweetness and light descend. Then he loves me, "Sure, Mum, I do!" Then he kisses me, and says, "Say, Mum, you're swell. Say, Mum, I'll take care of you now that Daddy's in Borneo again — like I did in Kuching, Mum! Remember, Mum? Say, Mum, do elephants squirt at people with their trunks? Did you ever shoot a big brown bear? Can a tiger eat a lion? Can a eagle kill a lamb? Can a whale swallow a jeep? Say, Mum . . ."

"Go to sleep, George, I'll tell you tomorrow." I look down on the long, fawn-colored head, on the cheeks round and brown, the lashes so long, on the grubby paws held in mine. Tears come. This is our son. He lives. God has been good.

*   *   *   *   *

I believe that:

While we have more than we need on this continent, and others die for want of it, there can be no lasting peace.

When we work as hard in peacetime to make this world decent to live in, as in wartime we work to kill, the world will be decent, and the causes for which men fight will be gone.

VICTORIA, BRITISH COLUMBIA — *November* 1946